Orby Shipley

Lyra Mystica

Hymns and verses on sacred subjects, ancient and modern

Orby Shipley

Lyra Mystica
Hymns and verses on sacred subjects, ancient and modern

ISBN/EAN: 9783337097684

Printed in Europe, USA, Canada, Australia, Japan

Cover: Foto ©Thomas Meinert / pixelio.de

More available books at **www.hansebooks.com**

Lyra Mystica.

BY THE SAME EDITOR,

Second Edition, price 7s. 6d.

Lyra Eucharistica:

HYMNS AND VERSES ON THE HOLY COMMUNION.

Lately Published, price 7s. 6d.

Lyra Messianica:

HYMNS AND VERSES ON THE LIFE OF CHRIST.

LONGMAN, GREEN, LONGMAN, ROBERTS,
AND GREEN.

1864.

Lyra Mystica:

HYMNS AND VERSES ON SACRED SUBJECTS,

ANCIENT AND MODERN.

EDITED BY

THE REV. ORBY SHIPLEY, M.A.

LONDON:
LONGMAN, GREEN, LONGMAN, ROBERTS,
AND GREEN.
1865.

Preface.

THE Lyra Myſtica owes its origin more to accident than to deſign; and a few words will ſuffice to explain the reaſon of its publication.

Whilſt arranging the Collections of Sacred Poetry which have been publiſhed under the titles of **Lyra Euchariſtica** and **Lyra Meſſianica**, by the kindneſs of Friends I was placed in poſſeſſion of many Poems of conſiderable merit which, from the conditions impoſed by allotted ſpace and ſelected ſubjects, I was obliged to deny myſelf the gratification of publiſhing in thoſe Books. The reſult, however, which attended the iſſue of the earlier Works led me to think that a Miſcellaneous Collection of Religious Poetry, which ſhould be written by the Contributors who ſecured the popularity of the former Lyræ, and which ſhould form at once a companion and a contraſting Volume to the Collections already publiſhed, would not be unacceptable to their Readers.

Preface.

With the obliging permission of the Authors of the several Poems, this plan has been carried into effect; and the Poems to which I allude form the nucleus of the Lyra Mystica. This nucleus of Sacred Poetry, however, has been much enlarged from the original selection. Many translations have been made by Friends; original Poems have been received both from former Contributors and from other Authors; privately printed pieces have been kindly placed at my disposal; and to these elements have been added, with a sparing hand, Poetry already published, chiefly by Contributors to the earlier Volumes.

The Title 'Mystica' was chosen as indicative of the mystical interpretation which has been given in many of the Poems in the following pages to the Sacred or Legendary Events, or to the doctrinal Statements of Holy Scripture, or to the other Subjects upon which the Hymns and Verses were composed.

I have not attempted to make any plan or arrangement of Subjects in the following Poems. The Hymns and Verses have been printed so as to produce as much variety in style and matter as possible. And the Collection, it is hoped, will be considered to be, as it was intended to be made, entirely miscellaneous in character and treatment.

ORBY SHIPLEY.

All Saints' Day, A.D. 1864.

Contents.

		Page
No. 1.*		
IN Natale SALVATORIS. *A Christmas Hymn of Adam of S. Victor.* XII. *Century.*	A.M.M	1
2. CHRIST in the Wilderness.	ALAN BRODRICK (*Bramshaw*)	3
3. Speciosus Formâ præ natis hominum JESUS. *A Sequence for the Transfiguration, from the Saltzburg Missal of the* XVI. *Century.*	H.R.B.	9
4. The Well of Bethlehem.	RICHARD FREDERICK LITTLEDALE	11
5. Hymn to CHRIST Crucified. *From the Spanish of Luis de Leon.*	ARCHDEACON CHURTON	15
6. The Communion of the Saints.	ARCHER GURNEY	20
7. Eucharistical.	PHIPPS ONSLOW	23

* The Hymns are not numbered in the Text; but by a reference to the Page they can at once be found both in the Table of Contents and Index of First Lines.

Contents.

No.		Page
8.	Soul-Gardening. . . . DORA GREENWELL	27
9.	The Ascension of CHRIST.	
	PHILIP STANHOPE WORSLEY	31
10.	After this the Judgment.	
	CHRISTINA G. ROSSETTI	33
11.	The Embracing of the Body of CHRIST by His Virgin-Mother.	
	Founded on a "Lament," translated from the Greek of Symeon Metaphrastes.	
	WILLIAM CHATTERTON DIX	36
12.	The Hymn of Aurelius Prudentius Clemens on the VIII. Day before the Kalends of January (Christmas Day) . . . HENRY THOMPSON	38
13.	The Two Covenants: an Allegory. R. E. J. A.	43
14.	Stanzas . . . . . AUBREY DE VERE	47
15.	Prayer of Hildebert the Venerable to the Holy TRINITY. . . . HERBERT KYNASTON	49
16.	The Vision of the Glory.	
	For the Feast of the Transfiguration, August 6.	
	GERARD MOULTRIE	53
17.	The Life of CHRIST.	
	A Latin Hymn of the XII. Century.	
	HENRY TREND	57
18.	Thy Daughter is dead, trouble not the Master.	
	CECIL FRANCES ALEXANDER	60
19.	The Shadow and the Substance. J. M. KING	63
20.	Surgit CHRISTUS cum Trophæo.	
	An Easter Sequence from the Missal of Tournay. XVI. Century.	
	JOHN WILLIAM HEWETT	65
21.	The Childhood of CHRIST. ANNA H. DRURY	67
22.	We would see JESUS.	
	CHARLES LAWRENCE FORD	70
23.	Faith. . . . . . MATTHEW BRIDGES	73
24.	In Youth I died. . . . . ANONYMOUS	76
25.	Stanzas . . . . . G. HUNT SMYTTAN	78

Contents.

No.		Page
26.	The Sacred Heart. ADELAIDE A. PROCTER	83
27.	Sanctæ Syon adsunt Encaenia. *A Sequence for the Dedication of a Church, from the Drontheim Missal of the XVI. Century.* . . . . P. ONSLOW	86
28.	Lays of Ancient Palestine. E. DUDLEY JACKSON	88
29.	Virginis in gremio. *A Sequence from the Saltzburg Missal of the XVI. Century* . . . . . A.M.M.	95
30.	Type and Antitype. EDWIN L. BLENKINSOPP	97
31.	Verses . . LADY GEORGIANA FULLERTON	101
32.	The Tomb of Joseph of Arimathea. DEAN NEWMAN	104
33.	Concerning the chief Spiritual and general Gifts of God. *An ancient Latin Hymn* . . . J.M.H.	106
34.	The Advent of the Divine Stranger. RICHARD TOMLINS	111
35.	The Heavenly Fatherland. *A Cento from the Rhythm of Bernard of Clugny.* . . . . . G. MOULTRIE	113
36.	Omnes Gentes plaudite. *A Hymn for the Ascension; from the Latin.* CHARLES INGHAM BLACK	117
37.	Bei stiller Nacht. *From the Hymn-Book of the Diocese of Treves.* FRANCES ELIZABETH COX	119
38.	Sonnets. . . . . . . DEAN ALEXANDER	123
39.	Verses. . . . . ORWELL	125
40.	Is there no Balm in Gilead ? . . . . C.S.	130
41.	Commendation of a Faithful Soul . . W.B.	133
42.	The Epiphany. FREDERICK W. KITTERMASTER	135
43.	Meditation of a Faithful Soul. *From the Latin* . . F. C. HUSENBETH	138

Contents.

No.		Page
44.	The CHILD-CHRIST on the Cross: an Anticipation of Calvary. HENRY NUTCOMBE OXENHAM	145
45.	The Signals of Levi. . . . R. S. HAWKER	148
46.	The Tree of Life. *From an old Latin Poem.* ARCHBISHOP TRENCH	152
47.	An Ode on the Nativity. *From the Italian of Manzoni.* C. B. CAYLEY	155
48.	Stanzas. . . . . . . D. GREENWELL	159
49.	A Legend of S. Peter. . MARY MOULTRIE	163
50.	An Easter Carol. . . R. F. LITTLEDALE	168
51.	Qui procedis ab Utroque. *A Sequence on the* HOLY SPIRIT *of Adam of S. Victor* . . . P. S. WORSLEY	170
52.	The Advent Antiphons. R. MEUX BENSON	173
53.	The Transfiguration. . . . . G. V. C.	178
54.	In Diebus Celebribus. *A Latin* Hymn *for the Holy Days of the Church; of the* XV. *Century.* H. TREND	182
55.	To CHRIST hanging on high. . . L. M. S.	186
56.	The Way-side Cross. . . C. E. KENNAWAY	186
57.	O quam Glorificum. *An ancient Latin Poem.* I. GREGORY SMITH	191
58.	After the Earthquake a Still Small Voice. ARTHUR BAKER	196
59.	The Three Enemies: a Colloquy. C. G. ROSSETTI	199
60.	Pentecostal Odes from the Service-Books of the Holy Eastern Church. . . W. C. DIX	201
61.	The Ascension. . . . . . A. M. M.	205
62.	Death. . . . . FREDERICK W. FABER	207
63.	Quam dilecta Tabernacula. *A Hymn for the Dedication of a Church; of the* XII. *Century.* WILLIAM B. FLOWER	211

Contents.

No.		Page
64.	In a Vision of the Night when deep Sleep falleth upon Man. . . . WILLIAM S. RAYMOND	214
65.	A Tradition of S. John the Evangelist. GEORGE W. COX	215
66.	Hymns of Novalis. . . . . HELEN LOWE	218
67.	Paradise. *From the Spanish of Luis de Leon.* ANONYMOUS	223
68.	The Incarnation. . . . . . C. L. FORD	224
69.	Jael. . . . . R. TOMLINS	229
70.	Funeral Hymn. . . . . G. MOULTRIE	231
71.	The Story of the Cross. . EDWARD MONRO	233
72.	The Passion. . . . . . . C. I. BLACK	237
73.	Thoughts from the Manual of S. Augustine. JAMES SKINNER	242
74.	Childlike Holiness. . . MANLEY HOPKINS	245
75.	The Advent. . . . . P. S. WORSLEY	248
76.	Colloquies between the Disciple and the Divine Master. . . . . ELIA	251
77.	In Domo PATRIS. *An Ancient Latin Poem.* . . . H. R. B.	254
78.	Thoughts in Lent. . F. MINDEN KNOLLYS	261
79.	Verses from the German. CATHERINE WINKWORTH	263
80.	Gethsemane. THE VOICE OF CHRISTIAN LIFE IN SONG	267
81.	Old Testament Hymns. . . H. KYNASTON	269
82.	An Allegory. . . MORNING THOUGHTS	274
83.	The Burial. . . . . . . A. M. M.	276
84.	The Power of Contrition. *An Ode from the Italian of Rossetti.* C. B. CAYLEY	281
85.	Lux advenit veneranda. *A Sequence for the Purification from the Breviary of Rennes of the XVI. Century.* H. R. B.	283

Contents.

No.		Page
86.	Verselets. . . . . R. E. J. A.	286
87.	Ad perennis Vitæ Fontem. *A Hymn of S. Peter Damiani on the Joys of Paradise* . . . R. F. LITTLEDALE	289
88.	She is not dead, but sleepeth. A. BRODRICK	293
89.	The Holy Sacrifice. . . . A. GURNEY	297
90.	God's Acre. . . . . . W. B. FLOWER	800
91.	The Five smooth Stones of David. J. M. KING	302
92.	Hymns for Whitsuntide: from the Latin. WILLIAM JOHN BLEW	307
93.	The Church. . . . . S. M.	312
94.	The Salutation of the Greek Church on Easter Day. . . . . . P. ONSLOW	316
95.	De Laudibus S. Scripturæ. *An ancient Latin Poem.* . C. I. BLACK	319
96.	S. Patrick's Coat of Mail. AFTER JAMES CLARENCE MANGAN	321
97.	Dies est lætitiæ. *Hymn on the Nativity: from the Latin.* F. C. HUSENBETH	326
98.	Go! and Come! . . . D. GREENWELL	329
99.	The Three Comings. . . E. D. JACKSON	333
100.	The Old-year's Blessing. . A. A. PROCTER	336
101.	Verses. . . . . S. B.	338
102.	Lætabundi jubilemus. *A Prose for the Transfiguration.* A. M. M.	342
103.	Paradise. . . . . C. L. FORD	344
104.	The Disciple whom JESUS loved. DEAN ALEXANDER	348
105.	In Sapientia disponens omnia Æterna DEITAS. *A Sequence from the Narbonne Missal of the XVI. Century.* . . J. W. HEWETT	350
106.	The Living Death. . . DEAN NEWMAN	352
107.	Thoughts in Verse. . . W. S. RAYMOND	555
108.	The Descent of the SPIRIT. *A Hymn for Whitsun-Day.* G. MOULTRIE	357

Contents.

No.		Page
109.	The Palimpsest: an Allegory. P. ONSLOW	360
110.	Via Sanctæ Crucis. . . . . A. BAKER	362
111.	Jerusalem, du hoch gebaute Stadt	
	A German Hymn on the Heavenly City; of the XVII. *Century* . . . F. E. COX	365
112.	I am the Rose of Sharon and the Lily of the Valleys. . . . FREDERICK GEORGE LEE	367
113.	JESUS CHRIST the Same yesterday, to-day, and for ever. . . . . . . A. GURNEY	368
114.	En Dies est Dominica.	
	A Latin Hymn for the Lord's Day; of the XV. *Century.* . . . . H. TREND	371
115.	Tria Dona Reges ferunt.	
	A Cento from an Epiphany Sequence of Adam of S. Victor. . . . R. F. LITTLEDALE	376
116.	Have mercy on me, O LORD, Thou SON of David. . . . . A. BRODRICK	378
117.	A Song which none but the Redeemed can sing. D. GREENWELL	380
118.	De Parente Summo natum.	
	A Sequence from Tournay Missal of the XVI. *Century.* . . . . J. M. H.	382
119.	Song of the early Christian Confessors. C. E. KENNAWAY	385
120.	Being in an Agony, He prayed more earnestly. C. S.	387
121.	The open Vision. . . . . . R. E. J. A.	389
122.	The Music of Heaven. . . . F. E. COX	392
123.	Holy Childhood. . . . . A. BRODRICK	394
124.	Stanzas. . . . . . . H. N. OXENHAM	396
125.	Sequence on the HOLY SPIRIT.	
	After Adam of S. Victor. . . W. J. BLEW	402
126.	Of the Gifts of GOD.	
	From the Latin. . . . . C. B. CAYLEY	405

Contents.

No.		Page
127.	Urbs beata Hirusalem.	
	On the Heavenly Jerusalem: *from the* Latin.	
	H. R. B.	409
128.	The Church, Militant and Triumphant.	
	Sir Archibald Edmonstone, Bart.	410
129.	Voices from the American Church:	
	Heart's Song.	
	A. Cleveland Coxe, Bishop Elect	412
	Song of Faith . . William Croswell	413
	As thy day, so shall thy strength be.	
	Bishop Eastburn	414
	The fashion of this World passeth away.	
	Bishop Doane	414
	The Glory Reserved.	
	W. A. Muhlenbergh	416
130.	The Prodigal's Return. . . . W. C. Dix	417
131.	Home. . . . . P. Onslow	418
132.	Stanzas. . . John Hoskyns-Abrahall	419
133.	Pro Christo Mortuus. . . E. D. Jackson	420
134.	Man.	
	A Hymn of Alanus, of the xii. *Century.*	
	P. S. Worsley	422
135.	Christ Triumphant. . Archdeacon Mant	424
136.	Martyr's Song. . . . . C. G. Rossetti	427
137.	The Starry Night.	
	From the Spanish of Luis *de Leon.*	
	Archdeacon Churton	430

Lyra Mystica.

Hymns and Verses on Sacred Subjects.

In Natale Salvatoris.

A Chriſtmas Hymn of Adam of S. Victor.

PON the SAVIOUR's Birthday bleſt
  Let all who ſhare this mortal ſtate
  Send up ſweet Hymns of joy and
    reſt
  To Angel-choirs ſubordinate,
That varying tones of many be
Made one in holieſt harmony.

This is a happy Day; on this
  The Co-eternal WORD made choice
For our cold world to leave His Bliſs—
  Let us be merry and rejoice;
The True SUN lights our darkened morn,
Of the meek Virgin GOD is born.

In Natale Salvatoris.

That man the guilty might not die
    God a **Redeemer** ſent below,
God in the Sole-Begot came nigh
    To thoſe He lovèd. Even ſo
He called us back to Life's loſt place
Not for our merit; of His Grace.

He lived before He ſought our clime,
    Tranſcending time and ſpace and ſenſe;
But now the Eternal dwells in time,
    And now doth place confine the Immenſe;
Our imperfections all He bore
That He might all things fallen reſtore.

It is not ſin He takes; it is
    Only the form which ſinners wear;
He comes a **Babe** of Holineſs
    To earth grown old with guilt and care,
Immortal to the mortal, Spirit
To fleſh, that fleſh might Him inherit.

Thus the Eternal **Word** hath lot
    With Fleſh in **One Bleſt** Perſon now,
And yet That Person changeth not,
    Nor is made Twain. Whene'er we bow
Our knees to our Incarnate Lord
One altogether is adored.

This is a Thing Divinely great,
    A Sacrament the crafty Foe
Might ſearch in vain by fraud or hate,
    All blind this Myſtery to know

Chriſt in the Wilderneſs.

What GOD's Eternal WISDOM True
Under the Veil of Fleſh would do.

The vaſt Enigma is not read,
  By eager ſearch it cannot be
(Or ſubtle ſpeech) illuminèd;
  To know the way is not for me,
But I believe that GOD can make
What human reaſon cannot take.

How deep His Counſels! how ſublime
  Of GOD-IN-FLESH the Myſtery!
The Fleece is wet like graſs at prime,
  The Rod doth bloſſom, all for me;
What Saints of old ſo craved is done;
The Virgin doth bring forth a SON.

Chriſt in the Wilderneſs.

IN the Camp where flares the watch-fire,
  In the lamp-lit ſtreet
I had wandered, O my Maſter,
  With what weary feet!

I had ſate at Monarchs' tables
  While the red wine ran,
And bright Beauty breathed her magic,
  A moſt lonely Man:

In the world's pale, reſtleſs market
  I had learnt to bend

To the golden Idol, Money;
   Trampled foe and friend,

Scrambled fierce for place and riband,
   Cringed and schemed and lied—
Hast thou found a worthy Master,
   O sad Soul?—I cried.

Let us seek some simpler pleasures:
   There's a home I know,
Lit by lanes of earliest primrose
   Where wild roses blow.

So we dwelt 'mid summer murmurs
   Of tall honied limes,
Heard across cool water-meadows
   Faint Cathedral chimes.

Ah! I felt a want, a longing
   E'en in earthly bliss,
Felt a nobler impulse stir me
   From a young Child's kiss.

Lord, where art Thou? from my Manhood
   Unto Thine, I sighed:
Not an answer came, but ever
   Boomed Thought's sullen tide.

Thus along Life's misty seashore,
   Tired of all, I strayed;
Heard Death's deep sea call me, call me,
   Of myself afraid.

Watched grey ſkies and ocean mingle;
  Nature kind replied—
He is not where thou haſt ſought Him;
  Seek Him in the Wild.

What fool praiſed Man's kindly Nature?
  Mad my Spirit ſpake—
Who can guide me o'er Grief's moorland,
  Through Care's thorny brake?

Devil's laughter rang around me,
  Moaned Doubt's hollow ſea—
Where's thy GOD? I know not any—
  Woe for me, for me!

Ah! a Hand ſo kind and gentle
  Touched my wicked lips!
Sorrow's ſunſet breathed a Bleſſing
  On Hope's fading ſhips:

I roſe up; He went before me,
  Such a wondrous King:
All my Soul did gladly follow
  Without queſtioning.

All the way grew bright beneath Him,
  Muſic ſtole around,
Such as Angels love to whiſper
  On Heaven's holy Ground.

Strange and dark the rocks frowned round us,
  Hoarſe the torrent's cry:

Christ in the Wilderness.

On He went; I could but follow,
  Half afraid to sigh.

Darkness fell, most weird and dreary,
  Sudden through the night
I heard holy Psalms uplifted:
  Then upon my sight

Loomed a Minster's lighted windows;
  On He went before,
I crept after wondering, dazzled
  Through the flashing Door.

White robed Figures silent, kneeling
  Thronged the sapphire Nave;
As I knelt, my Master turning
  One long Love-look gave.

All my Spirit worshipped weeping;
  When I raised mine eyes
He was standing at the Altar,
  And in lowly guise

All around, like Priests, the Angels
  Woke a joyous song :—
He has come, our wandering Brother,
  Looked for, oh, how long!

Through the Nave and Aisles and Arches,
  With triumphant roll,
Surged a deep of Heavenly Anthems,
  Flooding all my Soul.

Then I saw Him in His Glory
  Take my tear-stained prayers,
Place them in His golden Censer,
  Pass up Heaven's stairs.

As He went, I heard His Blessing—
  Come to Me, My Child!
If in crowds thou find'st no Master,
  Seek Him in the Wild.

Angel-faces came around me,
  Gladly on mine ear
Fell the Story of GOD's Gospel;
  With a reverent fear

I could see the Cavern manger,
  Roofs of Nazareth,
Learnt by Calvary's Wood-Altar
  Mysteries of Death.

I am Thine—I wept—O save me,
  I will stray no more:
Thou hast given me a Presence
  On the World's wild shore:

I shall find Thee in all places,
  For I wear the key
Which unlocks the Gate of Heaven
  When I pray to Thee.

Then a Voice spake fondly, slowly—
  Fear thou, lest thou fall!

Christ in the Wilderness.

Listen, when to inmost Conscience
  I, the Master, call!

In the world, if thou wouldst find Me,
  In its wildest Wild
Thou must seek Me, prayerful, fasting,
  O My Child, My Child.

From the Camp or City hurry,
  Pilgrim to God's Shrine;
Dally not with Pleasure's whispers,
  Fear not! thou art Mine.

From the Market and the Harbour
  Follow, follow Me:
I will be thy gentlest Master
  Through Eternity.

Then I rose up with my fellows;
  All the Minster fled,
Like a dream before God's morning
  Breaking overhead.

O sweet Dayspring! Thy great Glory
  Fills this wandering breast;
In Life's Wild I found my Master—
  He hath given Rest.

Speciosus forma prae natis hominum Jesus.

A Sequence for the Transfiguration.

JESUS, Beautiful in Form above the sons of men,
   On Whose Countenance distilling
Joy Divine, through Angels thrilling,
   Seraphim desire to look:
Who, for us Himself abasing,
All His Majesty effacing,
   King, a servant's likeness took:

The unapproachèd Light, to-day,
Which veils His GODHEAD's Form supernal,
Doth to His Chosen ones display,
As shadowed forth by Light external.

Upon a lofty Mountain crest
They saw His bright Transfiguration,
The Mountain high above the rest
Foreshown in Daniel's Revelation.

His Countenance was shining as the Sun,
   And as the Light
   His Raiment white
      To three alone
      This view Divine was shown.

By flesh and blood this Vision was not won;
By God in Heaven
The glimpse was given,
Whose awful Voice
Declared the eternal Choice—

This is My Beloved Son,
By all the world to be obeyed;
Now to Him be homage done,
Be reverence to His Teaching paid.

Oh, how blest, beyond all other,
Witnesses of this to be:
Peter, James, and John his brother,
Of the Chosen, chosen three.

Within the overshadowing Cloud
The Father's Voice proclaimed aloud
The wondrous Mystery to which ye hearkened;
That Cloud it bodes not fear to you,
It sheds a gracious, Heavenly dew;
With brightness glowing, not with vapours darkened.

Oh, sovereign Grace, oh, Dream of wonder,
Meet reward for Sons of thunder.
The Bearer of the Keys is sleeping;
But his heart is vigil keeping.

Ascend now this Mountain,
And follow those three,

From each of earth's quarters,
  His Glory to see:
A MAN above all men
  Exalted is He;
The Mountain is JESUS,
  Whom pure hearts shall see,

Reigning in the lofty Brightness
  Of the FATHER's Majesty,
Like as Moses and the Prophets
  Sang in constant harmony.

JESU, King of Glory, draw us after Thee.   Amen.

The Well of Bethlehem.

HERE is sound of war in Judah, and over Ephrath's plain,
  Though the fields are ripe for harvest, no Hebrew reaps the grain;

For the armies of the Heathen have come with flame and sword
To waste the pleasant dwellings of the People of the LORD.

In the Valley of the Giants Philistine tents are spread,
And their warriors are marshalled within the House of Bread.

The Well of Bethlehem.

No Chief goes forth against them, and no Champion
    comes to save;
For Israel's Hope, an exile, is pent within a Cave.

Around him still are gathered a chosen faithful few
Tried in full many a battle, and to his banner
    true.

Upon the cliffs of limestone rock the autumn sun-
    beams beat,
And glare upon the hunted band with all their
    parching heat,

Till David, faint and thirsty, in his longing speaks
    to them—
Would that I had but water from the Well of
    Bethlehem!

Then up arose three Chieftains from the places
    where they sate,
To bring their Master water from the Fount beside
    the gate.

They reck not of the thousand swords which fain
    would bar their way,
But calm in strength and valour straight address
    them to the fray.

Three men against an army vast, they have no
    thought of flight,
For each against a host of men hath stood alone in
    fight.

Too well Philistine widows have learnt those three
       names in woe,
Shammah, and Eleazar, and the peerless Adino.

Those mighty men have broken through all that
       opposing ring,
And have borne the cooling water in triumph to
       their King.

But David hath the Chalice out before JEHOVAH
       poured,
Saying—This is blood, not water, I may not drink
       it, LORD!

O 'Type of future story! O most deep and mystic
       sign
Of the longing of the Nations for Him of David's
       line!

There is sound of war in all lands, and through its
       cruel bane,
Though the Souls are ripe for harvest, no reaper
       stores the grain;

For the hosts of evil Spirits make war with flame
       and sword
Against the Gentile watchers who are waiting for
       the LORD.

Afar in every Country their countless legions
       spread,
To turn the poor and hungry from the blessed
       House of Bread.

And the scorching rays of sorrow on mourners ever
    beat,
No Rock is in the weary lands to shadow from the
    heat.

There is nothing to bring cooling, and naught may
    comfort them
Save the Well of Living Water that springs in
    Bethlehem.

But Three go forth to seek that Fount, in faith
    and valour strong,
Three who reck not of hindrances, nor of that
    travail long;

They go o'er hills and deserts with the guiding
    Star before,
Wise Caspar, true Baltasar, and the faithful
    Melchior.

In vain the hosts of Satan would beset their wan-
    dering,
For the mighty Men break through them to reach
    their new-born King.

They haste in eager worship to that long-expected
    sight,
To the Well of Life whose Glory gives all believers
    Light,

To the Chief Who comes to vanquish, the Cham-
    pion strong to save,

To Israel's Hope, an INFANT, now laid within a
    Cave.

And where the BABE is cradled, Whom the Three
    in awe behold,
They lay their three rich Offerings, Myrrh, Frank-
    incense and Gold.

Then they turn them back in triumph once more
    afar to roam,
Till they bear those Living Waters to thirsting
    hearts at home.

And that Chalice of Thy Passion, unto the FATHER
    poured,
Although It is Blood, not water, yet we may
    drink It, LORD!

O Pledge of future Glory! O most deep and
    mystic Sign
Of the Healing of the Nations by Him of David's
    line!

Hymn to Christ Crucified.

From the Spanish of Luis de Leon.

THOU Spotless LAMB of GOD,
    Bathed in Thine own dear Blood,
That flows to wash the world's deep
    guilt away,
  Who on the stubborn Tree
  Dost seem to call to me,

With Arms outstretched, to find the Grace I pray;
    Ere yet life's slow decay
    Makes pale the lustre bright
    Of that celestial Face,
    And Death's cold fingers trace
Their darkening shadows o'er those Orbs of light,
    O let one glance be thrown
From Thy meek Eyes on me, to mark me for
    Thine Own.

    Now when Thy Love profound
    Hath reached its utmost bound,
Nor mortal veil such Might may more confine;
    While on the painful Rood,
    With sharpest anguish bowed,
Thy thorn-crowned Head Thou dost to earth incline,
    With Mercy's glance Divine
    Thy Mother's gaze to meet;
    And Thy majestic Prayer
    E'en rebel Souls would spare,
Sent upward to Thy FATHER's Glory-seat;
    O let Thy Pardon free
Prevail for sins like mine. Now, LORD, remember
    me!

    Now while Thy suffering Hands
    Thy bounteous Grace expands,
As though in dying still outstretched to give;
    And as in balance weighed,
    The full account is paid,
Whereby poor slaves redeemed from bondage live;

Hymn to Christ Crucified.

  Thy captive, LORD, receive;
  While every vital pore,
  With flowing Mercy rife,
  Bursts out, and parting life
Drains from Thy Heart Love's ne'er-exhausted
   store;
  Fain would I first be there,
My loss, All-righteous SAVIOUR, earliest to repair.

  Thy Bedesman, LORD, behold,
  In thraldom dark and cold
Long laid, entangled long in Error's chain:
  Yet Hope, o'ermastering Fear,
  Still prompts, that Thou wilt hear,
My Advocate will not my prayer disdain:
  Since Mercy's highest strain
  Decrees, that pardon free
  E'en there should most abound
  Where deepest guilt is found;
And when the darkest stain is cleansed by Thee,
  Thy Blood with richest cost
Is lavished, and Thy Godlike Love rejoiceth most.

  What though with guilty load
  My drooping neck is bowed,
And my sad Spirit faints with toil and care,
  Because my rebel pride
  Cast Thy mild Yoke aside,
Doomed, justly doomed, a tyrant's bonds to bear:
  What though I might despair
  With weary steps and slow

Hymn to Christ Crucified.

  To reach Thee, Thou art nigh,
  And never more wilt fly;
Those royal Feet transfixed Thy Purpose show;
  Fixed on the firm-set Tree
In patient grief they tell how Mercy waits for me.

  I know it, O my GOD:
  As in a quiet road
My good desires may here at anchor ride;
  That Heart, in open sign
  Of pitying Love Divine,
Seen through the lattice of Thy wounded Side,
  Hath all my need supplied:
  That to the dying Thief
  Gave comfort; one brief word
  He spake, and he was heard:
E'en as a glad surprise the prayed relief
  Thy Answer gave; the night
Of darkness left his Soul in dawn of Life and Light.

  I come in happy hour
  To feel Thy Grace's power,
Now, when with Charter new, embracing all,
  Thy Gifts Thou dost prepare
  For all who seek to share:
Now, when to Thy sad Mother, bowed in thrall,
  Thy sovereign Voice doth call
  And bids her find a Son,
  Bids John a Mother find,
  The Thief of contrite mind
To look for promised Joy—shall I alone

Hymn to Christ Crucified.

Still pine for Grace denied?
No, Lord, each empty Soul with Thee is satisfied.

Behold me, Lord, a Son
In error's path undone,
My portion lost, did Justice speak my doom:
But Thy good Word hath said,
That Mercy's mildest aid
Turns, stays, and guides repentant wanderers home.
I come, Dear Lord, I come
To kiss Thy fainted Feet,
As on a rack, outspread
On Thy hard dying bed;
For here my sorrowing voice Thy Grace shall meet,
And Grace to Sons forgiven
Here speaks—O lost and found, thy portion rests
in Heaven.

For token of that Grace
To all who seek Thy Face,
E'en now Thy Head in death Thou dost incline:
I know that I have won
Of Thee that priceless Boon,
The earnest of my hope, in that dear Sign.
O Majesty Divine,
O Love of truth so pure,
Thy Bounty to bequeath,
That the Testator's death
Must pass to make the gift of Blessing sure!
O Mercy great and high,
That to confirm the bond e'en Mercy's Lord
must die!

My Song, we here muſt ſtay :
    Such theme to honour beſt
Not words, but flowing tears, ſhould ſpeak the reſt :
Sad ſilent muſings chaſe loud ſongs away :
    Our notes we cannot keep,
When Earth is huſhed, and Sun and Heaven in
    darkneſs weep!

The Communion of the Saints.

HEAVEN is no world of ſelf-ſufficing
    Bliſs ;
        Love is its radiance, Love its atmoſ-
            phere,
And Love the laſt and leaſt-beloved doth miſs
    And counts each Soul, Love's Blood was poured
        for, dear.
Did not our gracious Maſter tell us this,
    That Joy's vaſt thrill ſweeps through Heaven's
        ſplendour clear
When one poor ſinner turns that he may live,
And ſhall not Heaven bewail one fugitive ?

Think ye, each Saint who loved his brethren ſo
    He felt their ſorrows his, loves leſs above ?
Does joy make hearts leſs tender ? Surely, no.
    Heaven is the dwelling-place of deathleſs Love.
But your faint hearts, unconſcious of that glow,
    Paint a falſe bliſs : myſelf do I reprove

Who shared your doubts; but Faith its world of light
And sacred loveliness unbares to sight.

The Virgin Mother, highest raised of all,
　Who at her heart earth's Wondrous SAVIOUR bore,
Whose meek assent retrieved Eve's primal fall,
　Can she forget her brethren evermore?
That tender heart of pity rests the thrall;
　She cannot cease to love on that bright shore:
And JESUS' Foster-father mourns with her
The souls that mock, the loveless hearts that err.

And all that glorious Host no tongue can count,
　Apostles, Prophets, Martyrs, swell their moan.
Within each Soul still springs compassion's fount:
　Should human griefs and cares remain unknown?
Number the suns; then weigh the vast amount
　Of mortal woes! That can the Blest alone.
With tender yearning prayers for aye they seek
To bless the loveless and to cheer the weak.

And you, sweet Friends, who here partook our cares,
　Have you forgotten and forsaken quite?
Nay, HE Who shared the heart's fond yearning, shares
　Its tenderness and weakness infinite;
For weakness, strong in faith, is rich in prayers,
　And must be weak, while wrong contends with right.

He would not drain the care-benumbing gall;
Love, in the Highest, can be grieved by all.

He, on Heaven's Throne, their Lord and ours,
    Whose Heart
  Blends every Love, all human griefs in one!
O, that this world could know Thee as Thou art,
    Undying Lord, the All-loving Father's Son,
Yet ours, our Friend, our Own, Who mak'st Thy
    part
  To sue for ever hearts that scorn and shun:
Thou canst forget not—how should Thine forget?
Love pays, for ever pays Love's boundless debt.

O Thou, the Spirit of Light and Wisdom, pour
  Thy quickening rays into these hearts of ours,
That they may brim with grateful ardours o'er!
  O, earth's bare swamps shall yet be thronged
    with flowers.
Could we but know, we surely must adore;
  Where sunshine streams, in vain the twilight
    cowers.
Come Light! come Faith! 'our colder self destroy!
We only ask to love, and Love, we know, is Joy.

Eucharistical.

HE evening shadows thickly fall
O'er grassy slope and guarded wall,
Till darkness folds them in her pall.

But still, while darkness creeps around,
Linger the lights on holy ground,
On Zion's mountain, Temple crowned.

Like a rich garment's golden hem,
Or jewels in a diadem,
So gleam thy towers, Jerusalem.

And still the fading lights creep higher,
Till fretted roof and golden spire
Stand up, like lances tipped with fire.

And then the fleeting glories fly,
Massive and dark the towers lie,
Purple against a crimson sky:

While up and down, and round about,
As fireflies Eastern darkness flout,
The glimmering hearth-lights twinkle out,

And through the gathering darkness, yet
Gleam the white Tents, in order set
Adown the slopes of Olivet,

And ever from the busy street
Rise the quick sounds of pattering feet,
Where friends with friends in gladness greet.

For of the Jewish nation all,
Obedient to their Prophet's call,
Are met for their high Festival.

   * * *

But He, to Whom the Feast was due,
Sate sadly with the chosen few,
Among the faithless only true,

As friends who meet, and meeting know
That they must part, yet, lingering slow,
Would eat and drink before they go.

He sate within the Upper Room,
And told them of His coming Doom
Amid the evening's gathering gloom.

He told them of His Foemen's spite,
And of His yielding to their might—
Then one went out, and it was night.

He blessed the Cup, He brake the Bread,
And, 'This My BLOOD' for sinners shed,
And, 'This My BODY,' so He said.

Then out into the darkening air—
And then, the Agony of Prayer,
One holy Angel knoweth where—

Till, underneath the Olive shade
The hurrying torches gleaming played,
And by His Own He was betrayed—

And then, the scornful, cruel eyes,
The Cross, the Scourge, the bitter cries,
The All-sufficient Sacrifice.

   * * *

O Heavenly Food, O Living Bread,
Whereon of old Thy People fed,
Wherewith Thy Church is nourishèd!

O Blessed Wine, by Thee outpoured
When Thou wert present at the Board,
Then for Thy Church in mercy stored!

O blessed Presence, wherewith Thou
Dost feed Thy Church in mercy now,
While Saints and Angels reverend bow;

They who their glittering wings unfold,
And they who still Thy Face behold
Amid the flashing lamps of gold.

Silent they stand, those Words to hear,
And Heaven is filled with holy fear,
While fallen men on earth draw near;

They draw their wings before their face,
And silent for a little space
Adore The Mystery of Grace;

Adoring, while the Church they see,
Which sin had made in twain to be,
In Heaven and earth made One in Thee;

Then from their golden harps again
Peals forth the Church's rapturous ſtrain,
' Worthy the LAMB that once was ſlain.'

O broken Fleſh, O Blood outpoured,
By man and Angels both adored,
O Holy, Holy, Holy LORD,

Grant us to know with faithful eye,
As Saints and Angels know on high,
Thy Preſence in Thy Myſtery,

With John's deep love to Thee to cling,
Peter's warm faith to Thee to bring,
With Mary's tender ſorrowing;

Then, by the Sufferings keen and ſore
Which once that broken Body bore,
Draw near, and ſilently adore:

There, by our cares and troubles preſt,
There lean on Thee, and leaning, reſt,
As One that night, upon Thy Breaſt;

Caſt at Thy Feet our guilty fears,
The load of all our ſin-ſtained years,
And waſh them, as that Saint, with tears;

Till all its ſtrength Thy Love diſplays,
And troubled hearts Thy Comforts raiſe,
And mourners join in ſongs of praiſe,

In ſongs of praiſe that ſhall not ceaſe
Till Thou ſhalt grant the full releaſe
And call Thy Church to perfect Peace.

Soul-Gardening.

SO ſpake the hoary Thyme,
    Half hidden in the graſs—
" I watch from morning prime
    Until my LORD ſhall paſs.

" How bright beneath the Sun,
    How ſweet within the glade,
The flow'rets ope, each one
    Beloved by Him Who made
His Flowers that live in light, His Flowers that
    live in ſhade.

" The Primroſes are pale,
    Yet fair; the Violet grows
Beneath her leafy veil,
    And be ſhe pale none knows,
Or be ſhe fair, ſo ſweet her ſoul that overflows.

" But all my head is ſtrewed
    With aſhes gray; and bent
Beneath the footfall rude,
    Steals forth my timid ſcent
Cruſhed from a leaf that curls, its wound to hide
    content.

"Why should my Lord delight
  In me? Behold how fair
His Garden is! How bright
  His Roses blowing there;
His Lilies all like Queens that know not toil nor care,

"In white calm peace on high
  Each rears a blossomed rod;
The Gentian low doth lie,
  Yet lifts from up the sod
An eye of steadfast blue that looks up straight to God.

"I wait my Lord to greet,
  I can but love and sigh;
I watch His Eye to meet,
  He can but pass me by;
And if His hasty Feet
Should crush me, it were sweet
  Beneath His Feet to die."

*   *   *

My Love, my Lord, has gone
  Down to His Garden fair,
To tell o'er His Roses, one by one,
  And to gather Lilies there;
Now will I rise and sing
  A Song which I have made
Unto my Lord the King;
  Nor will I be afraid
To ask Him of His Flowers that spring in sunshine and in shade.

" Oh, what are these Roses bright,
   That in Thy Garland blow?
These Roses red as blood,
   These Roses white as snow?"

" These blood-red Roses grew
   On a field with battle dyed;
These snow-white Roses strew
   A path that is not wide;
None seek that path but they who seek Him Who
   was crucified!"

" Oh, what are these Lilies tipped
   With fire, that sword-like gleam?
Oh, what are these Lilies dipped
   As in the pale moon-beam,
That quiver with unsteadfast light and shine as
   through a dream?"

" These fiery Spirits passed
   From earth through sword and flame;
These quiet Souls at last
   Through patience overcame:
These shine like stars on high, and these
   Have left no trace nor name;
I bind them in one Wreath because their triumph
   was the same."

" Oh, what are these Flowers that wake
   So cheerful to the morn,
All wet with tears of early dew;
   And these that droop forlorn,

With heavy drops of night drenched through?"
" Thefe little Flowers of cheerful hue
Familiar by the wayfide grew,
 And thefe among the corn;

" And thefe, that o'er a Ruin wave
 Their crimfon flag, in fight
Were wounded fore, yet ftill are brave
 To greet the fcent and fight;
And thefe I found upon a grave all wet with drops
 of night.

" And fome I have that will unfold
 When night is dufk and ftill,
And fome I have that keep their hold
 Upon the wind-fwept hill;
Thefe fhrink not from the fummer heat,
 They do not fear the cold,
And all of thefe I know for fweet,
 For patient, and for bold."

" Thou beareft Flowers within Thy Hand,
 Thou weareft on Thy Breaft
A Flower; now tell me which of thefe
 Thy Flowers Thou loveft beft;
Which wilt Thou gather to Thy Heart
 Beloved above the reft?"

" Should I not love my Flowers,
 My Flowers that bloom and pine,
Unfeen, unfought, unwatched for hours
 By any eyes but Mine?

"Should I not love my Flowers?
　　I love my Lilies tall,
My Marigolds with constant eyes,
Each Flower that blows, each Flower that dies
　　To Me, I love them all.

"I gather to a Heavenly bower
　　My Roses fair and sweet;
I hide within My Breast the Flower
　　That grows beside My Feet."

The Ascension of Christ.

NOTHING now is left to do,
　　All the labour is gone through,
　　Christ hath bought us with His Blood,
　　Proved the work, and found it good,
Sealed, and writ with iron pen,
The unutterable Amen.

Look not for the fiery car
Borne above the winds afar,
Where the Angel-horses beat
Golden air with flying feet,
Flaming by a path untrod
In among the stars of God.

As to earth, with no high name,
Nor like earthly Kings He came,
Now rejected of His Own,
Grandly quiet and alone

He returneth to His Rest,
Back into the FATHER's Breast.

Only by a chosen few
Who believe His Promise true,
Eat His Bread, and drink His Cup,
He is seen as He goes up,
Till the cloud, that waiting lies,
Veils Him from their yearning eyes.

On the pure lips, ere He passed,
Words of Blessing were the last.
His receding Hands, outspread,
Pour Redemption on their head.
But the cloud comes in between,
And the Form is no more seen.

Spake beside them, in their sight,
Two Men robed in shining white—
Why in wonder thus do ye
Gaze, O Men of Galilee?
Hence! nor from the Work refrain
Till your CHRIST shall come again.

Then into the world they fare,
And His Love goes with them there;
To life's daily tasks they turn,
And His secret Presence learn;
While they do His gracious Will
All is good and nothing ill.

After this the Judgment.

Comes a Day when on the earth
The new Kingdom shall have birth,
And with many a wondrous Sign
Judah shall arise and shine;
But the season and the hour,
These are in the FATHER's Power.

Now let us new comfort draw
From the Vision which they saw,
And ourselves example take
From the word those Angels spake,
Nor from the good work refrain
Till our CHRIST shall come again.

And if here, in light so dim,
Toil itself is sweet for Him,
If, when under clouds we go,
From the Cross true pleasures flow,
What if ever we should stand,
Crowned in the Celestial Land,
With the Saints at GOD's Right Hand!

After this the Judgment.

AS eager homebound Traveller to the goal,
    Or steadfast Seeker on an unsearched
        main,
   Or Martyr panting for an aureole,
My Fellow-pilgrims pass me, and attain
That hidden Mansion of perpetual Peace
  Where keen desire and hope dwell free from pain:

That Gate stands open of perennial ease;
　I view the Glory till I partly long,
Yet lack the fire of love which quickens these.
　O passing Angel, speed me with a song,
A melody of Heaven to reach my heart
　And rouse me to the race and make me strong;
Till in such music I take up my part,
　Swelling those Alleluias full of rest,
One, tenfold, hundredfold, with Heavenly art,
　Fulfilling north and south and east and west,
Thousand, ten thousandfold, innumerable,
　All blent in one yet each one manifest;
Each one distinguished and beloved as well
　As if no second voice in earth or Heaven
Were lifted up the Love of GOD to tell.
　Ah, Love of GOD, which Thine own Self hast
　　　given
To me most poor, and made me rich in love,
　Love that dost pass the tenfold seven times seven,
Draw Thou mine eyes, draw Thou my heart above,
　My treasure and my heart store Thou in Thee,
Brood over me with yearnings of a dove;
　Be Husband, Brother, closest Friend to me;
Love me as very mother loves her son,
　Her sucking firstborn, fondled on her knee:
Yea, more than mother loves her little one;
　For earthly even a mother may forget,
And feel no pity for its piteous moan;
　But Thou, O Love of GOD, remember yet,
Through the dry desert, through the waterflood,

After this the Judgment.

(Life, Death), until the great White Throne is set.
If now I am sick in chewing the bitter cud
  Of sweet past sin, though solaced by Thy Grace
And oft-times strengthened by Thy Flesh and
    Blood,
How shall I then stand up before Thy Face,
When from Thine Eyes repentance shall be hid
  And utmost Justice stand in Mercy's place:
When every sin I thought, or spoke, or did,
  Shall meet me at the inexorable Bar,
And there be no man standing in the mid
  To plead for me; while star fallen after star
With Heaven and earth are like a ripened shock,
  And all time's mighty works and wonders are
Consumed as in a moment; when no rock
  Remains to fall on me, no tree to hide,
But I stand all creation's gazing-stock,
  Exposed and comfortless on every side,
Placed trembling in the final balances
  Whose poise this hour, this moment, must be
    tried?
Ah, Love of GOD, if greater Love than this
  Hath no man, that a MAN die for His Friend,
And if such Love of Love Thine own Love is,
  Plead with Thyself, with me, before the end;
Redeem me from the irrevocable past;
  Pitch Thou Thy Presence round me to defend;
Yea, seek with piercèd Feet, yea, hold me fast
  With piercèd Hands—Whose Wounds were
    made by Love;

Not what I am, remember what Thou waſt
  When darkneſs hid from Thee Thy Heavens
    above,
And ſin Thy FATHER's Face, while Thou didſt
    drink
  The bitter Cup of Death, didſt taſte thereof
For every man ; while Thou waſt nigh to ſink
  Beneath the intenſe, intolerable rod,
Grown ſick of Love : not what I am, but think
  Thy Life then ranſomed mine, my GOD, my GOD.

The Embracing of the Body of Chriſt by His Virgin-Mother.

THOU uncovered Corſe, WORD of the
    Living ONE,
  Self-doomed to be uplifted on the
    bitter Tree,
Thereon to die, Thy patient Will, Eternal SON,
  And thence in Love draw all men unto Thee.

Which of Thy holy Members is without a Wound?
  The thorny Wreath Thy bleſſed Brow embraces
    faſt ;
No place whereon to lay Thee, weary Head, was
    found—
  But Thou ſhalt reſt within a Tomb at laſt.

O Lips, which once with ſweeteſt Words did
    overflow,
  Freſh from ſharp vinegar and bitterneſs of gall ;

O Cheeks, how often turned to many a smiter's blow,
    And spat upon in Pilate's Judgment-hall.

By hands of men made helpless on the dreadful
    Beam,
  O Hands, of man creative, how were ye pierced
    through;
Yet all outstretched, ye reach e'en Hades to redeem,
    And give the first transgressor help anew.

O Mouth all sweet, no guile was ever found in Thee,
  And yet, alas! by traiterous kiss wast Thou be-
    trayed;
O blessed Feet, that walking on the stormy sea
    All water hallowed as the waves obeyed.

Where is the chorus of Thy sick ones, O my Son,
  All those infirm whom Thou didst heal, the
    upraised dead?
To draw the nails from Hands and Feet, there
    came not one
    Of all the crowds whom Thou hast comforted

Only came Nicodemus, he who sought by night,
  And Joseph kind, whose rocky Tomb Thy Bed
    shall be,
Whither, to sleep a Lion's sleep in awful might,
    My Son, how soon will they be bearing Thee.

Now Thou art borne to me from yon sharp Cross
    of pain,
    And heavily upon these Mother-arms art laid;

These arms which bare Thee long ago, and once again
   A lowly resting place for Thee are made.

I, who first swathèd Thee, Thy Grave-clothes now will bind,
   Giver of Life, Thou liest dead before me now:
Tears laved Thee at Thy Birth; far hotter tears I find
     To wash the Death-drops from Thy pallid Brow.

High in these arms Maternal Thou didst leap,
   Thou Who wast born of me, this weary world to save;
O bitter Funerals! that I who hushed Thy Sleep,
   Must wail this doleful Passion o'er Thy Grave.

The Hymn of Aurelius Prudentius Clemens,

On the Eighth Day before the Kalends of January,
(*Christmas Day.*)

HEREFORE doth the circling Sun
Cease the downward course to run?
Is it that the CHRIST is born,
Lengthening out the path of morn?

Ah, how swift the hurrying day
Seemed of late to fleet away!
Almost might the torch appear
Quenched, of the declining year!

Now the Heaven in livelier glow
Flames o'er gladdening Earth below;
Mounting now the daybeam shines
Gradual on the former lines.

Spring to light, All-lovely CHILD!
Spring from Mother undefiled,
Maid from spousal contact free,
Bearing GOD and MAN in Thee.

WORD of GOD! though Thou be sprung,
Uttered by the FATHER'S Tongue,
Yet in the Paternal Breast
WISDOM found an earliest rest;

She did heaven and earth ordain,
Night and day, and all their train;
At the Word their paths they trod,
Duteous—for the WORD was GOD.

But, the world's foundation laid,
All things in due order made,
He Who wrought them all at will
In His Father's Bosom still

Rested, till revolving years
Fill their thousandfold careers,

And **Himſelf** in mercy then
Seek this ſinful world of men.

For the tribes of loſt mankind,
Vanity-adoring, blind,
Worſhipped as their gods alone
Senſeleſs braſs, and wood, and **ſtone.**

While they thus unfaithful ſtrayed,
They the Spoiler's prey were made,
Prone their ſlaviſh life to ſteep,
Hopeleſs, in the fiery deep.

But the **CHRIST** would **not** that all
Nations **from** His **Realm** ſhould fall,
Leſt the glorious Structure wrought
By His **FATHER come to** nought.

He aſſumed a **mortal Frame,**
That, ariſing with the ſame,
He might rend Death's iron **ban,**
To His **FATHER** bear a **MAN.**

This is that great natal Day,
When amid the quickening clay
Warm the Informing Spirit ſtirred,
Breathing into Fleſh the **WORD.**

Feel'ſt thou not, imperial **Maid,**
All thy ſorrows overpaid,
All thy Maidenhood's pure bliſs
Overbleſt by Birth like This?

O what mighty Joys ſhall come
From that chaſte and holy Womb,
Whence the new-born ages bright
Forth proceed in golden light!

At that wondrous Infant-cry
Spring o'erſpreads the wintry ſky;
From her gloomy trance Thy Birth
Wakens up regenerate earth.

Well I ween that gracious morn
Saw unnumbered flowers new-born;
E'en parched Afric's ſandy ſhore
Fragrant nard and nectar bore.

All things barbarous, hard, and wild,
Felt Thy Birth, Celeſtial CHILD!
O'er her breaſt the dry rock drew
Flowery veil of vernal hue:

Honey from the cliff wells down:
Spicy gums the hard oak crown:
Mid the ſere and barren fields
Odorous balm the tamariſk yields.

O thrice holy humble ſtall,
Cradle of the King of all,
Ever to His Saints endeared,
By the ſpeechleſs race revered!

Yes! the unreaſoning kind adore,
Ignorant though of holy lore;

Thoughtful erſt of food alone,
Now their preſent LORD they own.

Yet, while Thee with faithful mind
Heathens, and the inferior kind
Seek, and on the unreaſoning race
Falls ſome glimmering of Thy Grace,

They, the Fathers' choſen line,
Hate and ſpurn the BABE Divine:
As with ſorceries dark inſpired,
Or demoniac frenzy fired.

Why thus headlong ruſh to ſin?
Own, if thought thy heart within
'Mid thy wild deluſion ſprings,
Here the King of all thy kings.

Him Whom humble cattle-ſtall,
Mortal Mother, cradle ſmall,
Weak and wailing Infancy,
Gave the Nations' LORD to be,

Sinner! thou ſhalt view on high
Throned upon the glittering ſky,
While with fruitleſs tears and ſore
Thou thy treſpaſs ſhalt deplore.

When through Heaven the Trump Divine
Gives for earth to burn the ſign,
And uptorn Creation rolls
Shattered from the blazing poles,

He shall from His Throne repay
Each man's doom for each man's way:
Heaven to these, and quenchless Light;
Hell to those, and rayless Night.

Then, Judæa! to thy loss,
Feel the thunder of the Cross:
Death his prey from hand of thine
Might receive, but must resign.

The Two Covenants: an Allegory.

ARISE! ye Children chosen of the LORD,
    And hasten for your life;
Nor tarry in the land of GOD abhorred,
    Where all His Plagues are rife;
Nor fondly gaze upon the accursèd spot;
Death lurks in Egypt's pleasures—touch them not.

But first with Sacred BLOOD be ye baptized,
  That in this awful night
The dread Destroyer, by that Sign apprized,
  May heed the holy sight:
Behold the LAMB! from the world's morning slain,
Make you His Pains your peace, His Grief your
    gain.

Aye, mark Him on your homes, your household
    ways,
  Him always, First and Last,

Who by His Love can such deliverance raise
  Till the death-stroke be past:
Then sheltered by that Love draw near, and take
Of the mysterious Feast such Love can make.

The bitter taste of penitential woe
  Makes pardoning Grace most meet
For cleansèd hearts that no ill leaven know,
  Only the savour sweet
Of meek obedience, and of constant will
That GOD in them His Purpose should fulfil.

And then, will shoe-clad feet and staff in hand,
  Stand ready for the flight
From dying Egypt to the living Land
  Of freedom and of light;
And while ye safely pass o'er sea and plain,
A much observèd night let this remain.

  *   *   *   *

Still are ye faring through life's middle space,
  The space of forty years?
Is the world's wilderness a dreary place
  Of perils and of fears?
Seems it a long way to the end of life,
A weary journey, and a ceaseless strife?

Children no more—but Chosen People still!
  GOD's Cloud is safest sorrow:
His Banquet lies outspread; take now your fill,
  And trust Him for to-morrow:

The Two Covenants.

Ye wist not what It is; but It is sent
To stay your famished Souls: be ye content.

O Marvel ever sweet, and ever new!
  To rise up morn by morn,
To wander forth, a Flock forlorn and few,
  Toil-stained and travel-worn;
To find the Wealth of Heaven on this bare earth,
And Canaan's plenty 'mid the desert's dearth.

What though the wondrous Thing should melt
    away
  Upon the scorching waste—
Have ye not stored a Blessing for to-day
  Whose joy ye still can taste?
All purest Pleasures that your Souls can need
Gathered in one—'tis Angels' Food indeed.

God's Measure is—Enough: enough of toil,
  Enough of rest and calm,
Enough of this world's care and fret and foil,
  Enough of His world's Balm:
E'en of Himself enough, in joy and woe,
Till Him in all His Fulness ye shall know.

   * * * *

O weary Pilgrims! nearly Home at last,
  Close upon Jordan's shore,
What are your troubles now that they are past?
  What are your joys in store?
Only keep closer yet beneath His Hand,
Who brings you to the borders of His Land.

Do ye look back upon the far-off days
   When firſt ye knew the LORD?
And went aſide from Egypt's evil ways
   Unto His Paſchal Board;
And gained a Guardian through the dangerous time
Of morning's early fluſh and golden prime?

Or think ye on the troublous wilderneſs,
   Its pitfalls and its ſnares;
Your faithleſs fears, your cries of deep diſtreſs,
   Your ſorrows and your cares;
And how the priceleſs Manna GOD-beſtowed
Lay, 'Meat enough,' along your Heavenward road?

Still to the laſt muſt your faint Souls be fed,
   GOD ſtill prepares a Feaſt;
Upon His Altar lies the Holy Bread,
   The portion of the Prieſt—
Yea, and of thoſe who, prieſtlike, ſtand and wait
Abſolvèd, cleanſèd, pure, within the gate.

GOD, Who through life hath fed you to this day,
   Defend you to the end;
His living Bread be ſtill your Staff and Stay;
   His Angel ſtill your Friend;
Till daylight fades, and hues of evening fall,
Till ſhadows ceaſe, and GOD is All in All.

Stanzas.

Persecution.

THERE was silence in the Heavens
    When the Son of Man was led
  From the Garden to the Judgment;
    Sudden silence, strange, and dread!
All along the empyreal coasts
On their knees the immortal Hosts
Watched, with sad and wondering eyes,
That tremendous Sacrifice.

There was silence in the Heavens
    When the Priest his garment tore;
Silence when the Twain accursèd
    Their false witness faintly bore:
Silence (though a tremor crept
O'er their ranks) the Angels kept
While that Judge, dismayed though proud,
Washed his hands before the crowd.

But when Christ His Cross was bearing,
    Fainting oft, by slow degrees,
Then went forth the Angelic thunder
    Of Legions rising from their knees:
Each bright Spirit grasped a brand;
And Lightning flashed from band to band:
An instant more had launched them forth
Avenging terrors to the earth.

Then from God there fell a Glory
　　Round and o'er that multitude ;
And by every fervent Angel
　　With hushing hand Another stood :
Another, never seen before,
Stood one moment and no more—
" Peace ! Brethren, peace ! to us is given
Suffering.　Vengeance is for Heaven !"

Law and Grace.

IT is not true that unto us, enrolled
　　Within Christ's Band, the Law exists
　　　no longer :
But this is true, that we, who sank of old
Oppressed beneath that armour's weight of gold,
　　Sustain it now in glory, being stronger !

The Form remains : but is a form no more
　　To eyes inspired, that see
　　Through bondage Liberty,
And in His earthly Shape their God adore.
　　To Love, all things are Love :
　　　To Grace, all things are Grace :
　　And humble Faith can never move
　　　In an unholy place !

Within, but not beneath the Law we dwell :
　　That wall, of old our prison's circuit, now,
　　Girding the citied mountain's sovereign brow,
Is but the bulwark of man's citadel :

Large views beyond are given;
Safe views of all the earth, and healing airs of
    Heaven.

Within the Temple of the Law we ſtand,
    As once without it ſtood
    That awe-ſtruck multitude;
And on the marble Tables lay our hand:
There, like the Prieſt of old, our GOD we meet,
And ſtand up boldly by the Mercy-Seat.

Prayer of Hildebert to the Holy Trinity.

To the Everlaſting Father.

FIRST and Laſt of faith's receiving,
    Source and Sea of man's believing,
    GOD, Whoſe Might is all-potential,
    GOD, Whoſe Truth is Truth's eſſential,
Good ſupreme in Thy Subſiſting,
Good in all Thy ſeen Exiſting;
Over all things, all things under,
Touching all, from all aſunder;
Centre Thou, but not intruded,
Compaſſing, and yet included;
Over all, and not aſcending,
Under all, but not depending;
Over all, the world ordaining,
Under all, the world ſuſtaining;

All without, in all surrounding,
All within, in Grace abounding;
Inmost, yet not comprehended,
Outer still, and not extended;
Over, yet on nothing founded,
Under, but by space unbounded;
Omnipresent, yet in-dwelling,
Self-impelled, the world impelling;
Force, nor Fate's predestination
Sways Thee to one alteration;
Ours to-day, Thyself for ever,
Still commencing, ending never;
Past with Thee is time's beginning,
Present all its future winning;
With Thy Counsel's first ordaining
Comes Thy Counsel's last attaining;
One the Light's first radiance darting
And the Elements' departing.

To the Eternal Son.

NEXT in Revelation's sequel,
Co-eternal SON, Co-equal,
FATHER's Light, and FATHER's Feature,
All-creating, yet a Creature,
With our flesh Thyself enduing,
All our righteousness ensuing;
With immortal Glory shining,
Yet to death and time declining;

Prayer of Hildebert.

Man and God united ever,
God in Man confounded never.
Not Thyself to flesh converting,
All the Godhead still asserting;
All the God to Manhood taking,
Yet the Manhood not forsaking;
One with God by conformation,
Less than God by Incarnation;
Man in substance of Thy Mother,
Yet than God Thyself no other.
Thus two Natures' wondrous union
Stands in unimpaired communion;
What He was ere worlds were dated,
That He was on earth created;
He our only Mediator,
None but He our Legislator;
Born for us, and circumcisèd,
Dead, and buried, and baptizèd;
Fell on sleep, to Hell descending,
Rose again to Life unending;
Thence to Judgment comes to call men
Who Himself was judged for all men.

To the Holy Spirit.

God, of Glory unabated,
Not begotten, nor created,
Spirit, Son nor Father neither,
Yet proceedest Thou from either,

From no Heavenly source exterior,
With no Quality inferior,
From Eternity no lower,
Substance, Majesty, or Power.

FATHER One in Gospel-story,
One the First-begotten's Glory,
One the HOLY GHOST's Procession—
Three, but One to Faith's confession.
Each Himself is GOD alonely,
Yet not Three, but One GOD only.
In this Oneness, worshipped truly,
Three in One I worship duly;
In their Persons ever Three,
In their Substance Unity;
None of Whom is less than Other,
None is greater than Another:
In each One no variation,
Into each no transmutation;
Each is GOD, and yet no blending,
Everlasting, without ending.

* * *

STRONGHOLD safe of Judah's Lion,
Take, O take me to thee, Sion!
Light's own GOD thy light's renewing,
From the Cross thy lintels hewing;
Living gems thy walls' foundation,
Praise thy gates, thy streets Salvation.
In that City sunshine vernal
Dwells for ever, Peace eternal;

There no taint of sin remaining,
No defect and no complaining;
Stunted none and none unsightly,
All conformed to Jesus brightly.
City of time-sainted Sages
Built upon the rock of ages,
O'er the stormy world's commotions
To Thee all my Soul's devotions
Waft I, for thy Love expiring,
Peaceful Rest and Joys untiring.
Feasts how bright thy Saints are keeping,
Without mixture, without weeping;
Heart to heart what love entwining;
With what stones the city shining,
Jacinth or Chalcedon be it,
They shall know who live to see it.

The Vision of the Glory.

For the Feast of the Transfiguration, August 6.

BRIGHT upon the vested Altar, partners of the early morn,
 Flame the Tapers in the stillness of the rosy August dawn;
Twin in number, twin in nature, earthly matter shining bright
With the flame which, uncommingled, sheds the radiance of its light,

Uncontained, yet cloſe united—undivided each,
   yet whole,
As the human fleſh is wedded with the reaſonable
   Soul:

While behind, diſtinct, myſterious, caſting ſhadow
   from above,
Spreads the Croſs its arms of **Mercy and of** all-
   embracing Love.

* * * *

Light of Light, from Heaven deſcending to thy
   earthly Altar-throne,
Lo! we call Thee, we receive Thee: Maſter, come
   unto Thine Own;

For on Tabor ſhone the GODHEAD through its
   Fleſhly Veil to-day,
And the darkneſs comprehends Thee, and the
   ſhadows flee away.

On the Mount, the miſts diſperſing, cleared the
   Viſion for a ſpace,
And weak man beheld the GODHEAD, unforbidden,
   Face to face;

Saw the Lowly MANHOOD kindle with a Glory
   not its Own,
As the GODHEAD, Uncreated, from its Human
   Veſture ſhone;

Saw Him there, but not in terror, as in olden time He came
In the blackneſs and the tempeſt and the mountain wrapt in flame;

Saw the covenanted meeting of the Old World and the New,
Every Word confirmed and witneſſed in the mouth of Three and Two;

Saw the Two of all the Old World, of the New World ſaw the Three,
Law and Prophets, chief Apoſtle, and the Sons of Zebedee.

Sounds the Voice through all the ages—Man has ſinned, and Man muſt die;
GOD has ſpoken in His Juſtice—Can the GOD of Juſtice lie?

Love takes up the Challenge, pleading—GOD is Love, and GOD has won
Pardon through the Blood-atoning of the Well-beloved SON.

GOD is Judge, and GOD the Ranſom: Heaven and earth in one rejoice;
Huſhed the earthquake; paſt the tempeſt; preſent is the ſtill ſmall Voice.

   * * * *

Bright upon the veſted Altar burns the Tapers' ſteady light,

For the Day-ſtar has ariſen through the ſhadows
    of the night,

And they ſhow in type and figure what the eye of
    faith may ſee
By the light of Tabor Mountain in an awful
    Myſtery :

In that Cloud we fear to enter : it is full of light
    within,
For the LAMB there kindles brightly the Burnt-
    Sacrifice for ſin :

And we tremble as we worſhip; for, behold! in
    lowly guiſe,
Under Form of earthly Subſtance, lies the bloodleſs
    Sacrifice ;

And the Soul flies back in memory to the Manger
    in the ſtall
Where in Form of earthly Subſtance lay the GOD
    and LORD of all :

GOD and MAN He willed for our ſakes in One
    PERSON to combine ;
GOD and MAN He comes for our ſakes under Form
    of Bread and Wine,

That His Pure and Sinleſs MANHOOD, raiſed
    from death, no more to die,
May appeal from earth to Heaven at the Throne
    of GOD on high.

Therefore on the vested Altar burns the Tapers'
    steady flame,
Setting forth the Two-fold Natures wherewith
    CHRIST the SAVIOUR came,

Setting forth the Heavenly Substance which the
    faithful Soul intent
Must discern beneath the Substance of the fearful
    Sacrament;

That the fainting may gain vigour, and the sickly
    be made whole,
If the hem of that bright Garment do but touch
    upon the Soul.

The Life of Christ.

From the Latin.

IN Wisdom, GOD the LORD,
    Who by His potent Word
        The Universe controls,
    Beheld us as we lay
To guilt and grief a prey,
    And pitied our lost Souls.
From His high Throne above
The FATHER sent in Love
    His Messenger to earth,
That all things might be done
As promised to the SON
    Before His wondrous Birth.

Soon as the Angel spoke
The Virgin's joy awoke—
    Hail! favoured One, for thou
(Said he) shalt bear a SON,
Both GOD and MAN in One,
    To Whom shall all things bow.
Nor was it long delayed
Before that Mother-Maid
    Embraced her Holy CHILD,
The Light of faithful men
Cheering the world again
    With Virtue undefiled.

The Eternal SON of GOD was born
A MAN, on that illustrious morn;
He Whom the boundless Heavens obey
Then in the lowly Manger lay,
And then awoke the exultant Hymn
From raptured choirs of Cherubim.
No proud ones saw the glorious light
That burst upon the Shepherds' sight,
But, Jesse's Rod in bloom, behold
With Myrrh and Frankincense and Gold,
Fit Gifts, the Magi come from far,
Led on by Bethlehem's Herald-star!

Born for men, He was indeed
Circumcised as Abraham's seed;
Him His Mother gladly brings
With the appointed offerings;
Simeon takes Him in his arms,
Spared to see the SAVIOUR's Charms,

The Life of Christ.

Who ere long in Jordan's river,
    In a glorious Mystery,
Washed away our sins for ever,
    If repentant we shall be,
If in the Baptismal wave
We shall own His Power to save.

Soon followed Acts of glorious Fame—
    See wine from water flowing;
Eyes for the blind, feet for the lame,
    Tongues for the dumb are growing:
The deaf find ears; diseases fly;
    The very dead show motion;
The Devils shun His piercing Eye;
    He calms the storm-tossed ocean:
Five thousand feast on what He gives,
    Five loaves and two small fishes;
Blood is staunched; and the poor child lives,
    As faith maternal wishes.

Now, as Holy Scripture reads,
On the Cross our Shepherd bleeds,
    Yielding up His precious Breath;
Spotless LAMB of GOD, He lies
Dying as our Sacrifice,
    Winning victory over death!
Dawns at length the appointed day;
Hell flies open; Death gives way;
    Christians see their Risen LORD:
Oh, the triumphs of that hour!
Miracles of saving Power
    Wait upon His gracious Word.

Having thus subdued His Foes,
Up to Heaven the SAVIOUR rose,
   Glory of our ransomed nature:
All Dominion is His own,
One with GOD upon the Throne,
   LORD and King of every creature.

Gift of His transcendent Merit,
Soon came down the Promised SPIRIT,
   Fount of living Consolation,
Fitting chosen men for teaching,
With new tongues and power of preaching
   Truth and Love to every nation.

Ye Saints, with faithful spirit sing
New songs to your exalted King:
The shades of night are melting fast,
And morning light will come at last—
   Raise your joyous eyes
   To the glowing skies;
   For He comes to bless
   With more than primal happiness.

Thy Daughter is dead, trouble not the Master.

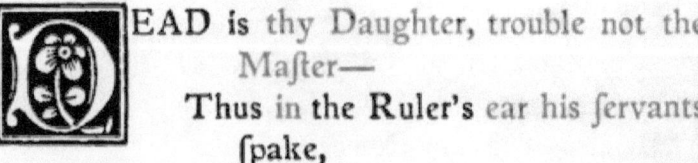

DEAD is thy Daughter, trouble not the
   Master—
   Thus in the Ruler's ear his servants
   spake,

Thy Daughter is dead.

While tremblingly he urged the SAVIOUR faster
  Up the green slope from that white margined
    Lake.

The soft wave weltered, and the breeze came sighing
  Out of the oleander thickets red;
He only heard a breath that gasped in dying,
  Or 'Trouble not the Master—She is dead.'

Trouble Him not. Ah! are these words beseeming
  The desolation of that awful day,
When love's vain fancies, hope's delusive dreaming
  Are over—and the life has fled for aye?

We need Him most when the dear eyes are closing,
  When on the cheek the shadow lieth strong,
When the soft lines are set in that reposing
  That never Mother cradled with a song.

Then most we need the gentle Human Feeling
  That throbs with all our sorrows and our fears,
And that great Love Divine its light revealing
  In short bright flashes through a mist of tears.

Then most we need the Voice that while it weepeth
  Yet hath a solemn undertone that saith—
Weep not, thy darling is not dead, but sleepeth;
  Only believe, for I have conquered death.

Then most we need the thoughts of Resurrection,
  Not the life here, 'mid pain, and sin, and woe,
But ever in the fulness of Perfection,
  To walk with Him in robes as white as snow.

Thy Daughter is dead.

When in our nurſery garden falls a bloſſom,
    And as we kiſs the hand and fold the feet,
We cannot ſee the lamb in Abraham's boſom,
    Nor hear the footfall in the golden ſtreet.

When all is ſilent—neither moan nor cheering,
    The huſh of hope, the end of all our cares—
All but that harp above, beyond our hearing,
    Then moſt we need to trouble Him with prayers.

Did He not enter in when that cold Sleeper
    Lay ſtill, with pulſeleſs heart and leaden eyes,
Put calmly forth each loud tumultuous weeper,
    And take her by the hand and bid her riſe?

Come to us, SAVIOUR! in our lone dejection,
    Speak calmly to our wild and paſſionate grief,
Bring us the hopes and thoughts of Reſurrection,
    Bring us the comfort of a true Belief.

Come! with that Human Voice that breaks in weeping,
    Come! with that awful Tenderneſs Divine,
Come! tell us that they are not dead but ſleeping,
    But gone before to Thee, for they are Thine.

The Shadow and the Substance.

AMARIA proud and glorious,
    Rival City of God,
Thou standest still victorious,
    Free from the Syrian's rod.

The horse and rider charge in vain,
    They hear a Phantom-shout;
A mighty army on the plain
    Flies, routed without rout.

The Spear-man fiercest in assault
    Flings spear and shield away,
And flees, as one fears to halt,
    The imaginary fray.

The Leper drinks from cups of gold,
    And lies where princes laid;
His loathsome fingers jewels hold
    For dainty nobles made.

'Tis rout, and shame, and ruin all
    With haughty Syria's men—
There's plenty in the leaguered Hall,
    Pale famine feasts again.

    *   *   *

Jerusalem, the Righteous,
    City of Christ and God,

Thou art in Heaven more glorious
    Thou art the Saints' abode.

I aſk Thee, God, the life to live
    Of holy Saints below;
I aſk Thee, Holy Ghost, to give
    The power of faith to ſhow;

I aſk Thee, Christ, on earth to fight
    Againſt the Powers of air;
I aſk Thee that in craven flight
    No Child of Thine may ſhare;

I aſk Thee that no Phantom-voice
    May ſhake my truſt in Thee;
I rather aſk the Champion's choice,
    The Martyr's conſtancy.

Jeruſalem, the Glorious,
    Theſe, theſe ſhall dwell and ſhine,
O'er ſin and ſelf victorious,
    True Citizens of thine.

Theſe, reſting on Thy Boſom, Lord,
    The Spirit's Jewels wear;
In Faith and Love they took the Word,
    And Faith and Love they are.

Surgit Christus cum Trophaeo.

An Easter Sequence.

CHRIST with mighty **Triumph** rises!
All the gates of Death surprises!
   From a **Lamb** a **Lion** strong:
Hell through all its depths is quaking;
Earth through all its graves is shaking;
   Raise on high the Victor's song!

Hail the LAMB! adore Him greatly,
Who upon the Cross but lately
   For His helpless Sheep was slain;
By His Death He brought Salvation,
To the lost of every nation
   Showed the Way of Life again.

He alone His Passion bearing,
None His mighty Grief was sharing
   Save repentant Magdalene—
Tell us Mary, 'mid thy weeping,
By the Cross thy station keeping,
   All the Woes that thou hast seen—

I beheld the LORD's Anointed
Bear the Stripes to sin appointed,
   Lifted on His Cross to die;
Saw the LORD His Thorn-crown wearing,
Grossest insult meekly bearing,
   Pale His Cheek, and sunk His Eye:

Through His Hands the nails were driven,
By the ſpear His Side was riven,
   Then He bowed His ſacred Head,
And His Soul to GOD commended,
All His bitter Paſſion ended—
   Lo! the LORD of Life was dead.

Tell us, Mary, all thy doing,
Still thy taſk of love purſuing,
   When the SAVIOUR's Soul was fled—
By the martyred Mother keeping,
While I ſoothed, I ſhared her weeping,
   Till unto her home I led:

Then upon the hard earth falling,
Mourned I o'er that Scene appaling,
   Mourned my SAVIOUR's bitter Doom;
Then the fragrant ſpices blending,
Love's laſt precious care attending,
   Hied me to the ſacred Tomb:

Search for my Beloved making,
Him for Whom my heart was breaking,
   All my ſearching proved in vain;
Then my Soul was newly troubled,
All my grief and care was doubled,
   And my tears burſt forth again.

Weep not, Mary, now unduly
CHRIST the LORD hath riſen truly,
   Broke the ſeal and 'ſcaped the ward—

The Childhood of Christ.

Words of comfort ye have ſpoken;
And indeed no ſingle token
   Saw I of the Riſen Lord:

Shining Angels told the ſtory—
Here is not the Lord of Glory,
   He is riſen, as He ſaid;
See unwound each linen Cerement
And yon token of endearment
   Which enwrapped His ſacred Head.

Yea, indeed, the Lord is riſen!
Burſting from His narrow Priſon;
   Hope in Him, ye Sons of men!
Riſen Saviour, leave us never,
Show us Love and Pity ever;
   Alleluia! Lord, Amen.

The Childhood of Christ.

WHAT earth appeared to Angel eyes
That Sabbath morn in Paradiſe,
When man before his Father
   ſtood,
And God beheld that all was good—

When Nature, guiltleſs yet of ſtain,
Returned her Maker's ſmile again,
And over all created things
Lingered the Spirit's brooding Wings—

So fair, ſo freſh, ſo free from taint,
Beyond all mortal ſkill to paint,
So calm in growing Strength ſerene,
The Holy Childhood muſt have been—

A Garden fed with Heavenly Dew,
Where all things lovely bloomed and grew,
Where Knowledge both of good and ill
But left the heart more holy ſtill.

But vainly would we ſeek to raiſe
The veil that ſhrouds CHRIST'S early Days,
Each wondrous Act, each Word ſublime
That beautified that glorious Prime.

A few brief lines of Sacred Writ
Contain the whole we know of it;
And there the eye of faith may ſee
The lowly Home in Galilee,

Where daily in His Mother's ſight
He grew in Wiſdom and in Might;
The path of meek Obedience trod,
In favour both with man and GOD.

He grew in Wiſdom! who can weigh
The meaning which thoſe Words convey;
Or trace the deep myſterious line
Between the Human and Divine?

We only know the daily growth
Was that of Mind and Body both,

Until the Perfect Childhood paſſed
Into the Perfect MAN at laſt.

Yet one recorded ſcene alone
A Glory o'er thoſe years hath thrown,
Revealing to His Mother's Soul
A Realm beyond her Love's control:

Teaching both her, who meekly heard
And treaſured every ſacred Word,
And all His Church, from age to age
Who read them in the Goſpel page,

That far above all earthly claim
Was that great Work for which He came,
As far beyond all earthly tie,
The Sonſhip of His DEITY.

And if to thoſe who love Him moſt,
His Preſence for awhile be loſt,
And on Life's crowded road they find
That they have left their LORD behind,

Let them each erring ſtep retrace,
And ſeek Him through His Means of Grace,
Who, in His FATHER'S Houſe of Prayer,
Still doth His Work of Mercy there.

We would see Jesus.

NCE, amid the wondrous Story of those
  thirty years and three,
 When the GODHEAD's veilèd Glory
  shone through our humanity,
Burst a sunlight transitory o'er that sorrow-darkened
  sea.

'Twas within the Holy City, briefest space ere
  He deceased,
In His world-atoning pity Paschal Sacrifice and
  Priest,
Chaunting psalm and solemn ditty, came the
  people to the Feast.

Branch of palm before Him flinging, marched the
  multitude along,
Little children with their singing joined the unpre-
  sumptuous throng,
Joyous Jubilates ringing filled Jerusalem with song.

Then it was from those far Islands dear to story
  and to fame,
From the classic vales and highlands dowered with
  a deathless name,
Breaking late the world's cold silence, Strangers
  with their question came.

We would see Him!—Him Whose Finger stills
  the storm upon the wave,

Him for Whom the thousands linger, health and
    benison to crave,
Him the glorious Godlike Bringer of corruption
    from the Grave.

Oh! then, for that bitter weeping o'er His own
    dear Nation's doom,
Came a smile of gladness creeping like a sunbeam
    on the gloom,
Like a radiant Angel keeping vigil o'er a dreary
    tomb.

For, beyond the darkening vision of that lordly
    Temple's fall,
Of the stern day of decision, and the Roman battle-
    call,
Rose a gleam of Light elysian, of a Day that
    dawned for all:

When from Sinim and from Thulé, from the
    Islands of the Sea,
With their Sacrifices duly, with their gold and
    silver free,
Owning His Allegiance truly, Princes to His
    House should flee.

And His Soul, through myriad ages, through the
    travail of the years,
Solved the riddle of the Sages, heard the music of
    the spheres,
In the glad advancing stages of a world that knows
    no tears.

He, Who, with His Sire Coeval, looked on Earth
 as firſt it ſtood,
Saw return the hours primeval, ſaw the Univerſe
 renewed
By the taming of the Evil, and the triumph of the
 Good :

Earth's great murmur huſhed for ever ; all the
 ſtrife, and all the pain,
All the fruitleſs wild endeavour for unſatisfying
 gain
Swallowed up in Joy's broad river, ſwelling to a
 boundleſs main.

But a Shadow dark and fearful ere that Light
 before Him lay,
Of an Agony all tearful, and a dark untrodden
 Way
With no friendly voices cheerful, brightened by no
 Heavenly Ray.

And His Human Soul was troubled, like the
 troubling of the deep,
When the gale, with force redoubled, laſhes in a
 ſudden ſweep
Wiſps of foam that danced and bubbled, to a wild
 and angry leap.

And, could the Unchanging waver, ſeemed it as
 the Fiend had power,
Working aye in our disfavour, man's bright Hope
 to overlower,

Should He say, the world's Sole SAVER—
    FATHER! save Me from this hour?

But, while listening Angels wonder, weeping o'er
    earth's sinful frame,
Though His Heart be rent asunder, stands GOD's
    Purpose without blame—
Hark! amid the answering thunder—FATHER!
    glorify Thy Name.

Be it so! Who suffers for us, answer to His
    Prayer be given!
By the universal chorus let the firmament be riven,
While the ages travel o'er us, glorified with Him
    in Heaven.

Faith.

AITH is the dawning of Day
        Where darkness was before,
    The rising of a solar ray
        To set in night no more.

Faith lights an Eye within the Soul
    From earth to Heaven that turns,
And there, where wheels of Glory roll,
    Admires, adores, and burns.

Faith plants an Ear that hears the Hymn
    Of everlasting praise,
Which sainted Souls and Seraphim
    In Alleluias raise.

Faith yields a Senſe of life and love
   Upborne on wings of prayer,
Swift as an eagle or a dove
   That cleaves the liquid air.

Faith gives a Hand, that holds the heart
   Within the myſtic veil,
Faſt by that Friend who will not part
   From thoſe who will not fail.

Faith feeds that Fire whoſe holy flame
   Illuminates my road,
With all the Glories of His Name,
   Who deigns to be my GOD.

Faith fans each phaſis of the fight
   Which ſin and ſelf deſtroys—
CHRIST changing weakneſs into Might,
   And ſorrows into Joys.

Faith leads me onward to the Croſs,
   And through it to a Crown,
When purified from all the droſs
   That weighs the Spirit down.

Faith lifts the Glaſs which ſhows ſo well,
   In lines of weal and woe,
Thoſe twofold worlds of Heaven and Hell,
   Above me, and below.

Faith is the Subſtance of my Hope,
   The Evidence of things

Faith.

Where Angels fathom not the scope,
   But shade it with their wings.

Faith is the Prop on which we lean
   In darkness or distress,
Far oftener felt and known, than seen
   Throughout this wilderness.

Faith opens amidst wastes of sand
   A Fountain fresh and fair,
Whose Waters, rising at Command,
   Annihilate despair.

Faith is a Compass never wrong,
   Nor swerving from its Pole;
It cheers the weak, directs the strong,
   And gladdens every Soul.

Faith is the Charm that keeps our sight
   From wandering by the way;
It studs with stars the brow of night,
   Or turns it into day.

Faith is the Talisman of Power
   No force can ever break,
No beasts of prey can e'er devour,
   Nor sorcery ever shake.

Faith is the Gem without a flaw
   Derived alone from GOD,
The Ransom of His broken Law,
   Bought with and bathed in Blood.

Faith is the Iris arching Heaven,
  Though gathering clouds are round,
The Token glad of guilt forgiven,
  Of bondage thus unbound.

Faith takes her Balances of gold,
  And weighs with skill sublime
Eternal Happiness untold,
  Against the dream of time.

O Lord, increase this Grace in me
  That with each fleeting breath
I more and more may know of Thee,
  And hail the hand of Death.

So Faith shall in Fruition end
  And Grace in Glory cease,
Where Praise her powers can never spend
  Nor aught disturb their peace.

In Youth I died.

IN Youth I died, in Maiden bloom;
  With gentle hand Death touched my
    cheek,
    And with his touch there came to me
  A Spirit calm and meek.

He took from me all wish to stay;
He was so kind, I feared him not;

In Youth I died.

My Friends beheld my slow decline,
    And mourned my joyless lot.

They saw but sorrow; I descried
The Bliss that never fades away:
They felt the shadow of the tomb;
    I marked the Heavenly Day.

I heard them sob, as through the night
They kept their watch: then on my ear,
Amid the sobbing, fell a Voice
    Their anguish could not hear.

Come! and fear not!—It softly cried—
We wait to lead thee to thy Home.
Then leaped my Spirit to reply—
    I come! I long to come!

I heard them whisper o'er my bed—
Another hour, and she must die!
I was too weak to answer them
    That endless Life was nigh.

Another hour, with bitter tears
They mourned me as untimely dead,
And heard not how I sang a Song
    Of Triumph o'er their head.

They bore me to the Grave, and thought
How narrow was my resting-place;
My Soul was roving high and wide
    At will through boundless space.

They clothed themselves in robes of black;
Through the sad Aisle the Requiem rang;
Meanwhile the white-robed Choirs of Heaven
    A holy Pæan sang.

Oft from my Paradise I come
To visit those I love on earth;
I enter, unperceived, the door;
    They sit around the hearth,

And talk in saddened tone of me,
As one that never can return;
How little think they that I stand
    Among them as they mourn!

But Time will ease their grief, and Death
Will purge the darkness from their eyes;
Then shall they triumph, when they learn
    Heaven's solemn Mysteries.

Stanzas.

The Armour of Christ.

LAD in the Panoply of Heaven
    What need I fear of Satan's power,
His cruel darts against me driven,
    Or artful wiles in evil hour?

If CHRIST have given me such array
    To save my Soul from hellish spite,

Stanzas.

Why should I dread to wend my way,
   Or fear to wage the holy fight?

For when with Truth my loins are girt,
   And Virtue's plate is on my breast,
No falsehood can my Spirit hurt,
   No vice within my bosom rest.

And if my feet be always shod
   With the defence of Gospel Peace,
No rugged path, that must be trod,
   Shall cause my zeal and love to cease.

And while I hold the shield of Faith
   To guard me from the wicked Foe,
I am assured, nor harm, nor scath,
   Can come to work me lasting woe.

And when Salvation's helm is mine
   To cheer me with a blessed Hope,
Why should my courage e'er decline,
   Or fear with evil powers to cope?

The SPIRIT's Sword is by my side,
   The Word of GOD, pure, undefiled;
Thus pride and error are defied,
   Though I am but a foolish Child.

Prayer, also, is a weapon sure
   Whereby temptation to withstand,
All Heavenly Graces to secure
   From my Redeemer's willing Hand.

And gives He not in very deed
 HIMSELF, His Sacrament of Love,
With more than Angels' Food to feed
 My ransomed Soul, from Heaven above?

Then shall I not sustain the fight,
 E'en though it be prolonged and sore;
And shall not I be clothed with Might
 To wear the Crown, when all is o'er?

Hereafter.

HOW feebly we adore Thee now;
 How lamely pay each holy vow;
Our Faith how weak, our eyes how dim,
How languid every laud and hymn!
When at Thy Altar, LORD, we kneel,
Thy Presence scarce our hearts can feel;
Not even those on earth who knew
Thy Form, Thy best-beloved, could view
On Tabor's solitary height
One glimpse of Thy Eternal Light:
They fell, o'erpowered with sight and sound,
Amazed and senseless to the ground.

But they who reach the Realms of Joy,
Where sin our bliss can ne'er alloy,
Shall look upon their Monarch's Face
Within His very Dwelling-place:

Shall all His Beauty fee and know,
Enraptured gaze—nor only fo—
But His effulgent Robe fhall wear,
And, one with Him, His Glory fhare.
Tranfcendent thought! that mortal men
The fecret things of Heaven may ken;
And GOD the LORD for evermore
With undivided Love adore!

The Redeemer.

WHAT, left my LORD the Realms of Light,
  His glorious Throne, for me?
Yes, Sinner, CHRIST in love forfook His FATHER'S
  Houfe for thee!

And was He clothed in mortal Flefh, in human
  Form for me?
Yes, Sinner, JESUS once became a little BABE for
  thee!

And did He faft, and fainting pray, afflict His
  Soul for me?
Yes, Sinner, CHRIST the LORD endured life's
  bittereft pangs for thee!

And was He fcorned, and fcourged, and mocked,
  and buffeted for me?
Yes, Sinner, JESUS oft-time bore moft cruel taunts
  for thee!

Stanzas.

Say, did He groan, and bleed, and die, upon the
   Croſs for me?
Yes, Sinner, He with joy poured forth His
   precious Blood for thee!

And went He to the Realms of Hell to vanquiſh
   Death for me?
Yes, Sinner, and on Eaſter-morn CHRIST roſe
   again for thee!

And is He gone to GOD's Right Hand to intercede
   for me?
Yes, Sinner, with His FATHER now, in Heaven
   He pleads for thee!

Then, there is hope of Life, and Peace, and Pardon,
   e'en for me?
Yes, Sinner, if thou go to CHRIST, Himſelf will
   give them thee!

With JESUS may I refuge take, to Him for ſuccour
   flee?
Haſte, Sinner, JESUS gladly hails, and Angels
   welcome thee!

Then, LORD, let me, a Sinner, come with contrite
   heart to Thee;
Forgive, O graciouſly forgive: in Mercy look on me!

O ſend Thy HOLY SPIRIT down, with Love to
   quicken me;
That ſo, for evermore, I may devote my life to
   Thee!

The Sacred Heart.

WHAT wouldſt thou have, O Soul,
    Thou weary Soul?
Lo! I have ſought for Reſt
    On the Earth's heaving breaſt,
  From pole to pole.
Sleep—I have been with her,
    But ſhe gave dreams;
Death—nay, the reſt he gives
    Reſt only ſeems.
Fair Nature knows it not—
    The graſs is growing;
The blue air knows it not—
    The winds are blowing:
Not in the changing ſky,
    The ſtormy ſea—
Yet ſomewhere in GOD's wide World
    Reſt there muſt be.
Within thy SAVIOUR's Heart
    Place all thy care,
And learn, O weary Soul,
    Thy Reſt is there.

What wouldſt thou, trembling Soul?
    Strength for the ſtrife—
Strength for this fiery war
    That we call Life.

Fears gather thickly round;
    Shadowy foes,
Like unto armèd men,
    Around me close.
What am I, frail and poor,
    When griefs arise?
No help from the weak earth,
    Or the cold skies.
Lo! I can find no guards,
    No weapons borrow,
Shrinking, alone I stand
    With mighty sorrow.
Courage, thou trembling Soul,
    Grief thou must bear,
Yet thou canst find a Strength
    Will match despair:
Within thy SAVIOUR'S Heart—
    Seek for it there.

What wouldst thou have, sad Soul,
    Oppressed with grief?
Comfort, I seek in vain,
    Nor find relief.
Nature, all pitiless,
    Smiles on my pain;
I ask my fellow-men,
    They give disdain:
I asked the babbling streams,
    But they flowed on;
I asked the wise and good,
    But they gave none.

The Sacred Heart.

Though I have aſked the ſtars,
    Coldly they ſhine,
They are too bright to know
    Grief ſuch as mine.
I aſked for Comfort ſtill,
    And I found tears,
And I have ſought in vain
    Long, weary years.
Liſten, thou mournful Soul,
    Thy pain ſhall ceaſe;
Deep in His Sacred Heart,
    Dwells Joy and Peace.

Yes, in that Heart Divine,
    The Angels bright
Find, through eternal years,
    Still new delight.
From thence his conſtancy
    The Martyr drew,
And there the Virgin band
    Their refuge knew.
There, racked by pain without,
    And dread within,
How many Souls have found
    Heaven's Bliſs begin.
Then leave thy vain attempts
    To ſeek for Peace;
The world can never give
    One Soul releaſe:
But in thy Saviour's Heart
    Securely dwell,

Sanctae Syon adsunt Encaenia.

No pain can harm thee, hid
   In that sweet Cell.
Then fly, O coward Soul,
   Delay no more,
What words can speak the Joy
   For thee in store?
What smiles of earth can tell
   Of Peace like thine?
Silence and tears are best
   For Things Divine.

Sanctae Syon adsunt Encaenia.

A Sequence for the Dedication of a Church.

LAD Zion's halls are sounding
   With song and festal lay,
And with bridal Joy abounding
   The Church is Bride to-day!

In robes of Grace excelling
   The glorious Bride is clad,
And the organ notes are swelling
   In anthems loud and glad.

Like rain and dew descending
   Is the FATHER's Heavenly ruth;
In a bridal Blessing blending
   Are His Mercy and His Truth.

Comes, all His Love revealing,
  The Bridegroom, Mary's SON;
Brings all the Grace of Healing
  Which He for earth has won,

Brings a glorious Bridal-dower
  For the Church which He has wed,
In the Grace of sevenfold Power
  From His HOLY SPIRIT shed.

With Mysteries life giving
  The Paschal Feast is rife,
Where the LAMB for ever living
  Is Himself the Bread of Life.

And to the LAMB's great Wedding
  His SIRE, the Heavenly King,
His chosen Saints is bidding
  With a gracious welcoming.

Comes Abel, witness bearing
  How innocence is blest;
Comes Noah, stern declaring
  How Justice is exprest.

In mystery confessing
  The great eternal Priest,
Melchisedec his Blessing,
  Gives ever to the Feast.

And Abraham the proven,
  Has brought his faith sincere,

With Israel the loving,
  And trustful Isaac here.

And Moses old and hoary,
  With light his forehead rayed;
And Joshua in his glory,
  Whose word the Sun obeyed.

And ardent David smiting
  In his youth the giant foe,
On his kingly throne delighting
  In the Psalms prophetic flow.

And the Law and Prophets greeting
  In union close rejoice;
While their strength and power completing
  Comes the Gospel's glorious voice.

And over earth and Heaven
  Great peace and stillness fall,
With the FATHER's Fulness given,
  And GOD is All in all.

Lays of Ancient Palestine.

Miriam.

OH, for that day, that day of bliss entrancing,
  When Israel stood, her night of bondage o'er,
And leaped in heart to see no more advancing

Egypt's dark host along the desert shore;
Or scarce a ripple now proclaimed where lay
The boasting Pharaoh and his fierce array.

Miriam! she silent stood, that sight beholding,
  And bowed with sacred awe her wondering head;
Till, lo! no more their hideous spoils withholding,
  The Depths, indignant, spurned their buried dead;
And all along that sad and vengeful coast
Pale corpses lay—a monumental host.

Miriam! she saw; then all to life awaking—
  "Sing to the LORD"—with a great voice she cried;
"Sing to the LORD"—their many timbrels shaking,
  Ten thousand ransomed hearts and tongues replied;
While, leading on the dance in triumph long,
Thus the great Prophetess broke forth in song—

> " Oh, sing to the LORD,
>   Sing His Triumph right glorious;
> O'er horse and o'er rider,
>   Sing His right Arm victorious;
> Pharaoh's horsemen and chariots
>   And captains so brave,
> The LORD hath thrown down
>   In the bottomless wave.
>
> " Man of War is the LORD,
>   And JEHOVAH His Name;

We trusted His Pillar
　　Of Cloud and of Flame.
Proud boasters, ye followed,
　　But where are ye gone?
Down, down in the waters,
　　Ye sank like a stone.

" O Lord, Thou didst blow
　　With Thy Nostrils a blast,
And upheaved the huge billows—
　　Like mountains stood fast.
Egypt shuddered with wonder,
　　That pathway to see—
Those depths all congealed
　　In the heart of the sea.

" ' I too will march onward,
　　(The Enemy cried)
I shall soon overtake;
　　I the spoil will divide,
I will kill'—O my God!
　　The depths fell at Thy Breath,
And like lead they went down
　　In those waters of death.

" But o'er us the soft wings
　　Of Thy Mercy outspread
To Thy own chosen Dwelling
　　Our feet Thou hast led.
Palestrina, affrighted,
　　The tidings shall hear,

And your hearts, O ye Nations,
    Shall wither with fear.

" Thus brought in with triumph,
    Safe planted and bleſt,
On Thy own holy Mountain
    Thy People ſhall reſt.
Shout! Pharaoh is fallen
    To riſe again never.
Sing! the LORD, He ſhall reign
    For ever and ever."

Gibeon.

OH! there were banners proudly dancing
    Round old Gibeon's royal walls;
Oh! there were war-ſteeds furious prancing
    To the battle-trump which calls.
On they come, five Kings in number,
    Oh, how ſtern their long array:
Up! brave hearts, nor dare to ſlumber,
    Life and death are on this day.

Men of Gibeon! like a river
    Hebron ruſhes from afar;
Jarmuth ſee! with bow and quiver,
    How he heads the burſting war:
Lachiſh ſhouts with ſcornful gladneſs;
    Eglon! who his waves ſhall ſtem?
Many a mother faints with ſadneſs
    At thy cry, Jeruſalem!

Onward! onward! buckler clashes,
    Lances shiver, helmet rings;
On! the roll of carnage dashes—
    Iron hearts are needful things.
Earth and air, with ghastly wonder,
    Start to eye that dreadful sight;
While each crash of martial thunder
    Shakes the crimson field of fight.

Hark! and tell me, heard ye stealing
    Footsteps through the dead of night?
Saw ye tread, their path concealing,
    Israel's chosen men of might?
Canaan's sons! no peace betiding,
    Moans that sullen night-wind's breath;
For upon its black wings riding,
    Lo! the Angel comes of death.

Thou, Bethoron! tell the story,
    How they died that banded host;
Bannered pomp and kingly glory,
    Where is now your swelling boast?
Speak, Azekah! say how o'er them
    Heaven its giant hailstones threw;
God, their Foe, above—before them;
    Israel's host behind pursue.

Conquerors! on; but, fast declining,
    See! the day is almost gone—
" Sun! stand still, on Gibeon shining:
    Stop, thou Moon! o'er Ajalon."

Wondrous sight! by Mortal spoken,
    Sun and Moon obeyed that word,
Till, the last proud foeman broken,
    Joshua triumphed and the LORD.

Gibeon's saved! ye Saints that languish,
    Crouched in sackcloth and in dust,
Rise! 'tis past, your hour of anguish—
    Perfect Peace awaits the Just;
You have sown in night of sorrow,
    Reap in joy your promised crown;
Happy, glorious, endless morrow,
    Sun and Moon that ne'er go down.

Deborah.

WAKE, Deborah! wake; and thou, Barak! arise,
And swell the proud chorus which gladdens the skies:
Attend, O ye Kings, and ye Princes, give ear—
I, Deborah, speak, but JEHOVAH is near.

O LORD, it was Thou with Thy People didst ride,
When they conquering burst from rough Edom's
    dark side,
The huge Mountains staggered along on Thy Way,
While the hearts of the Nations all melted away.

But forsaken by Thee, then how triumphed our foes,
Till I, Mother in Israel, Deborah, rose;

How silent our valleys, how wasted our plains,
While we sat down in sackcloth, and wept o'er
 our chains.

Speak, Deborah! speak; and thou, Barak! oh,
 say,
How captivity captive was led on that day;
All honour to you who, inspired by our breath,
So bravely did jeopard your lives to the death.

But curse ye the cowards, who, trembling with fear,
Resolved not the summons of rescue to hear;
Yes, bitterly curse them, who mocked at the word—
'Gainst the mighty, oh, come! to the help of the
 Lord.

Oh, that was a triumph, a glorious sight,
When ye came, O ye Kings! to Megiddo to fight;
Ah, Sisera! well may your chariots be nought,
When against you the stars in their bright courses
 fought.

Then tell me, O Kishon, then tell me, oh, whither
Hast thou swept all their glory, thou deep-flowing
 river?
Where has vanished so swiftly their boastful array?
O my Soul! down what strength hast thou trodden
 this day.

By the window she sat of her watch tower so high—
It was Sisera's Mother: she looked at the sky—
" Why tarries his chariot so long on the way?
Why thus, O my conquering Son! dost thou stay?"

Her wife **Ladies answered**—" The spoil to divide,
The glad **warriors rest on the** steep mountain's side;
They come"—Dreamers, hush! shall **I tell you
 the tale,**
How your **Sisera** died by the sharp-piercing nail?

Thus perish, consumed, **at the flash of Thy** Sword,
The madmen who challenge Thy Honour, O LORD!
But they who love Thee, on strong pinions unfurled,
Like suns shall **mount upward,** and tread on the
 world.

Virginis in Gremio.

A Sequence on the Incarnation.

WHEN of His Grace the SON of GOD
 the SON of Man would be
Then was a Bridal, GOD the Spouse,
 the Bride Humanity;
Our nature was not lost in Him, **nor** He defiled
 by clay,
So **let** all earth meet joyfully and keep the Bridal-
 day.

O blessèd end of enmity! O Peace which Angels
 tell!
O fairest fair Espousals! GOD with us, EMMANUEL!

This is the **Dew** on **Gideon's** Fleece, the Earth
    in opening **Spring,**
This is our **Aaron's Almond-rod** to **Glory** blof-
    foming.

Oh, once the Prophets **ſpake of Him,** and in the
    Fathers' day
The eyes which He had opened ſaw a **Gladneſs**
    far away;
But now their Voice is only love; He Whom
    they **ſaw** is nigh,
And dawns, a **Sun** of **Sinleſſneſs,** clear o'er the
    darkening ſky.

Then by **a** mortal **Mother's Arms** Immenſity was
    ſpanned,
Then was Humility moſt meek enthroned at **God's**
    Right Hand,
Then **God** was manifeſt **in** Fleſh, the Life would
    mortal be,
And **ſinners** recompenſed with hate **Divineſt**
    Charity.

There is a wondrous Story, of dim Tradition born—
There went **a** Virgin beautiful to ſnare the
    Unicorn;
She came upon his lair—oh then he laid his
    fierceneſs **by,**
And leaned for **ſlumber** at **Her Breaſt,** the am-
    buſh lurking nigh;

There is a Truth more wondrous yet; GOD's
    Wrath was waxing fell
When in the Pearl of Maidenhood He came as
    MAN to dwell;
Thither He came and thence He went even foes
    to seek and save,
Till through the Flesh He took of her the Nails
    of Death they drave.

So let us meet and kindle each in other Love's
    pure flame,
And send our lowly 'not to us' there whence
    the Merit came;
GOD breathed on earth His quickening Breath,
    then fell the SPIRIT's Shower,
And lo! in Mary's Garden sprang Salvation's
    votive Flower.

Type and Antitype.

The Tree of Life.

THE Tree of Life in Eden stood,
    With mystic Fruits of Heavenly Food,
    Which endless Life afford:
    That Life by man's transgression lost,
Cast out is man by Angel-host
    Until by MAN restored.

In vain the Lambs poured forth their blood,
In vain the ſmoking Altars ſtood,
   All unatoned was ſin :
Muſt greater be the Sacrifice,
Before the Gate of Paradiſe
   Can let the fallen in.

The LORD of Life His Life muſt give,
That man an endleſs Life may live,
   And Death's dark doom reverſe.
The Croſs is made the myſtic Tree,
The Blood that flowed on Calvary
   Hath waſhed away the curſe.

Now Eden's Gate is oped once more,
The guarding Angel's watch is o'er,
   And ſheathed the flaming ſword :
The Tree of Life now blooms afreſh,
Its precious Fruit the very Fleſh
   Of the Incarnate WORD.

Cain and Abel.

TWO Brothers each an Offering made,
   Two offerings on two Altars laid,
     Two differing hearts were there :
In one was faith and hope and love,
The other anger, malice move
     To murder and deſpair.

The bloodleſs Offering lies in vain,
The GOD moſt Higheſt will not deign
   To bleſs ſuch Sacrifice :
But ſoon that Offering's ſtained and red
With Brother's blood by Brother ſhed,
   Which loud for vengeance cries.

Again two Prieſts ſtand Face to face,
Two Brethren of one common race
   Within the Temple walls :
Again a BROTHER'S Blood is poured
An awful Offering to the LORD,
   But which for Mercy calls.

Upon our Altars now there lies
A bloodleſs, endleſs Sacrifice,
   Earth's fruits of Bread and Wine :
Our BROTHER brings His Blood to bleſs
And Conſecrate by Righteouſneſs
   An Offering now Divine.

Abram and *Melchizedek.*

WHEN conquering Abram Salem ſought,
   To GOD's High Prieſt his tithes he brought,
   His thankfulneſs to mark :
Melchizedek an Offering made
 Of Bread and Wine on Altar laid,
   And bleſſed the Patriarch.

A Victory nobler far we gain,
A nobler Sacrifice is ſlain,
 A better Bleſſing ſhed:
Our great High Prieſt in Heaven ſtands,
Who gives Himſelf with His own Hands,
 In myſtic Wine and Bread.

The Manna and the Rock.

FOR forty years was Iſrael fed
 With daily Manna, Angel's Bread;
 The Rock with Water flows:
That Water flowed, that Manna fell
Like dew on favoured Iſrael,
 Who like a lily grows.

CHRIST's Fleſh is now the Living Bread,
His riven Side the Rock which ſhed
 The Water and the Blood:
From Him the Church her life renews,
His Gracious Blood her Soul bedews
 With ever-ſtreaming flood.

The Paſſover and the Euchariſt.

IN anxious haſte at GOD's Command
 All Iſrael's hoſt prepare and ſtand
 To take its ordered flight:
With bitter herbs, unleavened bread,
And roaſted Lamb the Feaſt is ſpread,
 That memorable night.

Verses.

The awful Angel ſoars on high,
And Death is dealing far and nigh,
   Save where the Blood is found:
Supported by that Paſchal food,
The mighty hoſt paſſed through the flood
   Beyond the ſea's dark bound.

All girded for its coming flight
A Soul is paſſing hence to-night,
   And bids the world farewell:
Fed with the ſacred Nouriſhment
Of CHRIST's moſt Holy Sacrament,
   It burſts through ſin's dark ſpell.

All ſprinkled with the Precious BLOOD
It calmly paſſes through the flood
   Of Death's laſt agony:
It chants, while borne on Angel's wing—
O mighty Death, where is thy ſting?
   Where, Grave, thy Victory?

Verses.

Give me Children, or elſe I die.

IVE me Children, or elſe I die—
   'Twas wildly ſaid, and ſtill
  More wildly o'er the ſpeaker's heart
    Theſe words were doomed to thrill:

For they were uttered in an hour
   Of reckless love and pride,
By one who brooked not aught on earth
   To her should be denied.

The sound of that impassioned cry
   Ascended up to Heaven,
And to the loved and loving one
   A first-born Son was given.

Not in that hour did memory bring
   To that fond heart and weak
The echo of those frantic words
   That she had dared to speak.

Perchance, not until anguish came
   Returned their sound again,
Floating with fatal meaning through
   The dying woman's brain.

For Rachel now, a second time,
   Must meet her trying hour,
And Death, which she has once invoked,
   Now comes with fearful power.

' Ye know not what ye ask' is stamped
   On each unchastened prayer
That lays not at GOD's Feet its weight
   Of hope or of despair.

Comest Thou to me?

AND comest Thou to me, O Lord,
    When I have need of Thee?
Such was the Baptist's trembling cry,
    His self-denouncing plea.

But **none may shrink from work God sets**,
    From **high or** lowly task:
By thee **is** thine own part fulfilled?
    Is all **that** He will ask.

A sinner with **a** load **of** care
    And conscious sin opprest
Must sometimes act an Angel's **part**,
    And speak of God's Behest.

The highest place **may** sometimes **prove**
    A source **of** penance keen,
And self-abhorring pangs there are
    By all but God unseen.

His Gifts, through human hands and frail,
    Without defilement flow,
And Saints may kneeling claim the boon
    That sinners can bestow.

When Jesus **knelt** that wondrous hour
    At His own **Servant's feet**,
He taught proud hearts to bend **the** knee
    In lowly penance meet;

And in that hour the Sacred DOVE
　　Appeared to mortal eye,
And GOD'S own Voice in thunder spoke
　　A Blessing from the sky.

The Tomb of Joseph of Arimathea.

WAS night! still night!
A solemn silence hung upon the scene;
The keen, bright stars shone with un-
　　clouded light,
　　Calm and serene.

　　Hushed was the Tomb!
The heavy stone before its entrance lay:
No light broke in upon its silent gloom,
　　No starry ray.

　　The moonlight beamed;
It hung above that garden, soft and clear,
Around the watchful guard its radiance gleamed
　　From helm and spear.

　　The Tomb was sealed!
The watch patrolled before its entrance lone;
The bright night every passing step revealed;
　　None neared the stone.

　　Midnight had passed;
The stars their lustrous shining had decreased;
And day-break's earliest light was hastening fast
　　In the pale east.

The Tomb of Joseph.

    The morning-star,
Last in the silent Heaven, withdrew its ray,
And the white dawn spreading its spectre light
    Foretold the day.

    An earthquake's shock
Just at the break of morning shook the ground,
And echoed from that rent and trembling rock
    With startling sound.

    The guards, amazed,
Fell to the earth in wonder and affright;
And round the astonished spot in glory blazed
    A sudden Light.

    An Angel there
Descended from the tranquil sky;
The glory of his presence filled the air
    All-radiantly.

    He rolled away
From the still Sepulchre the massy stone,
And, watching silent till the risen day,
    He sat thereon.

    His garments white
Shone like the snow in its unsullied sheen;
His face was, like the lightning's gleaming light,
    Dazzlingly seen.

    All, all around
Was silence, and suspense, and listening dread;
The stirless watch lay prostrate on the ground,
    Hushed as the dead.

  At break of day
The SAVIOUR burſt that Cavern's ſtillneſs deep,
Riſing in conqueſt from Death's ſhattered ſway
  As from a ſleep.

  He roſe in Power,
In all the Strength of GODHEAD ſhining bright,
Freſh as that hallowed Morning's dewy hour,
  Pure as its light.

  He roſe as GOD,
Roſe as a mighty Victor ſtrong to ſave,
Breaking Death's ſilent chain and unſeen rod
  There in the Grave.

  He roſe on high,
While Angels hung around on ſoaring wing,
Wreſting from the dark Grave its victory,
  From Death its ſting.

Concerning the Chief Spiritual and General Gifts of God.

From the Latin.

I.

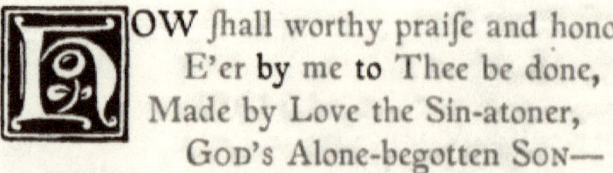OW ſhall worthy praiſe and honour
  E'er by me to Thee be done,
Made by Love the Sin-atoner,
  GOD's Alone-begotten SON—

Me, endowed, by such a Donor,
   Thus with every Gift in one?

For, since He to flesh hath deigned,
   I to live in Soul begin;
Through the stroke my LORD sustained,
   I with Him am dead to sin;
By this Bread of Life maintained,
   Oneness with my SAVIOUR win.

Where is such Divine Nutrition
   Found on earth 'twixt pole and pole?
Where so skilful a Physician,
   Raising up the languid Soul?
Holy hunger's glad fruition;
   Virtue's, Glory's perfect whole!

Me before ten thousand taking,
   Oh! how great Thy sovereign Love;
For my benefit forsaking
   All Thine Heritage above,
Till, with all Thy Saints awaking,
   I the full Redemption prove.

'Tis for me the tomb Thou quittest,
   Lifting up my Soul on high;
'Tis for me enthroned Thou sittest,
   Glorious in the upper sky;
'Tis for me that Thou remittest
   Thy Good SPIRIT ever nigh.

Now His soothing Smiles caress me
    With each prosperous delight;
Now He pleaseth to oppress me
    With the cloud of sorrow's night:
Yet, in either, He will bless me,
    If my loving heart be right.

At His withering Inspiration
    Carnal pleasures cease to bloom;
Burdens, by His Consolation,
    Lightsome to the flesh become:
Oh! how bright the Revelation
    When His Rays the sight illume.

Glories which our earthly senses,
    Dimmed by sin, can ne'er discern,
Through one Gift which He dispenses,
    Every faithful Soul may learn;
While with all Divine defences
    From them evil He doth turn.

No poor speech of man availeth
    Good so great as this to tell:
Faith attempteth, but she faileth—
    Grace and Love unsearchable!
When desire the Soul assaileth,
    This alone its thirst can quell.

Lo! a train of Heavenly Blessing,
    (Numbers fail the sum to give)

Are the holy, this poſſeſſing,
  Fitted ever to receive:
Their Beſtower, without ceaſing,
  Laud while endleſs ages live.

Be Thou raiſed all heights tranſcending,
  FATHER, Fount of Grace and Might!
Be Thy Glory ſtill extending,
  SON, of men both Life and Light!
Be Thy Praiſes never-ending,
  COMFORTER in ſorrow's night!

II.

SHOULD Creatures all their voices raiſe
  In one high ſong to Thee,
It were not worthy of Thy praiſe,
  Thrice Holy TRINITY.

The Riches of Thy bounteous Grace
  We happy mortals prove;
Made in Thine Image is our race,
  And dowered with Thy Love.

Oh! matchleſs Love to meaneſt worth!
  Our FATHER gave His SON
To ſave from death the ruined earth,
  And lift us to His Throne.

Light of all Light, and WORD of GOD,
  He deigned the Virgin's Womb,

To snatch our forfeit brotherhood
   From sin's eternal doom.

Thou (be Thy gracious Power adored!)
   From Hell hast set me free,
My long-lost Dignity restored,
   My likeness, LORD, to Thee.

Hadst Thou not made me all Thy Care,
   And rich Oblation given,
For me remained but grim despair,
   Shut out from Hope and Heaven.

Most faithful Advocate and Friend,
   Unfailing SAVIOUR Thou,
Thy free Bestowments know no end,
   No need they disavow.

Thy wondrous Birth the Price procured;
   Thy Death the Ransom paid;
Thy Rising the result assured,
   And full Salvation made.

How full of joy to me Thy Birth!
   How full of fruit Thy Doom!
How Glorious Thy Going forth
   Triumphant from the Tomb!

My poor desire Thy Love repays,
   It is my wish supreme;
And, though the effort fail, Thy praise
   Shall be my constant theme.

Let praiſe the Maker FATHER greet;
  Honour, the Saviour SON;
And Glory to the PARACLETE,
  Renewer GOD, be done!

The Advent of the Divine Stranger.

HE Chriſtmas Eve is **waning**,
  The Morning ſtreaks the ſky,
Earth ceaſes her complaining,
  Redemption draweth nigh!

But Who ſo ſwiftly moveth?
  Who on the mountains ſtands,
To earth, as One that loveth,
  Stretching His gracious Hands?

Whence cometh **He** Whoſe Geſture
  Infant-like **doth invite**,
Yet glorious in **His** Veſture,
  And travelling in His Might?

Who for our greeting waiteth?
  Who waiteth **us** to greet?
Walking **a** world that hateth—
  How beautiful His Feet!

Whoſe **is the** Face that gloweth,
  And lighteth **up the Sun**?
Whoſe is the Voice that floweth
  Like many waves in one?

Whose are the Accents ringing,
    Like far, faint, holy Chimes,
Like Childhood's Carols bringing
    Their tones to exile climes?

Now from a lowly Manger,
    Now from the Throne on high,
O Meek and Mighty Stranger,
    Thy Voice fills earth and sky.

But lo! He draweth nearer,
    And full upon His Brow
The eastern lights fall clearer—
    My God! What see I now?

'Tis not day's crimson gleaming,
    'Tis not morn's dewy gold,
That in His Locks is beaming,
    Too glorious to behold.

'Tis not the winter's treasure,
    The holly's blood-red beads,
Strung for a wreath of pleasure—
    His tender Visage bleeds.

'Tis not the Tyrian glory,
    His Raiment hath imbued,—
His Head and Feet are gory,
    His Hands are red with Blood.

But decked with Light He shineth,
    Brightly, more brightly yet,

With Light that ne'er declineth,
  With Beams that never set.

Ring out, ye Chimes, your greeting,
  Ye Carols, mount on high,
For Heaven and Earth are meeting
  In Him Who cannot die.

The Heavenly Fatherland.

The Rhythm of Bernard of Clugny.

HERE we have many fears, this is the vale
  of tears, the land of sorrow:
    Tears are there none at all in that
    Celestial hall, on life's bright morrow.

Oh, for the Joys in store; but one short moment
  more, then Life for ever:
Oh, for the Joys in store, at the glad Heavenly
  door of the Life-giver.

What is the Prize? for whom?—Heaven for the
  sons of doom; Life for the winner;
Bliss for the nothing-worth; Gold for the dross of
  earth; GOD for the sinner.

Loud sounds the battle-cry; whence comes the
  victory seek you to guess?—Hence,
Full-streamed, without alloy, flows everlasting Joy
  from His bright Presence.

I

Hope here we live upon; here we see Babylon
  Sion invading.
Now grief is all our lot; then Joys which wither
  not—garlands unfading.

    *   *   *   *

O Sion bright with gold, flowing with milk thy
  fold, City of gladness,
Tongue cannot tell thy bliss, heart sinks opprest
  with this, even to sadness.

I cannot strain my sight to that intense delight,
  nor tell the story,
What throbs of ardent love thrill through the
  courts above, how vast their glory.

My ears may strain to hear, they cannot reach the
  sphere, for full before it
Beams of surpassing light fall on my dazzled sight;
  mute I adore it.

For Sion's halls along echoes the voice of song:
  there the Departed,
Fresh from the deadly fight, throng round the
  LORD of Light, jubilant-hearted.

There is eternal Rest; there after toil the Blest
  cease from life's fever:
There in Heaven's banquet-hall sounds the high
  festival of the Receiver:

There round the LORD of Might, vested in garments white, on that bright morrow

Musters their vast array; tears have all fled away;
    vanished all sorrow.

For Sion's courts within Death may not tread,
    nor sin, nor guilt's endeavour;
Thus without fault are they; peaceful, without
    dismay; at rest for ever.

        *   *   *   *

O Sion glorious, City victorious, tower of Salvation,
Thee I seek and desire; to thee I aye aspire in
    contemplation.

Good works I offer none; I have no pardon won
    by my own merit;
Firstborn of wrath am I; sold to iniquity, body
    and Spirit.

I can bring nought at all, bondsman of sin and
    thrall, scarred in each feature,
In life and Soul I faint, under the poison-taint of
    my lost nature.

Yet day and night I cry—FATHER, Thy Help is
    nigh when we beseech it;
I see the Prize above, stretch forth Thy Hand of
    Love, aid us to reach it.

Thou to life call'st us forth out of the dust of
    earth; Thine own Ablution,
When we were born in sin, washed our Souls clean
    within from all pollution.

Thine is the Salve ordained for thoſe whom guilt
      has ſtained, who by compunction
Claim what no Soul can claim, unpurged by grief
      and ſhame—the Heavenly Unction.

From David's fount apace flows the pure ſtream
      of Grace ever deſcending,
Through it ſin's leproſy ſoon fades and dies away,
      and has its ending.

O Grace of GOD, on high I ſee beyond the ſky;
      the clouds are riven:
As through a glaſs I ſee, dimly and miſtily, the
      gates of Heaven.

O Sion, bright with gold, dear home of Joys untold,
      in GOD's Light burning;
I ſtretch my arms—my Soul; ſhall I e'er reach
      the goal of all my yearning?

O bleſſed Fatherland, I ſee the happy Band—the
      miſts grow lighter—
I ſee the light of day round their fair garlands play
      brighter and brighter.

O bleſſed Fatherland, ſay ſhall I ever ſtand where
      I can ſhare thee?
Say but—' The time ſhall come when to this happy
      Home Angels ſhall bear thee.'

Is it a trance, a dream? Oh, do theſe things but
      ſeem? Is it a viſion?

Omnes Gentes plaudite.

Let me but graſp it fair! No: 'twill not melt in
    air, in vain deriſion.

O my duſt, triumph thou! GOD is thy Portion
    now—thine now and ever!
O my duſt, triumph thou! GOD is thy Portion
    now—thine now and ever!

Omnes Gentes plaudite.

A Hymn for the Aſcenſion.

HUMAN-KIND, your voices raiſe
    In loud and ſweet accord,
And tune each feſtal Choir to praiſe
    The Triumph of the LORD;
And let the joyous trumpet tell
    How He returns to-day,
Leading the captive ſpoils of Hell
    On His victorious way.

Ah, Bliſs of GOD! to note how fair,
    How glorious, and how bright,
The Divine Shoot of the ancient Root
    Is burſting into light:
Above the thrones of the mortal ones,
    And Powers that dwell on high,
The growth to which earth to-day gives birth
    Is lifted to the ſky.

Within a veil which can never fail
    Has our better Moses passed:
And a great amaze draws the wondering gaze
    Of His People first and last;
With uplifted eyes, in that dread surprise,
    Stand the Galilean men,
Watching the Cloud which must cover the crowd
    And hide Him from their ken.

When away from earth Elias broke
    In his chariot of flame,
A twofold Spirit with the Prophet's cloak
    Upon Elisha came:
But when our LORD with His lingering Feet
    Did the upward pathway trace,
He sent to His Own, in the PARACLETE,
    A universal Grace.

O'er Jordan must our Israel go,
    The stream that He must quaff,
Burdened with His prevailing Love,
    The Cross His only staff;
With a twofold Band He is now at hand,
    With the treasures of all time,
With the unincarnate Spirits and
    The Souls that shall reign sublime.

This is the Conqueror true and brave
    Who in Glory sweeps afar,
Who from the portals of the grave
    Did rive every bolt and bar:

Bei stiller nacht.

Over all Virtues Sovereign King,
    Whoſe mighty Will and Sway
The world, and every living thing,
    In Heaven and earth obey.

To ſhare His own eternal Throne
    The FATHER calls the SON,
Till every foe is overthrown
    And willing hearts are won:
In the Heaven of Heavens He ſits in Bliſs;
    But He comes again in the end
To judge, by a Power that is only His,
    The foe alike and the friend.

LORD of all Retribution, come!
    But let Thy Mercy reign
Till we learn by Grace to win our place
    And look on Thee again:
Oh, in that final future morn
    Let Thy Pity fill our ears;
And let us be unto Glory born
    For the everlaſting years.

Bei stiller nacht.

A Hymn on the Paſſion of Chriſt.

WITHIN a Garden's bound,
    Where ſtill Night reigned around,
  A mournful Cry of bitter anguiſh
    wailed;

There, hid from mortal gaze,
  ONE knelt in deep amaze,
A Heart oppreſſed beneath its burthen quailed.

That ONE, in travail ſore,
  Was our Dear LORD, Who bore
Our ſins' great burthen that on Him was laid;
  While none could bring relief
  To that exceeding Grief,
The Grief that made His Human Soul afraid.

But lo! from thoſe hot Veins,
  Forced out by Mental pains,
Great drops of Blood adown the verdure fall;
  Such whelming fears aſſail,
  That heart and courage fail,
As firſt eſſays of ſin's ſtrange load appal.

No other gaze but His
  Could fathom that abyſs,
Whoſe loweſt depths to Him ſtood all revealed;
  The ſins of Adam's race,
  Againſt GOD's Love and Grace,
His Thought embraced them all as thus He kneeled.

Ungodly counſels then,
  And deeds of evil men,
All ſins of each degree, of every kind,
  Not as to human eyes,
  But in their helliſh guiſe
Were then all bared to His omniſcient Mind.

Bei ſtiller nacht.

  The ponderous weight of all,
  From Adam's grievous fall,
Till earth's Laſt Day and ſolemn Reckoning Time,
  Of all GOD's Books record,
  The Curſe, the due reward,
The iniquity of all now laid on Him!

  That high-filled Cup of Woes
  His preſcient Mind foreknows,
From firſt approach of Judas' torch-led hoſt;
  That falſe Diſciple's kiſs,
  And all that followed this,
Till on the Croſs He yielded up the Ghoſt.

  Each furrowed, bleeding gaſh
  From cruel ſcourge's laſh,
And ſharpeſt pricks of that mock thorny Crown;
  The inſults, blows, and ſcorn
  That muſt be meekly borne,
Theſe weigh the SON of Man's ſad Spirit down.

  He ſees with Viſion clear,
  (And ſhrinks with human fear)
The Croſs with Curſe o'erlaid and angry Doom;
  The hours of racking pain
  He muſt, nailed there, ſuſtain
While lingering death Life's marrow ſhall conſume.

  Maker and LORD of all!
  Behold Him proſtrate fall,
And humbly kneel in ſilent anguiſh there;

  Till, with an inward groan,
  Towards the Heavenly Throne,
With earneſt pleading He directs His Prayer.

  Father, to Thee I pray,
  O take this Cup away:
Thou haſt all Power to do Thy Will Divine;
  Remove, if it may be,
  This Cup away from me:
Yet, Father, not My Will be done, but Thine.

  Thus thrice our Suffering Lord,
  With proſtrate Form, implored
That even then that Hour might paſs away;
  Until from Heaven at length
  An Angel brought Him ſtrength,
And healing balm His troubled Soul to ſtay.

  O well for us indeed,
  He took, as was decreed,
And drained the Cup His Heavenly Father
   gave;
  And therefore Songs of praiſe
  We ranſomed ſinners raiſe
To Him Who meekly died our Souls to ſave.

Sonnets.

The Love of God: from S. Augustine.

I.

WHAT love I, when I love Thee, O my God?
Not corporal beauty, nor the limb of snow,
Nor of loved light the white and pleasant flow,
Nor Manna showers, nor strains that stream abroad,
Nor flowers of Heaven, nor small stars of the sod.
Not these, my God! I love, who love Thee so.
Yet love I Something sweeter than I know,
A certain Light on a more golden road,
A Somewhat not of Manna, nor the hive,
A Beauty not of summer or the spring,
A Scent, a Music, and a Blossoming,
Eternal, Timeless, Placeless, without Gyve,
Fair, Fadeless, Undiminished, never dim,—
This, This is what I love, in loving Him.

II.

This, This is what I love, and what is This?
I asked the beautiful Earth who said, 'Not I;'
I asked the Depths, and the immaculate Sky,
And all the Spaces said, 'Not He, but His.'
And so like One who scales a precipice,
Height after height, I scaled the flaming wall
Of the great Universe; yea, passed o'er all
The world of thought, which so much higher is.

Then I exclaimed—To whom is mute all murmur
Of phantasy, of nature, and of art,
He, than articulate language hears a firmer
And grander meaning in his own deep heart,
No sound from cloud or Angel. Oh, to win
That voiceless Voice, 'My Servant, enter in!'

In My Father's House are many Mansions.

THE stars are out in their eternal youth,
  That such a wealth of fancies nightly yield,
The golden corndrops call them of a field
Where the moon glideth like the gleaner Ruth;
And some look on their company in sooth
For poesy, some for love of loving eyes,
Who see the same things in the same blue skies;
And some in search of Hope and some of Truth.
I have my starry thought: the Twelve are up,
The door is opened, and they linger yet:
CHRIST's Wine is in the Eucharistic Cup;
CHRIST's Chalice waiteth Him in Olivet;
While He, His Eye on the star-sown expansions,
Saith—' In My FATHER's House are many
    Mansions.'

God is a Sun and Shield.

GOD is a Sun and Shield: why both, or either?
  Why? peradventure that those strains
    soul-drawn,
Those songs of gold, of lilies, and the dawn,

Cluster their mystic epithets together,
As boughs do blossoms in the sunny weather,
A waste of beauty meaninglessly fair?
Not so. I deem there is a purpose there
And both the words are true, and lost is neither:
And one Divinely silvers o'er the psalm,
And one awakens some far battle boom.
The Shield is for the land that knows no calm;
The Sun for that blue country o'er the tomb:
This for GOD's Garden is, that for His Fray;
The Sun for Home, the Shield is for the Way.

Verses.

In the Beginning was the Word.

ETERNAL WORD! GOD's True and
    Only SON,
  Maker, and Lord, and Heir, and
    Judge of all;
First-born of every creature; Holy ONE!
  We praise Thy Name, and on Thy Name we
    call.

JEHOVAH dwells from everlasting years
  In silence and in solitude concealed;
And yet from Everlasting He appears
  In Thee to all His Universe revealed.

And life and love and truth and joy and might,
  And all the Creature lieth incomplete,

Some darkness lingering in their purest light—
  Only in Thee doth all their fulness meet.

Nothing so dark as the pure Light of GOD;
  Nothing so far from us and strange and high;
Nothing so weary as the grievous load
  The burdened Creature bears until he die.

But in the SON of Love and Sacrifice
  Nothing so near and clear as GOD appears;
And lightly on the heart the burden lies
  Of all our imperfections and our fears.

True SON of GOD, our Sonship is in Thee;
  True Light of GOD, our Wisdom too Thou art;
O LAMB from earth's foundation slain for me,
  Thou bringest Life and Peace into my heart.

Ever in Thee the FATHER is revealed,
  Ever in Thee all things are reconciled,
Ever in Thee our sins and wounds are healed,
  Glory to Thee, the Pure and Undefiled.

I have finished the Work Thou gavest Me to do.

NO work of Man was e'er complete before,
    With sinless, faultless, holy beauty graced;
But when his task was ended, evermore
The faithful Servant sadly must deplore
    It was a fair shortcoming at the best.

Never did Limner paint up to his thought;
  Nor Sculptor chisel in the marble white

The visioned model after which he wrought;
Never was Song from sweet melodious throat
   The perfect utterance of the Soul's delight;

Never did Hero wholly yet achieve
   The feats of glory which he had designed;
Nor thoughtful Sage the absolute pattern weave
Of GOD's great Universe, which he might leave
   A wonder and a faith to all mankind.

Still our best work is only partly done,
   And grows from man to man, from age to age,
Some failure lurks in every triumph won;
Others will mend whate'er we have begun,
   And blot some matter from our fairest page.

One only Life there is without a stain,
   Accomplishing the FATHER's perfect Will;
With highest aim—and never aimed in vain,
Attempting nought which must be tried again,
   But all the Thought of GOD it did fulfil.

Perfect the sinless Beauty of His Ways;
   Perfect the Wisdom of His faithful Love;
Perfect the Trust that walked with GOD always;
Perfect in Suffering; perfect in the Praise
   Which still like incense rose to Heaven above.

O fairer Thou than sons of men; and yet
   Not terrible Thy Beauty! In sweet accord
All tender Graces in Thy Being met;
And of their fulness all Thy People get
   Still growing to the Fulness of their LORD.

Behold! thy King cometh.

LO! He cometh, meek and lowly,
  Strew the palm-branch on His road,
Son of David, Pure and Holy,
  King of Zion! Christ of God!

He hath healed our sore diseases,
  Purged the eyeballs of the blind,
And the dumb have sung to Jesus,
  Vexed with demons in their mind.

And He spake, as never mortal
  Spake before, with Truth and Grace,
Words which are the glorious portal
  Into Wisdom's holy Place.

Lo! He comes, grand Foot-prints leaving
  All along the path He trod—
Each a Miracle, and giving
  Token of a Present God.

Gospel to the poor He preacheth,
  Will not break the bruisèd reed,
And with holy Power He teacheth—
  Is not this the Christ indeed?

He will heal us and enlighten,
  He will teach us Wisdom's ways,
He will calm the storms that frighten,
  He will give us songs of praise.

Lift the high Gates everlasting,
 O ye Doors, be opened wide,
CHRIST, the LORD, to us is hasting,
 In our hearts He would abide.

God forbid that I should glory, save in the Cross
of our Lord Jesus Christ.

CROSS of shame! our boast and glory,
 Darkest, brightest scene in story:
Through hatred fellest, love the purest,
Best of Blessings thou securest.

Strange, mysterious contradiction!
Death of sin in Crucifixion
Of the Sinless! and Salvation
In the Just ONE's condemnation!

Joy expressed from Love's heart-bleeding!
Peace and rest from wrath proceeding!
Out of gloom the true Light springing,
And from the Tomb the new Life bringing!

His Cross from shame all shame hath taken,
His Cross from wrath doth Hope awaken,
His Cross the power of Death hath broken;
O Cross, of Love divinest token!

K

Is there no Balm in Gilead?

S there no Balm in Gilead then, is there no Healer nigh?
No freshening Spring to cheer the waste so desolate and dry?
Hath Hope's dear vision vanishèd for ever from thy sight,
And darkness fallen around thee, the very gloom of night?
And seems thy Soul forsaken, her every Blessing flown,
No soothing for her sorrow, and nowhere to make her moan?
Yet, stay: the Cross thou bearest thus hath first been borne for thee;
JESUS Himself did hang thereon, thy Life and Cure to be.

For thine own ease He bare it all, the Scourge and piercing Thorn,
The Nailing and the Bruising, the Denial, Shame, and Scorn,
Darkness and Desolation deep, and Pangs beyond thy thought,
And all for thy Soul's healing these sad Agonies were wrought.
Upon His Cross He yearned for thee, for thee His Heart-strings brake;

Is there no Balm in Gilead?

Himself of all forsaken, He could not thee forsake.
Then ever more, when chastenings sore thine
    inmost spirit wring,
Say—My Beloved is crucified, and I to Him will
    cling.

How shall I sing thy holy Love, dear Passion of
    my Lord?
Or how thy mystic Virtue shall I worthily record?
Thou art the Spring of all our hope, the Balsam
    of our woes,
The Solace of our yearnings, and the Bower of
    our repose:
True Paradise of all delights, since joy of grief is
    born;
For as the flowers but close at night to ope more
    fresh with morn,
So He Who wept and bled for us, and bowed in
    earthly gloom,
Now makes those Sorrows our bright Bliss, those
    Wounds our joyous Home.

Here is a Covert from the storm when winds and
    waves arise,
A Shadow in the scorching noon, a Light in star-
    less skies,
A Staff upon the rugged road, a Shield when foes
    assail,
A Charm Divine against Whose Might no evil
    can prevail;

For where the Cross of Jesus is, is Peace, and
    there alone;
And 'neath that Banner of His Love He gathereth
    His Own:
And thou who wilt be Jesus', must not grudge
    thy portion small
In His own bitter Chalice, Who once for thee
    drained it all.

Thou know'st He went not up to Joy, but first
    He suffered Pain,
And all the selfsame Path must tread, who that
    His Bliss would gain:
Is aught too wearisome or hard for Jesus' sake to
    bear?
While He is crowned with Thorns, wilt thou a
    crown of roses wear?
Lo! this good Cross He offers thee, it is thy very
    Life;
Anoint with holy Unction, it will aid thee in the
    strife;
'Tis hallowed by thy Saviour's Touch, Who
    hung on it for thee,
And Love's sweet might shall make it light, and
    win the victory.

Draw near, thou reft and drooping Heart, draw
    near, and lift thy gaze
To Him Who yearns with outstretched Arms thee
    from thy grief to raise:

Commendation of a Christian Soul.

Draw near, and clinging close beneath thy
 SAVIOUR'S Bleeding Heart,
Tell o'er each throb of that deep Woe in which
 thou haſt a part;
Tell o'er each Drop of dear Life-Blood which
 ebbs for thee ſo faſt,
And all thy weary heart-aching upon that true
 Love caſt:
In JESUS' Croſs and Paſſion is the Medicine of
 thy Soul,
Yea, there is Balm in Gilead, and a Healer to
 make whole.

Commendation of a Christian Soul.

UNTO Thy Hands, O LORD,
 This precious Soul we give,
 A jewel, 'mid Thy gliſtening Hoard
 Of quickened ſtones to live;
Now let Thy mild Fraternal Eyes
Our darling deign to recognize,
A work of Thy creative Mould,
A Sheep of Thine Apoſtles' Fold,
A Sinner from the fiery flood
Redeemed by Thine own Fleſh and Blood.

Receive, with Arms outſpread,
 A Prize that coſt Thee dear!
'Tis Eaſter round this dying bed
 When our true Life draws near!

The **thought of** Thy forsaken Tomb
With brightness cheers this awful gloom;
The stifling, sickening airs of death
Are freshened **by** Thine odorous Breath;
And Hades' gates are glorified
At sight of **Him** that lives, and died.

Out of this world of tears,
  O Christian Soul, depart!
Farewell **to pain** and grief and fears,
  And wants that rend the heart!
Go thou where these can come no more,
Within the Cherub-guarded door,
Nor dread to change a world like this
For quiet deepening into Bliss,
For Eden's dwellings calm and fair—
Pass **forth** and take thy portion there!

Out of this world of sin,
  O Christian Soul, depart!
The Stainless call thee; pass thou in,
  Full-pardoned as thou art!
O Crown of joys! no more to stray,
No more to take thy own wild way,
No more thy dearest Friend **to** leave,
No more His Loving SPIRIT grieve,
What promise sweet **or boon** secure
Can match those Words—' I make thee pure?'

Now let the LORD arise
  And put thy foes to flight!

The Epiphany.

Let all the immortal Panoplies
   Array thee in their might!
Fenced round about by holieſt things,
From Satan`ſcreened by Angel-wings,
To GOD Who made thee, GOD Who bought,
And GOD Whoſe Grace thy cleanſing wrought,
That Hell no part in thee ſhould claim—
Go forth, ſweet Soul, in JESUS' Name!

The Epiphany.

BEYOND the barren Mountain-range
   Where Hor lifts up its ſacred head,
And buried lies in myſtery ſtrange,
   As years work out their ſilent change,
      The City of the dead.

Where proud Euphrates day by day
   Winds through the plain, or ſleeping lies,
The watching Magi nightly pray,
And ſeek the future's hidden way
      From planet-lighted ſkies.

Through the unclouded midnight air
   On vaſt Infinity's dark page,
With deepeſt ſkill and conſtant care,
They read the golden letters there
      That wax not old with age.

Lo! as they gaze with deep intent,
    A Star more brilliant than the reſt,
The Herald of ſome great Event,
Moves through the gilded firmament
       Onward towards the weſt.

Then came the ſound Tradition brought
    From Peor's top in days of old,
What time the Seer entrancèd caught
Prophetic Power, and Spirit-taught
       The future did unfold.

A Sceptre ſhall from Iſrael riſe,
    A Star from Jacob doubly bleſt,
And now before their wondering eyes
The brilliant Meteor walks the ſkies
       Still onward toward the weſt.

Where'er it leads, that fiery Light
    Unhidden by the blaze of day,
And marking with intenſer might
The darkneſs of the deeper night,
       They follow on the way,

With morning's bluſh, when ſunſets fade,
    On over rock and ſteep and wild,
By Palm and Cedar tree and ſhade,
Till in the homely Manger laid
       They find the Royal CHILD.

The Epiphany.

Intruding doubts away they fling,
  Unheeding the unwonted stir,
They from their costly treasures bring
Free Offerings for the Infant King,
    Gold, Frankincense and Myrrh.

Gold shadows forth His Royalty,
  While Frankincense His Priesthood shows,
And Myrrh that He shall buried be—
And so the wondrous Mystery
    With deeper meaning grows.

Oh! for some Heavenly Light enshrined
  In God's dark Ways, or holy Word
To break upon each erring mind
With Spirit power, that all might find
    The Saviour, Christ, the Lord.

Till walking in a living way
  To holier purpose we arise,
And on His Altar day by day
Our thoughts and best affections lay,
    A willing Sacrifice.

Meditation of a Faithful Soul: from the Latin.

Of Contempt of the World.

HEN I see with heartfelt pain
All this world defiled remain,
All this world but makes my heart
With concern and anguish smart.

When the Spirit pure and fair
Thinks how vain is earthly care,
For its safety it will sigh
And from worldly care will fly.

When the mind serene and pure
Finds no worldly things secure,
Lest with them the mind should fall,
Carefully it flies from all.

When in earnest thought I find
Worldly hope so false and blind,
To a firmer hope I turn,
Earthly hope I scorn to learn.

Worldly care when I regard,
How depraved it is, how hard!
Him who owns its power I find
Callous both in heart and mind.

Meditation of a Faithful Soul.

When the world's applause I meet,
Think of all its vain deceit,
Fraud and worldly praise and fame
Ear and heart will deem the same.

When I think of this world's fruit,
Grief and woe in each pursuit,
All its fruit is but a curse,
Nothing than the world is worse.

When the world's gay flowers are spread,
And I think what scent they shed,
In them so much grief I see,
Perfumes none they yield to me.

When I think of life's short days,
And their vain and giddy ways,
Light grows weighty then and strong,
And the short is found full long.

Of the Fear of Death.

WHEN I dwell on Death's dread day,
Calling me from life away,
With deep fear am I possessed,
Then my Soul can take no rest.

When I think I am but dust,
And that quickly die I must,
Then with anxious fear possessed
Cold as ashes turns my breast.

When I think, condemned to die,
What will be my deſtiny,
Well may I be filled with fear,
Unprepared to view it near.

How I dread that wrathful Day,
Day of terror and diſmay,
Day of anguiſh, grief and woe,
Vengeful Day on ſin below.

Of the Coming of the Judge.

HOW I tremble, filled with fear,
 As the future Judge draws near;
All ſhall be laid open, plain,
Nought ſhall unavenged remain.

Who amongſt us ſhall not fear,
When he ſees that Judge appear,
And before Him raging Fire,
Scathing ſinners in His Ire?

From the Heavens He comes to view,
Judge and Witneſs, faithful, true;
Nor ſhall He, approaching near,
Hold His Peace, nor pauſe, nor fear:

Juſtly judge, nor will He ſpare,
Favour none may hope to ſhare,
Not with gold can He be bought,
Nor by prayer may then be ſought.

He shall judge the Nations round,
He shall save men guiltless found;
But the strong shall feel His Power,
Slaves to riches dread that hour.

All who pleasure sought and proved,
Then shall curse those joys they loved;
All who worldly lived and vain
Shall with Souls condemned remain.

What shall then the sinful do?
What shall then self-love pursue?
O what works shall then avail
When all power to work shall fail?

Then shall hidden deeds appear,
All past works be plain and clear,
All shall tremble, high and low,
Till their final doom they know.

Then will sorrow come too late
To avert the sinner's fate,
And to weep for sins and wail
Then will prove of no avail.

Of the Sinner's Punishment.

HOW dreadful when that Word
On the Left ' Depart' is heard,
While the great King on the Right
Shall with ' Come' the Just invite.

Meditation of a Faithful Soul.

Then shall every hope be past,
And 'to-morrow' end at last;
Each to torments doomed to go,
No release shall ever know.

Burnt in Flames, yet not consumed,
Food for worms and reptiles doomed,
He in pain shall writhe and turn
Who Salvation would not earn.

O what foul Tormentors then
Tear and torture sinful men,
And unsparing Demons dire
Sins avenge in endless Fire.

O how sad, that then too late
Sinners moan their hopeless fate,
None can then their anguish heal,
When Hell's quenchless Flames they feel.

* * *

O Thou great Celestial King!
Grace and succour to us bring,
From these tortures save us free,
May we ever rest in Thee.

Of the Joy of the Blessed.

WHEN I think what shall befall
After death the Virtuous all,
And how firm will stand the Just,
Greatly I rejoice and trust.

For the Day is near when those
Just and Good shall find repose,
When their persecutors cease
And the Patient reign in peace.

O that Day of Life and Light,
Day of unheard Glory bright,
When grim Death itself shall die,
And the dismal night shall fly.

Lo! the great, long wished for King
Now Salvation hastes to bring,
Now will at the just One's prayer
Heavenly Bliss for him prepare.

Heavenly King, He hastens now;
At His Coming all must bow,
Judge and Witness, great and free,
He Whom every eye shall see.

He will come and not delay,
And His Glory will display,
To reward the suffering Just,
Who in Him have placed their trust.

O how happy! O how sweet!
When those Souls shall Jesus meet,
Whom in life they truly loved,
And His faithful Servants proved.

Then with gracious Look and Word,
Speaking, Jesus shall be heard;

Thus His Love ſhall utterance find
In the ſight of all mankind—

You who have your Faith maintained,
And with Me have firm remained,
You who bore for Me and fought,
See the good you long have ſought.

See the Kingdom promiſed you,
Though concealed till now from view;
Behold, poſſeſs, and reign ſecure,
Ever ſhall your Joy endure.

Then the Juſt ſhall in amaze
Speak with holy joy and praiſe,
And reply exultingly,
Praiſing what they wondering ſee—

To our GOD be thanks and praiſe!
What we hoped for all our days,
Now we ſee and now poſſeſs;
CHRIST our LORD we praiſe and bleſs!

O how ſweet, how bleſt our fate,
Throughout life the world to hate;
Sad and bitter would it prove
If the world had gained our love.

Happy thoſe who mourned and wept,
And their Souls in patience kept,
Thoſe to whom the world gave pain
Now in endleſs Bliſs ſhall reign.

There shall dwell no grief, nor fear;
None shall ever shed a tear;
Nor shall want; nor age, nor care,
Nor defect be ever there.

There shall reign eternal Peace,
Holy Joy shall never cease,
There shall be the flower of youth,
There Salvation's crown and truth.

None the Rapture can conceive,
Nor the perfect Joy believe
In Heaven's Glory to remain,
And with Angels ever reign.

* * *

To that Realm Thy Children call,
O Thou righteous Judge of all;
Thee we seek, on Thee rely,
Thee implore with frequent cry.

The Child-Christ on the Cross: an Anticipation of Calvary.

HIS Face is flushed with Boyhood's glow,
His earnest Eyes are raised to Heaven,
No thorn has scarred that bloodless Brow,
Nor Hands nor Feet by nails are riven.

The Child Christ on the Cross.

They have not bared His Limbs in scorn,
    Nor stripped Him of His seamless Vest;
No scourge His Virgin Flesh has torn,
    No soldier's spear has gashed His Breast.

No crowds press round with ribald cry
    To mock the Helpless SAVIOUR's woes;
Why bides He there so patiently?
    Why hangs the CHILD-CHRIST on the Cross?

Not yet are poured the bitter Tears,
    The Blood to save a world undone,
And of those three and thirty years
    Scarce the first twelve their course have run.

Oh why that Self-made Cross embrace?
    Why antedate the coming strife?
Why blend with Boyhood's dawning grace
    Dread shadows of a tortured Life?

The Chalice steeped in this world's sin,
    The Sweat of dark Gethsemane,
The burning Thirst our Souls to win,
    The Baptism of the bleeding Tree;

The Traitor in the midnight gloom,
    The guilty Herod's murderous fears,
The shout that hails the unrighteous doom
    Creep onward with the creeping years;

They come, they come, my SAVIOUR LORD,
    The snares around Thy path are set,

The foeman's darts againſt Thee ſtored,
  They come, but oh, they come not yet.

Not yet in pride, or hate, or ſcorn
  A tyrant world has riſen to ſlay;
Oh, wherefore ſhroud Life's early morn
  In ſtorms that wrap the ſetting day?

Victim of Love, in Manhood's prime
  Thou wilt aſcend the Croſs to die;
Why hangs the CHILD before His time
  Stretched on that Bed of agony?

   *   *   *

No thorn-wreath crowns My Boyiſh Brow,
  No ſcourge has dealt its cruel ſmart,
In Hands and Feet no nail-prints ſhow,
  No ſpear is planted in My Heart.

They have not ſet Me for a Sign
  Hung bare beneath the ſunleſs ſky,
Nor mixed the draught of gall and wine
  To mock My dying Agony.

The livelong night, the livelong day,
  My Child, I travail for thy good,
And for thy ſake I hang alway
  Self-crucified upon the Rood.

To witneſs to the living Truth,
  To keep thee pure from ſin's alloy,
I cloud the ſunſhine of My Youth:
  The MAN muſt ſuffer in the BOY.

Viſions of unrepented ſin,
  The forfeit crown, the eternal loſs,
Lie deep My ſorrowing Soul within,
  And nail My Body to the Croſs.

The livelong night, **the livelong** day,
  A CHILD upon that Croſs **I** reſt;
All night I for My Children pray,
  All day I woo them to My Breaſt.

Long years of toil and pain are **Mine**
  Ere I be lifted up to die,
Where cold the Paſchal moonbeams ſhine
  At noon on darkened **Calvary.**

The thorn-wreath then will pierce My Brow,
  The nails **will fix Me to the** Tree;
But I ſhall hang, as **I** do now,
  Self-crucified for Love of thee.

The Signals of Levi.

Signal the Firſt.

THERE is light on Hebron now,
  Hark to the trumpet-din!
Day dawns on Hebron's brow,
  Let the Sacrifice begin!

The Signals of Levi.

Hear ye the gathering sound?
   How the lute and harp rejoice,
'Mid the war of Oxen bound,
   And the Lamb's beseeching voice!

This day both the Prince and Priest
   Will hold, at Salem's shrine,
A high and a haughty Feast
   Of Flesh and the ruddy Wine.

For a perilous hour is fled,
   And the fear is vain at last,
Though foretold by Sages dead,
   And sworn by the Prophets past.

They said that a mortal Birth
   Even now would a Name unfold
That should rule the wide wide earth,
   And quench the Thrones of old.

But no sound, nor voice, nor word,
   The tale of travail brings;
Not an infant-cry is heard
   In the Palaces of Kings.

Blossom and Branch are bare
   On Jesse's stately Stem;
So they bid swart Edom wear
   Fallen Israel's diadem

How they throng the cloistered ground!
   'Mid Judah's shame and sin;
Hark to the trumpet sound,
   Let the Sacrifice begin!

Signal the Second.

THERE is light on Hebron's towers!
    Day dawns o'er Jordan's ſtream,
And it floats where Bethlehem's bowers
    Of the bleſſed morning dream.

Yet it wakes no kingly halls,
    It cleaves no purpled room,
The ſoft calm radiance falls
    On a cavern's vaulted gloom

But there, where the Oxen reſt
    When the weary day is done,
How that Maiden-Mother's Breaſt
    Thrills with her Awful Son!

A Cave! where the Fatlings roam,
    By the ruddy Heifer trod,
Yea, the Mountain's rifted home
    Is the Birth-place of a God!

This is He! the myſtic Birth
    By the Sign and Voice foretold;
He ſhall rule the wide wide earth
    And quench the Thrones of old!

The Child of Judah's line,
    The Son of Abraham's fame,
Ariſe, ye Lands! and ſhine
    With the Bleſſed Jesus' Name.

This is the glorious dawn;
　So fades the night of ſin;
Lo! the gloom of Death is gone,
　Let the Sacrifice begin!

Signal the Third.

O! Watchman, what of the night?
　Tell! Chriſtian Soldier, tell!
Are Hebron's towers in ſight?
　Haſt thou watched and warded well?

Yea, we have paced the wall
　Till the Day-ſtar's glimmering birth,
And we breathed our trumpet-call
　When the ſunlight walked the earth.

What ſaweſt thou with the dawn?
　Say! Chriſtian Warder, ſay!
When the miſts of night were gone,
　And the hills grew ſoft with day?

We beheld the morning ſwell
　Bright o'er the eaſtern Sea,
Till the ruſhing ſunbeams fell
　Where the weſtward Waters be!

City and bulwark lay
　Rich with the orient blaze;
And rocks, at the touch of day,
　Gave out a ſound of praiſe!

No hill remained in cloud,
    There lurked no darkling glen;
And the Light of God is loud
    Upon every tongue of men!

There shall never more be night
    With this eternal Sun!
There be Hebrons many in sight,
    And the Sacrifice is done!

The Tree of Life.

From an old Latin Poem.

THERE is a spot, of men believed to be
    Earth's centre, and the place of Adam's grave,
    And here a slip that from a barren Tree
Was cut, Fruit sweet and salutary gave—
Yet not unto the tillers of the land;
That blessèd Fruit was culled by other hand.

The shape and fashion of the Tree attend:
    From undivided stem at first it sprung;
Thence in two arms its branches did outsend,
    Like sail-yards whence the flowing sheet is hung,
Or as a yoke that in the furrow stands,
When the tired steers are loosened from their bands.

The Tree of Life.

Three days the slip from which this Tree should
   spring
  Appeared as dead—then suddenly it bore,
(While earth and Heaven stood awed and won-
   dering)
  Harvest of vital Fruit; the fortieth more
Beheld it touch Heaven's summit with its height,
And shroud its sacred head in clouds of light.

Yet the same while it did put forth below
  Branches twice six, these too with fruit
   endued,
Which stretching to all quarters might bestow
  Upon all nations medicine and food,
Which mortal men might eat, and eating be
Sharers henceforth of Immortality.

But when another fifty days were gone,
  A Breath Divine, a mighty storm of Heaven
On all the Branches swiftly lighted down,
  To which a rich nectareous taste was given,
And all the heavy leaves that on them grew
Distilled henceforth a sweet and Heavenly dew.

Beneath that Tree's great shadow on the plain
  A Fountain bubbled up, whose lymph serene
Nothing of earthly mixture might distain;
  Fountain so pure not anywhere was seen
In all the world, nor on whose marge the earth
Put flowers of such unfading beauty forth.

And thither did all people, young and old,
  Matrons and Virgins, rich and poor, a crowd
Stream ever, who, whenas they did behold
  Thoſe branches with their golden Burden bowed,
Stretched forth their hands, and eager glances
    threw
Towàrd the Fruit diſtilling that ſweet dew.

But touch they might not theſe, much leſs allay
  Their hunger, howſoe'er they might deſire,
Till the foul tokens of their former way
  They had waſhed off, the duſt and ſordid mire,
And cleanſed their bodies in that holy Wave,
Able from every ſpot and ſtain to ſave.

But when within their mouths they had received
  Of that immortal Fruit the guſt Divine,
Straight of all ſickneſs were their Souls relieved,
  The weak grew ſtrong; and taſks they did
    decline
As overgreat for them they ſhunned no more,
And things they deemed they could not bear they
    bore.

But woe, alas! ſome daring to draw near
  That ſacred Stream, did preſently retire,
Drew wholly back again, and did not fear
  To ſtain themſelves in all their former mire,
That Fruit rejecting from their mouths again,
Not any more their Medicine, but their bane.

An Ode of Manzoni on the Nativity.

Oh blessèd they, who not withdrawing so,
   First in that Fountain make them pure and fair,
And who from thence unto the Branches go,
   With Power upon the Fruitage hanging there:
Thence by the Branches of the lofty Tree
Ascend to Heaven—The Tree of Life oh, see!

An Ode of Manzoni on the Nativity.

AS when from off some precipice
    A mass of rock goes sounding,
   O'er long and steep declivity
    From mountain summit bounding;
O'er crags and hollows leaping,
A course resistless keeping,
   It strikes the dale, and stays;

And where it stopped, immoveable
   Its bulk inert remaineth
Across the lapse of centuries,
   And never more regaineth
Its former lofty station,
If gracious ordination
   The fallen shall not raise:

So lay the wretched progeny
   Of man, that by transgression
Had braved an Anger Infinite—
   When under that oppression

The nethermost of evil
He reached, and from its level
    Could rear his neck no more.

Who then among the inheritors
    Of malison from Heaven
Durst move the far-off Holy ONE
    That they might be forgiven?
Who made new Leagues eternal?
Who forced the Foe infernal
    His prizes to restore?

Behold! a CHILD is born for us;
    A SON to us is granted:
If but His Eyelid quivereth
    The hosts of Hell are daunted:
His Hand to man He tenders,
He raises him to splendours
    Beyond his former lot.

From Palace-courts ethereal
    A Fountain is descending,
And through the fissures briary
    Its living stream extending:
Trunks are with honey flowing,
And flowers there are blowing
    Where life or sap was not.

O SON, to Whose Original
    No age an epoch setteth,
Eternal, Whom the Eternal ONE
    Like unto Him begetteth,

Who art, Whose Comprehension
Exceeds the world's extension,
   Whose Word the world hath made—

Didst Thou Thyself humiliate
  To wear this nature earthy?
What excellence could render it
  Of so much Bounty worthy?
O Thy deep Counsels grounded
On Mercy, what unbounded
   Compassion they displayed!

This Day He's born: to Ephrathah
  That place foretold, the Maiden,
The Glory unto Israel,
  With Him ascended laden:
She to the Same doth owe Him,
Who promised to bestow Him
   Thence, when He comes on earth.

The Mother incomparable
  In Swaddling clothes enlaced Him
Of poorest sort, and tenderly
  Within the Manger placed Him:
Then worshipped, O the greatly
Favoured, That GOD That lately
   From her pure self had birth.

The Messenger Angelical,
  That had to bear to mortals
These wondrous tidings, halted not
  At rich or great men's portals:

But Shepherds world-neglected
And fervent he respected;
　　And showed a sudden blaze,

In which, around him clustering
　From all the nighted region,
They saw Celestial Ministers,
　　A flying, flaming Legion,
That in their Heavenly measure,
And fired with zeal and pleasure,
　　Were heard to sing God's Praise.

Returning to the Firmament
　They ceased not from their singing,
Which through the clouds was issuing
　Fainter and fainter ringing;
Till higher yet ascended
The sacred Hymns, and ended
　　For those Believers' ears.

Now rise the watchers fortunate,
　And seek without delaying
For that abode of poverty,
　Which well they find displaying
The Truth foretold, where swaddled
And in the Manger cradled
　　The Lord of Heaven appears.

Sleep, Heavenly Babe, sleep quietly:
　No storms shall murmur o'er Thee,
That went like Thy Van-cavalry
　O'er guilty earth before Thee,

Stanzas.

Let flumber ftill poffefs Thee,
And waking not diftrefs Thee,
    Nor weeping gall Thine Eye.

Sleep, Heavenly ONE: the multitudes
  Have heard not yet Thy Story,
But they fhall be Thy Heritage
  Hereafter and Thy Glory;
And in abode fo lowly,
And hid in duft, their holy
    Lawgiver fhall defcry.

Stanzas.

Thou gaveft me no Kifs.

HOU gaveft me no Kifs,
  JESUS, my Mafter, oft I fadly thought!
  Perchance Thou choofeft to be found
    unfought
And I was ever feeking! Yet in this
Methought, I cannot change; and fhould I mifs
Thee on Thy Way, yet there I will abide
And track Thy Foot-prints to the dark ftream's
    fide.

    Thou gaveft unto me
No Sign! I knew no loving Secret told
As oft to men beloved, and I muft hold

My peace when these would speak of converse
    high;
Yet would I, Jesus, Master, still be nigh
When these would speak, and in the words rejoice
Of them who listen to the Bridegroom's Voice.

    Thou gavest unto me
No goodly Gift, no Pearl of price untold,
No Signet ring, no Ruby shut in gold,
No Chain about my neck to wear for pride,
For love no Token in my breast to hide;
Yea! these perchance from out my careless hold
Had slipped; perchance some robber shrewd and
    bold
Had snatched them from me! So Thou didst pro‑
    vide
For me, my Master kind, from day to day,
And in this world, Thine Inn, thou badst me stay
And saidest, "What thou spendest, I will pay."

    I never heard Thee say,
"Bring forth the Robe for this My Son, the best!"
Thou gavest not to me as unto guest
Approved, a festal Mantle rich and gay;
Still singing, ever singing, in the cold
Thou leavest me without Thy Door to stay,
And the night draweth on, the Day is old,
And Thou hast never said, "Come in, My Friend:"
Yet once, yea! twice, methinks, Thy Love did
    send

A secret Message, " Blessed unto the end
Are they that love and they that still endure :"
JESUS, my SAVIOUR, take to Thee Thy poor,
Take home Thy humble Friend!

Declension and Revival.

DIE to thy root, sweet Flower!
　　If so GOD wills, die even to thy root,
Live there awhile an uncomplaining, mute
Blank life, with darkness wrapped about thy head.
Oh, fear not for the silence round thee spread;
This is no Grave, though thou among the dead
Be counted, but the Hiding-place of Power:
　　Die to thy root, sweet Flower!

　　Spring from thy root, sweet Flower!
When so GOD wills, spring even from thy root;
Send through the earth's warm breast a quickened
　　　　shoot,
Spread to the sunshine, spread unto the shower,
And lift into the sunny air thy dower
Of bloom and odour; life is on the plains
And in the woods a sound of birds and rains
That sing together; lo! the winter's cold
Is past, sweet scents revive, thick buds unfold.
Be thou, too, willing in the Day of Power;
　　Spring from thy root, sweet Flower!

Stanzas.

Death.

IN Spring the green leaves ſhoot,
  In Spring the bloſſoms fall,
With Summer falls the fruit,
The leaves in Autumn fall;
Contented from the bough
They drop; leaves, bloſſoms now
And ripened fruit, the warm earth takes them all.

Thus all things aſk for reſt,
A Home above, a Home beneath the ſod:
The Sun will ſeek the Weſt,
The Bird will ſeek its neſt,
The Heart another Breaſt
Whereon to lean; the Spirit ſeeks its GOD.

Vespers.

WHEN I have ſaid my quiet ſay,
  When I have ſung my little ſong,
How ſweetly, ſweetly dies the day
  The valley and the hill along;
How ſweet the Summons " Come away"
  That calls me from the buſy throng!

I thought beſide the water's flow
  Awhile to lie beneath the leaves;
I thought in Autumn's harveſt glow
  To reſt my head upon the ſheaves;

But, lo! methinks the day was brief
And cloudy; flower, nor fruit, nor leaf
I bring—and yet accepted, free,
And bleſt, my LORD, I come to Thee.

What matter now for promiſe loſt,
    Through blaſt of Spring or Summer rains?
What matter now for purpoſe croſſed,
    For broken hopes and waſted pains;
What if the Olive little yields,
    What if the Grape be blighted? Thine
The Corn upon a thouſand fields,
    Upon a thouſand hills the Vine.

Thou loveſt ſtill the Poor; oh, bleſt
    In poverty beloved to be!
Leſs lowly is my choice confeſſed,
    I love the rich in loving Thee!
My Spirit bare before Thee ſtands;
    I bring no gift, I aſk no ſign;
I come to Thee with empty hands
    The ſurer to be filled from Thine.

A Legend of S. Peter.

ALL of you ſhall ſoon forſake Me—One
    already hath betrayed—
So the LORD addreſſed His loved Ones;
    only One an anſwer made.

Simon Peter, self-reliant, yet the strongest in the
    Faith,
Answered—Master, I go with Thee both to prison
    and to death.

Soon, too soon, he rued that answer! Now, by
    GOD'S great Mercy blest,
Clings he closer to the SAVIOUR thrice denied, yet
    thrice confessed.

And for Him Who knoweth all things, knows he
    loves Him, will he keep
Until death that last Injunction, CHRIST'S Com-
    mand, to feed His Sheep.

Toils he on with patient labour through the work
    and wail of years,
But though still in CHRIST rejoicing, sheds he
    still repentant tears.

Still whene'er the bird of morning, ere the day
    break, sounds his call,
Up S. Peter at the summons rises—kneels to
    weep his fall.

So, though holiest aspirations on life's work our
    hearts may fix,
Still the tears of deep contrition with the noblest
    aims must mix.

Now at length, his mission ended, in a prison he
    must lie,

Where the foes he braved have thrown him, captive, and condemned to die.

But the brave and faithful Servant, eager yet to work for all,
Cannot reſt in patient waiting 'neath that dreary dungeon-wall.

Stealthily he leaves his priſon in the ſilence of the night,
Though no Angel now attends him ſent from Heaven to aid his flight :

Yet the maſſive gates of iron yield unto his trembling hands—
What is this? Can ſight deceive him? Christ, his Lord, before him ſtands.

Joy and wonder overwhelming, heart and head before Him bow,
Scarce his lips can form the queſtion—Maſter, whither goeſt Thou?

Falls the hope that erſt had thrilled him, Christ with him might there abide—
Peter, I to Rome am wending; there, I muſt be crucified!

Then, as once when at Emmaus in the Breaking of the Bread,
He before His two Diſciples ſpake the Word and vaniſhed,

So e'en now He ſpake to Simon, ſpake, and
	vaniſhed at the Word,
Leaving him transfixed in wonder at the tidings
	he had heard.

Ponders he—Though He redeemed us by His
	Death of ſhame and pain,
Though ſubdued is Death's dominion muſt He
	ſuffer all again?

No! 'Twas once for all He ſuffered, by His
	Death to make us free;
But His Followers ſtill may bear Him: He muſt
	die again in me.

I who late have left my priſon, feared to ſuffer for
	His Name,
Have I thus again denied Him? Coward ſpirit!
	bluſh for ſhame.

Have I then in deed belied Him, ſpurned the holy
	Truth's defence?
Oh, the act of ſinful weakneſs! Satan! Tempter!
	get thee hence.

Now, O LORD, would I confeſs Thee with no
	ſelf-confiding breath;
LORD, I love Thee: take me with Thee both to
	priſon and to death.

Humbled, yet in hope exultant, ſtricken, yet of
	fear bereft,

A Legend of S. Peter.

Turns he back a willing captive to the dungeon he had left.

With the iron chain they bind him, bear him prisoner into Rome:
Ah! they little reck they lead him unto his eternal Home.

One more Victim stands beside him, fellow-witness to the Faith,
Who, for love of his Dear SAVIOUR, will endure the pains of death.

Saints of GOD he persecuted till he heard his Master's Call,
Then with holy Zeal he laboured more abundantly than all.

Now before the Cross S. Peter stands confessing bold and free,
Speaks the thought that seethes within him—Is this privilege for me?

No! myself I will not liken to the LORD Whom once I spurned;
Of His Death I am not worthy; downward let my head be turned.

Thus he suffers—yet, who knoweth what Divine Support is nigh?
Who shall say what golden Visions float before that closing eye?

Who shall guess what inward **rapture** stays that
 short and gasping breath,
While the pallid brow is moistened with the chilly
 dews of Death?

Who shall doubt, the **warfare over,** on his Master's
 Breast he lies;
Face to face doth there confess Him 'mid the Joys
 of Paradise!

An Easter Carol.

THEY bound him well in the dungeon
 cell,
  His father's best-loved son,
 And the iron dole into Joseph's soul
  Its bitter way hath won:
But faith and truth have gained him ruth
  And loosed the tyrant's chain,
And the exile lone to Egypt's throne
  From prison comes to reign.
The SON of the FATHER, Almighty to save,
Was laid for three days in the heart of the grave,
But the fetters which held Him no longer may
 bind,
And He reigneth to-day over ransomed mankind.

  He laid him down in Gaza town,
   The forceful Nazarite,
  And the heathen guard kept watch and ward
   To slay him at morning-light:

An Easter Carol.

But at midnight he rose from the midst of his foes,
    No longer would he stay,
And to Hebron's hill of his own strong will
    He carried their gates away.
The Nazarene Captive Whom Hell had ensnared,
Around Whom the hosts of the Evil One glared,
Hath gone from among them in conquering state,
And broken in pieces their bars and their gate.

    O now His rolling chariot wheels
        Lead bound captivity,
    And where His Presence He reveals
        His people bow the knee.
    He takes to Him a priestly Bride,
    And He Himself is glorified,
        And clad in white and gold:
    He sitteth on the royal seat,
    And all the nations at His Feet
        Lay tribute manifold.

    The riddle erewhile spoken,
        May now be read with ease,
    The slaughtered lion's token,
        The honey and the bees.
    To-day in full completeness
        The mystery stands good,
    Since from the strong comes Sweetness,
        And from the eater, Food.

Hearken to Him as He comes in His Might,
Monarch of monarchs, victorious in fight:

Qui procedis ab Utroque.

Speaks He in anger, the sinner to blame?
Speaks He in sorrow, the dastard to shame?
    With no reproach for blindness
      He meets His own to-day,
    In perfect Loving-kindness
      Thus only will He say—
The winter time away is past, the rain is gone
    and o'er,
The flow'rets bloom again at last, the birds are
    heard once more,
And in our land we list afresh the cooing of the
    dove,
The figs and vines are green and lush, O come
    away, My Love!

Qui procedis ab Utroque.

A Sequence of Adam of S. Victor to the Holy Spirit.

THOU from FATHER, SON, proceeding,
Sanctify our praise and pleading,
    PARACLETE, enthroned above;
Lips of Inspiration lend us,
And responsive ardours send us
    To Thine own rich flames of Love.

    Hail by FATHER, SON, belovèd!
    Equal unto Each, approvèd
      Peer of Perfect DEITY;

All things filling, all sustaining,
Warder of the stars, and reigning
   Moveless o'er the moving sky.

Light the clearest, Light the dearest,
Who our inward darkness cheerest
   With Thy cloud-dissolving Ray:
By Thine Advent men are mended,
Sin departs, her empire ended,
   And sin's rust is wiped away.

Knowledge of the Truth Thou sowest;
Thou the road of Justice showest,
   And the pleasant paths of Peace:
Far from hearts perverse Thou fliest,
But, where Goodness is, suppliest
   Access to Thy Mysteries.

Nothing dark where Thou explainest;
Nothing foul where Thou remainest;
   Thy pervading Presence bright
Wakes exultant Spirit-voices;
Conscience feelingly rejoices
   In the cleanness of Thy Light.

Thou canst render heart-strings tender,
And expellest, where Thou dwellest,
   Clouds of heaviness and gloom:
Flaming ever, burning never,
Hallowed fires from pain deliver
   Human Souls, where Thou dost come.

Qui procedis ab Utroque.

Intellects that erewhile slumbered,
With a deadening crust encumbered,
   Quicken in Thy glorious Light :
Into Speech-divine Thou mouldest
Tongues, and lovingly upholdest
   Hearts made ready for the right.

Help of Souls for succour groaning,
Comforter of mourners moaning,
   Refuge of the friendless poor,
Teach us to cast off the leaven
Of this earth : to Thine own Heaven
   Every erring love restore ;
Clear from taint what wrong hath blighted,
Reconcile the disunited,
   Be our safeguard evermore !

Thou who once, in visitation,
Strength and lofty Consolation
   To Thy trembling Church didst send,
Visit, if it be Thy Pleasure,
Even us, and in like measure
   All who at Thine Altars bend.

Equal Majesty and Power
Stand the everlasting Dower
   Of the GODHEAD—THREE in ONE :
Thou, the Third, art rightly reckoned
Equal with the First and Second ;
   Ordered scale existeth none.

Wherefore, in Thy mighty Prefence,
Sharer of the FATHER's Effence,
   Humbly do Thy Servants fue:
We to GOD the FATHER ever
And to GOD the SON deliver
   And to Thee our praifes due.

The Advent Antiphons.

O Sapientia.

THOU, the Effential WISDOM, Who
   doft proceed
Eternal from the Eternal, in the Breaft
Of the Great FATHER dwelling, ever
   bleft,
Firft Caufe of all, and Crown of time's laft deed!
Love's Sovereign purpofe fhines in Thee decreed
Through void of ages making manifeft,
In meafured Might harmonioufly expreffed,
The unfeen Infinite, which does all things lead.
Come! Quickly come! Thy Touch bids WISDOM
   fpring,
A ftream of Grace from Nature's barren rock,
To fpread rich paftures for Thy wandering Flock.
Come! Quickly come! enable us to bring
Thanks meet for Heaven, to be accepted there:
Thy WISDOM crowns us, if Thy Grace we fhare.

O *Adonai.*

 THOU who **ever** ruleſt Iſrael's Race
With Love ſtill pledged to Abraham's
faithful prayer :
In Sinai's buſh, the Flame revealed Thy Care :
Thy Voice gives Light which clouds **can** ne'er
efface.
Thy **WORD** calls forth a people full of **Grace** :
Why **doubt** we Thy Commands ? Thy **Might** we
bear,
Called from earth's chains **Thy Laws** pure robes to
wear :
Cleanſed in **Thy** Name, we **claim** the children's
place.
Come ! Quickly come ! Through ſin's foul touch
we pine :
And diſobedience, wailing o'er **her** dead,
Finds pleaſures wither whereſo'er ſhe **tread.**
Come ! Quickly come ! ſtretch forth the Arm
Divine !
In years of grief Obedience didſt Thou learn :
Redeemed Obedience waits for Thy Return.

O *Radix Jeſſe.*

 THOU, the Root of Jeſſe ! Many an age
Has trampled **down** Thy Stock with heed-
leſs mood !

Yet was GOD's Truth Thy Guard: and aye,
   renewed,
Thy Bloom ſhall cheer earth's briar-grown or-
   phanage:
Kings ſhall fall proſtrate and forget their rage,
In ſilence by Thy fragrant Power ſubdued:
Nations ſhall flock to Thy bleſt ſolitude,
And claim in prayer GOD's promiſed Heritage.
Come! Quickly come! ſpread wide Thy ſhelter-
   ing Grace!
Meek violets fed with tears are all our wealth:
Love brings Thee all, and ſeeks Thy balmy
   Health.
Come! Quickly come! Let Hope's impriſoned
   race
Riſe free and vigorous, taſting Thy ſoft Gale,
And Love's bright form outſhine Time's cloudy
   veil!

O Clavis David.

THOU That beareſt David's wondrous
   Key,
The Sceptre of united Iſrael!
No foe ſhall enter where Thy Saints ſhall dwell:
Heaven's gates unfold their bliſs to none but Thee:
Men murmur at Thy Voice, but Thy Decree,
Supreme in Power each ſtubborn heart to quell,
Builds here on earth the Saintly citadel
To ſhine with Thine own Self for ever free.

Come! Quickly come! ſin ſhall be ours no more,
Safe in Thy Sanctity! when ſcorners fly
Shut out in darkneſs, hope and fear ſhall die.
Come! Quickly come! through Thee, Heaven's
　　myſtic door,
For Death's dark exile gain we God's true Light,
For ſpace-bound ſenſe, exiſtence infinite.

O Oriens.

 THOU, the central Orb of righteous Love,
　　Riſing in fulneſs of Eternal Light
On this our wintry world! Thy Radiance bright
Wakes the glad ſhout of Faith! Hope dwells
　　above;
Thy Saints with holy luſtre round Thee move,
Stars of a new Creation, in the height
Of God's ordaining Counſel, as Thy Sight
Gives meaſured Grace to each, Thy Power to
　　prove.
Come! Quickly come! and let Thy Beams diſ-
　　perſe
The lingering taint of primal ſin's defiling,
With kindling touch, transforming, reconciling.
Come! Quickly come! diſpel fallen manhood's
　　curſe,
Till all our nature feels the eternal ray
In Fellowſhip Divine of ſpotleſs Day

O Rex Gentium.

THOU, the King of Nations, throned
　　　ſupreme
On bliſsful height of bounteous Providence,
The Long-deſired, Long-promiſed! Man's offence
Broke off a world from GOD: do Thou redeem!
Now glows Thy Majeſty with nobler beam,
The Corner-ſtone of true Love's triumph, whence
The flaſh of multiform Magnificence
Thrills through the ſhrine of Life with jewelled
　　　ſtreams!
Come! Quickly come! our cold dark ſtains efface!
Thy Breath to GOD's pure Beauty raiſed our clay:
Renewing Love ſhall that ſame Breath diſplay.
Come! Quickly come! raiſe up Thy new-born
　　　race
From ſlumbrous apathy! let Zeal conſume
Each trace of earth, and Godlike gild the gloom.

O Emmanuel.

THOU, EMMANUEL, Who now doſt hide
　　　In Subſtance of dependant Infancy
Thine All-ſufficing GODHEAD, ſinners flee,
Our King and SAVIOUR! to Thy gentle Side.
Hence burſts the Fount of Manhood Deified,
Making us meet for GOD. O CHRIST, to Thee
The gathering of the nations ſoon ſhall be,

To own as Judge the SAVIOUR they denied.
Come! Quickly come! Bid their blind raging
　　ceaſe,
Joy of Thy Saints and Terror of Thy foes!
Ariſe to ſave us and Thy Power diſcloſe!
Come! Quickly come! Thy Preſence gives us
　　Peace!
The bond of Saints Thy lonely Cradle brings,
And Hoſts unſeen adore Thee King of kings.

The Transfiguration.

WHO would not burn with ſtrong deſire
　　To mount up with the favoured
　　　three?
　Whate'er the height, whoſe feet
　　would tire
On Tabor's top that ſight to ſee?
　　Words are too faint
　　That ſcene to paint;
Language can give no fit narration
Of CHRIST our LORD's Transfiguration.

Who were thoſe choſen ſons of men
　Who climbed the path where JESUS led,
Who ſaw what baffles tongue or pen,
　Who trod where Angels feared to tread?
　　　Beſt of the beſt
　　　(Though good the reſt)
Of all the Twelve the ſafeſt, ſureſt,
The foremoſt three, the braveſt, pureſt.

The Transfiguration.

O pass not by their honoured names;
   Peter the prompt to do and dare,
The loving John, the faithful James
    Breathe with their LORD the mountain air.
       But mountain air
       And prospect fair,
All, all are lost in wondrous gazing
At JESUS' Form in brightness blazing.

For, while he prayed in accents low,
   That Human Form became Divine;
His Raiment glitters as the snow,
   With Heavenly Glow His Features shine,
       Transfigured, bright,
       White as the light.
But lo! while bending they adore Him,
Two forms in Glory stand before Him;

Moses the meek—from Sinai's height
   Who gave the Law 'mid thunders loud;
Elias—who in chariot bright
   Ascending pierced the opening Cloud;
       The glorious two,
       Now sent to view
JESUS the Radiance here resuming,
Which erst He wore, ere Man's sad dooming.

But not alone to view they came;
   High converse with their LORD and ours
They held of suffering, death, and shame,
   Of triumph too o'er Satan's powers.

The Transfiguration.

      But where are ye
      Apostles three?
A dizzy dimness o'er them creeping,
They sank awhile, unconscious, sleeping.

Awaking soon in wondering fear
   Peter, his brethren's mouth-piece, cried—
'Tis good, 'tis blessed to be here,
   Where, Lord, Thou deignest to abide;
      With prayer and praise
      Three Tents we'll raise;
Three structures, reared with labour pious,
For Thee, for Moses, and Elias.

The random words escaped his tongue,
   (For he and they were sore afraid)
Such Mystic Wonders round him hung,
   He scarce was conscious what he said.
      While yet he spoke
      A bright Cloud broke
In overshadowing gleams around them,
And from the Cloud these Words astound them—

This, This is My Beloved Son,
   To Whom, well-pleased, all Power I give;
Hear Him (for He with Me is One)
   And from His Lips learn how to live—
      Down to the ground
      (As that high sound
Passed from the Cloud, with tones o'erpowering)
The listeners fell, in wonder cowering.

The Transfiguration.

How strange their thoughts what tongue can say?
  Their terrors who can understand?
Till Jesus viewed them as they lay,
  And touched them with a tender Hand—
      Arise, my Friends,
        The Vision ends;
Arise (He cried) and fear no longer,
Arise with faith and courage stronger.

With wakened sight in vain they ranged
  The sainted Two again to see;
Alone with Jesus! all is changed:
  Yet found they all, Good Lord, in Thee;
      As down He led—
        Tell none (He said)
This wondrous Scene, till from Death's prison
The Son of Man again is risen.

Down from the Mount, fresh work of Love
  Soon claimed the Saviour's healing Power;
But John and James and Peter strove
  With hearts more zealous from that hour,
      To keep that Word
        They now had heard
In solemn charge—with rapt reflection
On Death, the Grave, the Resurrection.

In Diebus Celebribus.

A Hymn for the Holy-Days of the Church.

HE Christian must on **Holy-days**
Abstain from all unlawful ways;
From things forbidden he must cease,
As hurtful to his Spirit's peace.

Repressing all desires to roam,
The Mind must keep itself at home;
And, earthly thoughts expelling thence,
Must bar the doors of flesh and sense.

Who sees not that such calm repose
A concentrated power bestows
To worship, on His glorious Throne,
The LORD, Who is our GOD alone?

The Intellect, the Memory,
The Will, moreover, then so free,
With every faculty of Soul,
Must yield to His entire Controul.

We must rejoice alone in GOD,
And grieve to have provoked His Rod;
And turn, with hope and holy fear,
His gentle Words of Love to hear.

His Influence let us realize;
His Absence fear; His Presence prize;

To Him, whate'er may happen, bring
Each adverse and each prosperous thing.

More deeply cherished be the thought
Of what our Blessed LORD has wrought
In Gifts bestowed, or claimed again;
And what His Promises contain.

He has our numerous sins forgiven;
And, from His boundless Store in Heaven,
Our Souls, renewed in Righteousness,
He will with endless Riches bless.

The Gifts of Nature and of Grace
Our Souls must now in silence trace;
Think on the wicked's doom of woe,
And what reward the Just shall know.

We must reflect what wondrous loss
Our SAVIOUR suffered on the Cross,
That we, redeemed from endless flame,
Might be rewarded in His Name.

So also, in this thoughtful state,
The mind must love to meditate
With what serene and glorious rest
The Citizens of Heaven are blest.

The very purpose of this Day,
When servile works are put away,
Is that the Soul may use her wings,
And rise to gaze on Heavenly things.

Thus let us now afcend on high,
And pierce by faith the orient fky;
And fee the Saints' rich Joy and Love,
In the Jerufalem above.

With plenitude of Grace fupplied,
Their happy Souls are fatisfied,
Poffeffed of all they wifhed below,
And freed from every mortal woe.

Within, without, and everywhere
Celeftial Glory fills them there;
From God, their All, around them all
Rays of immortal Splendour fall.

In freedom there, through wondrous Grace,
They fee His Beauty Face to face;
And, filled with rapture at the fight,
They love Him with intenfe delight.

From His bleft Countenance alone
The Light of Glory is their own:
The whole Celeftial Company
Hence gather all they wifh to be.

O happier far than tongue can tell
The blifsful City where they dwell,
And where, in purity, they fee
The Glory of the Trinity!

Hence all the radiance of the fky,
With all its focial harmony;

In Diebus Celebribus.

The Angels and the Saints above
Drink from one Fount of glorious Love.

To praise with all their Spirit's might
The FATHER of Eternal Light
Is all their action—to be blest
In Him for ever, all their rest.

From this the thoughtful mind will see,
In rest or movement, it must be,
Throughout the hours of Holy-days,
Devoted to JEHOVAH's Praise.

For Blessings given while he lives,
For those which GOD in promise gives,
The Christian now in lively song
Must praise the LORD with heart and tongue.

Who thus on holy Festival
Is free upon His GOD to call,
Knows best within himself the way
To celebrate a Holy-day.

To us this knowledge while we live,
King of Eternal Glory, give;
Then we in Heaven Thy Name will praise
With Angels in immortal lays.

To Christ hanging on high.

OW with **vivid** desire
In thine **accents** of fire,
Voice in my Heart weeping,
A new measure **try**;
No longer lie sleeping;
He heareth on high.

Mid vain talking merely,
Distinguished most clearly
The words of emotion
Contrite and sincere,
The song of devotion
He loveth to hear.

This Wood is the token
Of Faith never broken,
Of Love never told,
Faith crying to me—
Draw near **and** behold
Where He hangeth for thee.

Here, sin ever hated
Thou hast expiated,
Thou, **Lamb ever purest**,
Of sin's misery
The burden endurest,
Hope giving to me.

To Christ hanging on high.

I living, adore Thee,
I loving, implore Thee,
Lamb ever faireſt,
  Beſtow upon me,
Of all Gifts the rareſt,
  A Heart turned to Thee.

Make calm by a Word,
This Heart tempeſt-ſtirred,
The guilt far removèd,
  May I cry unto Thee—
I have ſinned, moſt Belovèd,
  Have pity on me.

Raiſe up cleanſed in brightneſs,
This Soul in Death's likeneſs,
Sublime and ſet free
  In Thy Goodneſs immenſe,
I groaning implore Thee
  For true penitence.

If fully beſtowing
Thy Grace to o'erflowing,
Even here may the Spirit
  Enraptured unfold
Her wings, to inherit
The Palace of gold.

Thou, bleſſed Salvation,
Doſt give invitation,

To unending Pleasure
  Dost draw me above,
Where I beyond measure
  May joy in Thy Love.

Thus while I behold Thee,
Sweet Peace doth enfold me;
I hope for the conquest,
  And ever to be
In the rapture of Rest
  Abiding in Thee.

The Way-side Cross.

SILENT we rested where a towering Cross
    On the dry fields of far Bavaria
      stands;
    And wide as man's illimitable loss,
  Its all-embracing arms, like Love, expands.

Upon the wondrous fixture drooping low
  Its wooden weight, a Human Figure hung!
That melancholy Form, I mark it now;
  That ghastly Look, from dread endurance wrung.

Its Brow was crowned in mockery with thorn,
  That dimmed its calm composure all with Blood;
So deep, so difficult the Passion borne,
  That suffering seemed to fill the impassive wood.

Age had not yet its heavy honours hung
　　Upon that Aspect meek, and Godlike Form;
Youthful, not His the vigour of the young,
　　The foot to flee, or breast to brave the storm—

O great Example!—superhuman tie
　　Fashioned in Heaven! love-chant of many parts
By Angel chorus sung, while glad reply
　　Echoes on earth from thousand bleeding hearts!

Ah matchless Beauty! what compared to Thine
　　The chiselled grace of young Antinous' form?
What wreath so graceful as the cruel spine?
　　What chisel like Heaven's dreadful anger-storm?

Still is that patient Head in love reclining
　　When evening hangs her silver lamps on high;
And still, when morning in the East is shining,
　　That great white wondrous Figure marks the sky.

No Rizpah wipes that cold and clammy Brow;
　　No shield is thine against the fiery sun;
Thou that o'ershadowest all, unshaded Thou
　　Bear'st the great ills of the fallen world alone!

Hard were it on such picture long to gaze,
　　And not believe it Very CHRIST to be—
True Sun, though shooting through a mist its rays;
　　Dread Avatar, Incarnate DEITY.

And Memory treasures still the mournful Figure;
　　And Fancy opens wide her half-shut eye;

And Faith herself recruits her failing vigour
  At sight of that immortal Constancy.

There still It stands: no friendly form is nigh;
  Only the way-worn Pilgrim kneeling down
With head reclined, but tearful upward eye,
  Forgetting in that Sorrow all his own.

There through the changing year the stars look
    forth,
  And each above in silent glory sings;
Both when the winter strips the cold blue north,
  And when the west wind spreads its summer
    wings.

And sometimes haply as the pilgrim passes,
  While the dark wind pipes loud, the shadowy
    Form
Seems all to swell and sigh, while mournful masses
  Come through the pauses of the driving storm.

Peace to such thoughts—

*   *   *

           And yet be pardon mine,
  If sometimes all too fondly I may fix
My pensive gaze where Love has set her shrine,
  Within thy blood-streaked boughs, mysterious
    Crucifix!

O quam Glorificum.

An Ancient Latin Poem.

BLISS beyond telling,
   To muſe all alone,
When the Spirit is dwelling
   Serene on its throne;
When the Bridegroom is near,
   Diſcerned through a glaſs,
Where no ſhadows of fear
   Caſt a gloom as they paſs.

Alas! that this gladneſs
   Comes ſeldom, ſoon flies;
O'erclouded by ſadneſs
   It fades and it dies:
For life till the end
   Is a weariſome ſtrife,
And Man muſt contend
   Againſt ills that are rife.

Lo! Sin is prevailing,
   And waxes more bold;
While Love unavailing
   Grows faithleſs and cold.
From far and from near
   Comes the Foe with a ſhout:
Within there is fear;
   There are fightings without.

O quam Glorificum.

Oh! why 'mid my sorrow
   Are gleams thus allowed,
Which the grief of to-morrow
   Shall veil in its shroud?
What is life at the best
   But a burden of care,
With seldom a rest
   From the weight of despair?

O Speck in creation,
   How can'st thou complain,
Though sore thy probation
   Of sorrow and pain?
Forgetting that life
   Is no season of ease,
But of watching and strife,
   Till the battle shall cease.

As gold is made purer
   By trial of flame,
My Son, so grows surer
   Thy faith in My Name.
I chastise whom I love,
   It is writ in My Word,
Nor are Servants above
   The lot of their LORD.

Say, hast thou forgotten,
   How all My Life long,
I, the ONLY-BEGOTTEN,
   Bore anguish and wrong?

O quam Glorificum.

How I wandered forlorn,
   With no place of repose,
No shelter from scorn
   In My manifold Woes?

Be patient; be lowly;
   And so shalt thou be
In feature more wholly
   Made like unto Me,
Who came from on high,
   True God and True Lord,
To live and to die
   Despised and abhorred.

And she, as thou knowest,
   From whom is My Birth,
Was counted the lowest
   And least upon earth;
Was proved and was tried
   By a chastisement sore,
But is now glorified
   And exalted the more.

Those whom I hold dearest
   I chasten and prove
By trials severest
   The sign of My Love:
By the sharpness of pain
   Their faith is made sure,
Till the joys they attain
   That for ever endure.

The poor and the lowly
  Find grace in My Eyes,
While all the unholy
  And proud I despise:
In the world they have fame
  And renown for a day,
But are covered with shame
  When I spurn them away.

Oh! could'st thou but ponder
  The Joys of the Blest,
Thou never would'st wonder,
  Though sorely distrest,
In hope to attain
  The Joys that are stored
For those who bear pain
  And reproach for their LORD.

For nought can'st thou tender
  More dear to thy LORD
Than thus to surrender
  Thyself to His Word:
With never a moan
  All thy sufferings bear;
Bring those to His Throne,
  As thine Offering there.

When all things are beaming
  With peace and delight,
There are whose fair seeming
  Proves false in the fight:

When ſuccours are few,
   In the moment of need,
'Tis ſhewn who are true,
   And who faithleſs indeed.

Too often Man chooſes
   To own ſin's control;
Then ſweet are the uſes
   Of pain to the Soul:
For this is the way
   That My Servants have trod
To the Realm far away,
   To the Courts of their GOD.

O JESU, Thy SPIRIT,
   I pray Thee, impart,
That I may inherit
   This patience of heart:
And in every woe
   Enable me ſtill
Chief ſolace to know
   In doing Thy Will.

Thus nearer, oh! nearer,
   LORD, draw me to Thee;
And make Thy Croſs dearer
   Than all things to me:
By Thee let me ſtand
   In Thy Torture and Shame—
By Thee 'mid the Band
   That rejoice in Thy Name!

To Thee, UNBEGOTTEN,
  Creator of all,
To Thee, SOLE-BEGOTTEN,
  Who heareſt our call,
To Thee, SPIRIT Bleſt,
  THREE PERSONS ONE LORD,
Be praiſes addreſt
  With eternal accord!

After the Earthquake a Still Small Voice.

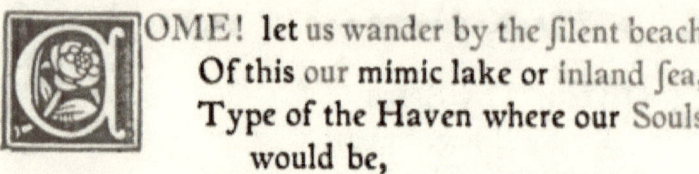

COME! let us wander by the ſilent beach
  Of this our mimic lake or inland ſea,
  Type of the Haven where our Souls
    would be,
And learn the leſſons which its waters teach,
As all GOD's voiceleſs Creatures uſe to preach.

We need not travel to the Holy Land,
  To trace the ſacred print of JESUS' Feet,
  Where, without ebb or flow, the wavelets beat
With myſtic murmur o'er the level ſand
Of Galilee's world-venerated ſtrand.

Sweet are the Fountains of fair Jordan's Lake,
  Bitter the ocean-ſprings of yon Sea-bay;
  O'er both, moſt bright, moſt blue, the ſun-gleams
    play,
While fitful breezes ſolemn echoes wake,
And oft the encircling crags in terror quake.

God's Voice is heard in thunder underground;
   The rumbling, reeling earth, man's laſt ſole ſtay,
   Labours with gape and heave to roll away;
The ſeething billows, one huge tidal mound,
Pour their volcanic torrent far around.

Woe to Bethſaida! to Chorazin woe!—
   Sad dirge of men's hearts failing them for fear
   At roaring ſea and waves—thy doom is near;
Repent, or elſe expect thine overthrow;
Though high as Heaven, as Hell thou ſhalt ſink
    low.

Then all is calm and ſmiling as before;
   The river cleaves the interlacing hills
   With gentle flow, made muſical by rills
From yonder ſnowy peak's perennial ſtore,
Where many a graſſy ſteep o'erhangs the ſhore.

And many a Ti-palm, many a tufted buſh
   With bloſſoms glimmering red through pendant
     leaves
   Of creeping paraſites, a garland weaves;
And giant trunks their feſtooned branches puſh
Above the tangled ſcrub and feathery ruſh.

And many a Fern-tree rears its lofty creſt,
   Embowering leafy nooks of paler green
   Than the deep umbrage of the foreſt ſcreen,
Where birds of varied plumage ſhun their neſt
To baſk in that ſweet ſunny realm of reſt.

Their notes, like silver chimes, fill all the grove
   With modulated music, rich and clear,
   Cheering the lonely fisher on the mere,
Or where his net upon the rock is hove,
While sportive shoals glance harmless through
   the cove.

Here Jesus might have fed the famished host;
   Here wrought the Miracle of frantic swine;
   On yonder Mount, Transfigured, shone Divine;
O'er yon calm waters roamed from coast to coast,
Or hushed them with His Word, when tempest-tost.

The Gospel is not written in a book,
   A tale that may be read and then forgot;
   Its work of Love and Truth endureth yet,
Or in the silence of this desert nook,
Or in the busy hum we late forsook.

Jesus is everywhere, is very nigh;
   The Holy Land is in us and around;
   Grace blends with Nature, Earth with Heaven
      profound;
To them of loving heart and single eye
Deep Sacraments all Creatures underlie.

Whoso is wise, like Jesus' Self, will blend
   The Active with the Contemplative Life;
   Leave for awhile the city's cares and strife,
In solitude his proud heart's knee to bend,
And in the wilderness seek One True Friend.

In calm or storm, in sunshine or in shade,
  His Presence will go with thee and give rest,
  Soothing the stormy passions of the breast;
Lo! I am with you always—so He said—
Even to the end; 'tis I, be not afraid.

The Three Enemies: a Colloquy.

The Flesh.

SWEET, thou art pale.—More Pale to see
  Christ hung upon the cruel Tree,
  And bore His Father's Wrath for me.

Sweet, thou art sad.—Beneath a rod
More heavy, Christ for my sake trod
The Winepress of the Wrath of God.

Sweet, thou art weary.—Not so Christ,
Whose mighty Love of me sufficed
For Strength, Salvation, Eucharist.

Sweet, thou art footsore.—If I bleed,
His Feet have bled: yea, in my need
His Heart once bled for mine indeed.

The World.

SWEET, thou art young.—So He was Young
  Who for my sake in silence hung
  Upon the Cross, with Passion wrung.

Look, thou art fair.—He was more Fair
Than men, Who deigned for me to wear
A Viſage marred beyond compare.

And thou haſt riches.—Daily bread:
All elſe is His; Who Living, Dead,
For me lacked where to lay His Head.

And life is ſweet.—It was not ſo
To Him, Whoſe Cup did overflow
With mine unutterable woe.

The Devil.

THOU drinkeſt deep.—When CHRIST would ſup
He drained the dregs from out my cup:
So how ſhould I be lifted up?

Thou ſhalt win Glory.—In the ſkies:
LORD JESUS, cover up mine eyes
Leſt they ſhould look on vanities.

Thou ſhalt have Knowledge.—Helpleſs duſt,
In Thee, O LORD, I put my truſt:
Anſwer Thou for me, Wiſe and Juſt.

And Might.—Get thee behind me! LORD,
Who haſt redeemed and not abhorred
My Soul, oh, keep it by Thy Word.

Pentecostal Odes of the Holy Eastern Church.

An Ode of an unknown Author.

E keep the Feast of Pentecost,
The Coming of the HOLY GHOST;
Our hope is now fulfilled, and we
Receive the mighty Mystery.

The Day of Promise long foretold,
The time appointed we behold,
And therefore gladly now we sing,
To Thee be praise, Creator, King.

O wondrous Gift of CHRIST the LORD
On His Disciples newly poured,
That they to all might Grace proclaim,
And publish far the Saving Name.

Thy Love immortal, WORD of GOD,
In foreign Tongues they found abroad,
And all the wounds of sin to heal,
Thy signal Mercy they reveal.

The HOLY SPIRIT all things leads,
From Him all Prophecy proceeds,
His Priests He ever sanctifies,
He makes the poor and lowly wise.

On Fishers He hath poured His Grace;
He rules the Church, His Dwelling-place;
He welds her Order, and His Might
Protects her Children in the fight.

Thee, ONE in Nature, ONE in Throne,
Eternal COMFORTER, we own,
With GOD the FATHER and the SON,
The Ever-blessed THREE in ONE.

An Ode of S. John Damascene.

THE tuneful sound of music
    Burst sweetly forth of old,
In honour of the Idol,
  The lifeless form of gold;
We cry, with awe adoring
  The SPIRIT'S radiant Flame—
Sole TRINITY, we bless Thee,
  For evermore the Same.

They who the Voice Prophetic
  Knew not as Word of Thine,
The Unknown Tongues regarded
  As drunkenness of wine;
But we, in faith devoutly,
  Give GOD the honour due—
Sole TRINITY, we bless Thee,
  Who makest all things new.

'The Prophet Joel looking
  Upon the Face of GOD,
Aſtonied heard Him ſpeaking,
  And told His Words abroad—
They whom I give My SPIRIT
  Shall cry, thus filled with Might—
Sole TRINITY, we bleſs Thee,
  O everlaſting Light.

The Third Day-hour abounded
  With Grace, that we might know
The Source of Bleſſing, Threefold,
  Whence Benedictions flow:
And now, on this glad morning,
  The beſt and chief of Days—
Sole TRINITY, we bleſs Thee
  In Hymns of grateful praiſe.

An Ode of S. Coſmas the Melodiſt.

HE Who with His mighty Hand
  Breaks the battle and the brand,
Now hath buried in the tide
Egypt's chariots and her pride.
Songs of victory we ſing,
Periſhed are her hoſt and King,
Tell the triumph far and wide,
GOD the LORD is glorified.

  Thou a Light on earth haſt ſhined,
  CHRIST, the Lover of mankind;

Thou the COMFORTER haſt ſent,
All hath found accompliſhment,
Which the Law and Prophets old
In the ages paſt foretold ;
Every Promiſe, every Word
Which Thy dear Diſciples heard.

For the HOLY SPIRIT'S Grace
On the true and faithful race
Freely hath to-day been poured,
From the world's foundation ſtored :
Gladly then theſe Hymns we lift,
Thankful for the wondrous Gift,
Praiſing, as is right and meet,
GOD the Bleſſed PARACLETE.

An Ode of S. John Damaſcene.

UNTO the fiery Furnace flung,
   The Holy Children ſweetly ſung,
  And ſinging, turned the fire to dew
   Which quenched each flame that leapt anew :
And this the ſtrain their love expreſſed,
GOD of our fathers, Thou art Bleſſed.

  What time the Twelve inſpired of GOD,
   Redemption's Story ſent abroad,
  The Working of the Breath Divine,
   The unbelievers deemed new wine :
But we, through this ſame SPIRIT ſee
The THREE in ONE, the ONE in THREE.

The Ascension.

The Nature One we praise and bless,
The Glorious Trinity confess;
Co-equal, Co-eterne, the Same,
We lift on high the Threefold Name,
And laud the Faith of old professed—
God of our Fathers, Thou art Blessed.

The Ascension.

'TWAS on the Mount of Olives,
    Nigh where the faithful Three
Had bid the Master welcome
    So oft at Bethany,
'Twas there the Man we cherish,
    The Mighty God we praise
Among His Chosen ended
    The wondrous forty days.

There was not ought about Him
    The coming change to say,
Only a cloud was o'er them
    As on a common day;
He stood with Hands uplifted;
    He blessed; that Blessing o'er,
After that earthly pattern
    He will not bless them more.

For while He spake, the Saviour
    Passed from this world of ill
Far o'er the sacred village,
    Far o'er the ancient hill;

The Ascension.

Love unto Love returning,
   Light to Its kindred Light,
The cloud o'erhead He entered
   And paſſed from mortal ſight.

Then Angels came foretelling
   That He ſhall come once more
In clouds that we may follow
   Where He has gone before;
And then His Own deſcending
   Haſtened with joy where lay
The towers of Sion City
   Diſtant a Sabbath-day.

So God went up to Heaven;
   But many an age has paſſed,
And ſtill the Angel's promiſe
   We wait, in this, the laſt,
And oft our Souls expectant
   Send up the cry of pain—
Too long, too long He lingers;
   When will He come again?

Be huſhed, life-weary Spirits!
   Not ſlack the Work proceeds;
On earth He ſtrives and quickens,
   In Heaven His Death He pleads,
With Kings for nurſing-fathers
   Shall we the Servants fail?
Not without Blood Divineſt
   The Maſter paſſed the Veil.

Death.

Wishes about Death.

I WISH to have no wishes left,
    But to leave all to Thee;
And yet I wish that Thou shouldst will
    Things that I wish should be.

And these two wills I feel within,
    When on my death I muse:
But, Lord! I have a death to die,
    And not a death to choose.

Why should I choose? for in Thy Love
    Most surely I descry
A gentler Death than I myself
    Should dare to ask to die.

But Thou wilt not disdain to hear
    What those few wishes are,
Which I abandon to Thy Love,
    And to Thy wiser Care.

Triumphant Death I would not ask,
    Rather would deprecate;
For dying Souls deceive themselves
    Soonest when most elate.

All Graces I would crave to have
    Calmly absorbed in one—

Death.

A perfect sorrow for my sins,
   And duties left undone.

All Sacraments and Church-blest things
   I fain would have around,
A Priest beside me, and the hope
   Of Consecrated ground.

I would the light of reason, LORD,
   Up to the last might shine,
That my own hands might hold my Soul
   Until it passed to Thine.

And I would pass in silence, LORD,
   No brave words on my lips,
Lest pride should cloud my Soul, and I
   Should die in the eclipse.

But when, and where, and by what pain—
   All this is one to me:
I only long for such a death
   As most shall honour Thee.

Long life dismays me by the sense
   Of my own weakness scared:
And by Thy Grace a sudden death
   Need not be unprepared.

One wish is hard to be unwished—
   That I at last might die
Of grief for having wronged with sin
   Thy spotless Majesty.

The Paths of Death.

HOW pleasant are thy Paths, O Death!
   Like the bright slanting west,
 Thou leadest down into the glow
Where all those Heaven-bound sunsets go,
   Ever from toil to rest.

How pleasant are thy Paths, O Death!
   Back to own dear Dead,
Into that Land which hides in tombs
The better part of our old homes;
   'Tis there thou makest our bed.

How pleasant are thy Paths, O Death!
   Thither where sorrows cease
To a new Life, to an old past,
Softly and silently we haste
   Into a Land of Peace.

How pleasant are thy Paths, O Death!
   Thy new restores our lost;
There are voices of the new times
With the ringing of the old chimes
   Blent sweetly on thy coast.

How pleasant are thy Paths, O Death!
   One faint for want of breath—
And above thy promise thou hast given:
All, we find more than all in Heaven,
   O thou truth-speaking Death.

How pleasant are thy Paths, O Death!
   E'en children after play
Lie down, without the least alarm,
And sleep, in thy maternal arm,
   Their little life away.

How pleasant are thy Paths, O Death!
   E'en grown-up men secure
Better manhood, by a brave leap
Through the chill mist of thy thin sleep—
   Manhood that will endure.

How pleasant are thy Paths, O Death!
   The old, the very old,
Smile when their slumberous eye grows dim,
Smile when they feel thee touch each limb—
   Their age was not less cold.

How pleasant are thy Paths, O Death!
   Ever from pain to ease;
Patience, that hath held on for years,
Never unlearns her humble fears
   Of terrible disease.

How pleasant are thy Paths, O Death!
   From sin to pleasing GOD;
For the pardoned in thy Land are bright
As Innocence in robe of white,
   And walk on the same road.

How pleasant are thy Paths, O Death!
   Straight to our FATHER's Home;

All loſs were gain that gained us this,
The **Sight** of G<small>OD</small>, that ſingle Bliſs
   Of the grand World to come.

How pleaſant are **thy Paths, O Death**!
   Ever from toil to reſt—
Where **a** rim of ſea-like ſplendour **runs**,
Where the days bury their **golden ſuns**,
   In the dear hopeful **weſt**.

Quam dilecta Tabernacula.

A Hymn for the Dedication of a Church.

HOW loved **Thy Halls and** Dwelling-
     place,
   O L<small>ORD</small> of Hoſts moſt **High**!
  Selected are the Architects,
  Secure the Buildings lie!
Untouched by ſtorm, or wind, **or rain**,
Nay, e'en for theſe they firmer ſtill remain.

How **rich in** beauty and in ſtrength
   Is the Foundation-ſtone!
Of old in Sacramental **type**
   And ſhadow oft foreſhown;
Eve ta'en from ſleeping Adam's ſide,
Type **of** an everlaſting Race ſupplied.

For Noah was ſalvation wrought
   In Ark compoſed of wood,

Quam dilecta Tabernacula.

Which, piloted, did safely ride
    Above the world's vast flood :
And Sarah laughed in joyance wild
When late in life she bore the promised Child.

Rebecca standing by the well
    With Abraham's servant nigh,
To quench the Camels' thirst and his
    The water doth supply;
Bracelets and earrings weareth she,
That for her husband she prepared may be.

Jacob supplants the Synagogue
    Which wanders far away,
Whilst in the letter of the Law
    It is content to stay.
To weak-eyed Leah hid must be
What Rachel, wed in equal bond, doth see.

And by the way-side, as she sits
    With closely veilèd face,
Long widowed Thamar twins conceives
    From Judah's fond embrace.
Here in an Ark, by rushes bound,
By Maid who came to bathe is Moses found.

Here is the blessèd Offering made,
    The sacred Lamb is slain—
And Israel, sated with its blood,
    May ever safe remain.
Here too is passed the Red Sea wave
'Neath which the Egyptians found a watery grave.

Quam dilecta Tabernacula.

Here is the Urn with Manna filled;
 And here the Law's Commands
Stored in the Ark of Covenant
 (The Law which GOD demands;)
Here are the Ornaments Divine
The glorious robes of Aaron's Prieſtly line.

And here Uriah is condemned,
 And Bathſheba is known
As one to higheſt honour raiſed,
 The ſharer of a throne.
In gold-embroidered garments dreſſed
She ſtands, as daughter of King's houſe confeſſed.

Attracted by his wiſdom rare
 King Solomon to ſee
The Queen of Sheba hither comes,
 All black, yet comely ſhe—
As when commingled to the ſkies
The fragrant clouds of myrrh and incenſe riſe.

To us the day of Grace reveals
 Whatever was foretold,
Whate'er in ſhadow and in type
 Enveilèd was of old;
And we at length are given to reſt
All ſafely on our own Beloved's Breaſt.

Uplift we then the ſong on high
Since now the Marriage-feaſt is nigh,
Which trumpets did inaugurate—
Its end ſhall pſalteries celebrate.

Let thousand thousand voices raise
The joyous strain, the Bridegroom praise;
And as in harmony they blend
Repeat they ever without end—
                      Alleluia! Amen.

In a Vision of the night when deep Sleep falleth upon Men.

N dreams I slept, where Israel wept of old,
    Her walls down-torn, her altars shorn of gold:
And in my dream Euphrates' stream rolled by
With sullen pride, in ocean's tide to die.
At first, how bright, how clear the night had seemed—
Sweetly at even the lamps of Heaven had beamed;
All toil was stayed, the winds were laid in calm—
From dells and bowers, went up of flowers sweet balm.
Sudden, on high was heard a cry of woe;
Heaven's darkest pall fell over all below.
With flashing flame God's thunder came—that sound
Whose echoes hold faint hearts or bold spellbound.

      *   *   *   *

So on that shore, long years before he lay
In Heavenly trance, and upward glance alway

A Tradition of S. John.

Daniel, that Seer whoſe holy fear and love
Gained a bleſt ſight of Saints' delight above;
When from the ſeas a fourfold breeze had blown,
When **Beaſts** on wings, and myſtic things were
    ſhewn.

      *   *   *   *

So from my view ſlowly withdrew the veil:
Full on my ſight a Form of Light I hail.
A wondrous power in that dread hour was mine:
Scathleſs to hear thoſe Words of fear Divine—
" No anſwer give if thou would'ſt live—be ſtill—
Where'er I go theſe thunders ſhow GOD's Will;
At Whoſe Command I ſweep the land of ſin
Till ye, like us, be glorious within.
O! happy thoſe when night ſhall cloſe whoe'er
Spotleſs have worn their robes; for morn is near."

A Tradition of S. John the Evangeliſt.

TWO thouſand years have wellnigh paſt
  Since he, the gentleſt and the laſt
    Of all that holy band,
  That with their LORD and SAVIOUR
    bore
  The weary toil and labour ſore,
    Led by His guiding Hand,

Hath paſſed unto his reſt away,
Where Love can never more decay

And Faith and Hope are o'er;
All gently closed his eyes in sleep,
E'en while his Children round him weep,
   That he may stay no more.

They laid him in the hallowed ground,
And many a day they watched around,
   And deemed the earth did wave
At every breath of slumber sweet,
And gently heave beneath their feet
   Upon his lowly grave.

And long they watched the glad flowers grow,
And deemed that still his breath below
   Did heave that little mound;
For aye they thought to hear once more
The tones of Love oft heard before,
   And lift their peaceful sound.

They thought upon his last farewell,
How with faint voice he still would dwell
   On Love and Love alone;
How, while his Children all stood near
Fondly his parting words to hear,
   Love breathed in every tone.

And when they asked why that one word,
From him so long, so often heard,
   Was all he uttered still,
He said, as faint his accents fall—
That Love, and Love alone, would all
   Our SAVIOUR's Words fulfil.

Then as his eyes in ſlumber cloſed,
They deemed he now awhile repoſed,
   And laid him in the grave;
And, as they watched long years around,
They ſtill would think that graſſy mound
   Did gently heave and wave.

And thus would they long vigil keep
Over the place of his laſt ſleep,
   And aye in Love would dwell.
Thoſe early days of Peace are o'er:
Do we of later ages ſtore
   His peaceful Words as well?

How tread we now the paths of old,
With Faith all faint and Love grown cold,
   With feeble ſteps and ſlow;
Our very Souls cling fondly fixed,
With ſcarce a nobler longing mixed,
   On fancied joys below.

Yet oft in glowing words we ſpeak
Of Love all holy, pure and meek,
   While ſtrange the ſenſe they claim;
For, joined in an unholy tie,
Falſe Creeds and Faith all ſheltered lie
   Beneath this ſpecious name.

It is not thus; for faint from far,
Soon as we heed it not, the ſtar
   Of Truth more dimly gleams

With wandering and uncertain ray—
So to our eyes it seems who stray
   Far from its nearer beams.

O Love, so prized in days of yore,
While all the Cross before them bore,
   How faint and low the tone
That comes from forth thy holy shrine;
Far other is thy glance benign
   Than that which we would own.

O early dawn of Christian Love,
Enkindled by the Holy Dove,
   O days of glowing Faith,
When hearts beat high to suffer here,
When Faith and Hope prevailed o'er fear,
   And Weakness conquered Death.

Hymns of Novalis.

The Desire of God.

I KNOW not what I could desire
   Wert Thou, dear Being, only mine;
   Wert Thou to crown my Soul with
      gladness,
  And still be near and call me Thine.
The vext crowd to and fro are hurrying,
   With eager glance they search around;
They call themselves the wise, the prudent,
   And yet this Treasure have not found.

One thinks his hand the Prize now grasping—
  Lo! what he hath is nought but gold;
Another, earth and sea exploring,
  Hath for a Name his quiet fold.
One for the Crown of victory striveth,
  One for the Poet's wreath of bay,
And thus the ever-changing glitter
  Attracting all doth each betray.

To you Himself hath He revealed not?
  Can you forget Who died for you?
Who for your sakes from Life departed—
  Yea, Scorn and bitter Anguish knew?
Have ye not read, have ye not listened?
  Of Him, from Him ne'er heard a word?
How He brought down Divinest Mercy,
  What endless Good on us conferred?

How from high Heaven He descended,
  The exalted Son of Mother blest?
What Tidings to the earth He carried—
  How many healed by Him find Rest?
How, by pure Love drawn down, He offered
  Himself for us, a Victim free?
Low laid in earth, of God's own Temple
  The eternal Corner-stone to be?

And shall not such a Message move you?
  Is not This Man sufficient found?
Your doors to Him will ye not open
  Who passed for you Hell's dismal bound?

Will ye not then lose all things gladly,
   Forego with joy each idle thought,
Your hearts for Him alone reserving
   Whose Grace is promised you unbought?

Lift Thou me up, Thou Gentle Saviour!
   Thou art my world, my life is Thine;
Though nought of earthly hope were left me,
   I know my Recompense Divine.
Thou all my love with Love returnest;
   Thy Truth for ever shall endure;
The Heavens bow down in adoration;
   Thou dwellest still within me sure.

The Desire of Death.

AWAY, below the earth's broad breast,
   Far from light's realms descending!
Storms of woe and wild unrest
   Departure glad portending;
The narrow bark shall waft us o'er
Full soon to land on Heaven's calm shore.

Blest be that everlasting night;
   Blest, never-broken slumber:
Day with toils hath worn us quite,
   Cares too long encumber;
Now vain desires and roamings cease,
We seek our Father's House in peace.

What should we do in this cold world
  With Love and Truth so tender?
Old things are in oblivion hurled,
  The new no gladness render:
O sorrowful his heart and lone
Who reverent loves the past and gone!

Those ages past, whose purer race
  High thoughts with ardour fired,
When Man beheld our FATHER's Face,
  And knew His Hand desired;
While many a simple mind sincere
Resembled still His Image clear.

Those days of old, when flourished wide
  Stems of Patriarch story;
When even Children joyful died
  And suffered for Heaven's Glory;
While though life laughed and pleasure spake,
Yet many a heart for strong Love brake.

Those times of yore when GOD revealed
  Himself in young life glowing;
With early death His Passion sealed,
  His precious Blood bestowing;
Nor turned aside the stings of pain
Us nearer to Himself to gain.

Through deepening mists how vainly gaze
  Our fond thoughts, backward turning:

Nought in this dreary age allays
  The thirſt within us burning:
We muſt arrive our home within
That ancient Holineſs to win.

What ſtill delays our wiſhed return?
  The Loved have long been ſleeping;
Their grave our earthly journey's bourne—
  Enough of fear and weeping!
With fruitleſs ſtriving long annoyed
The heart is weary, the world a void.

Strange rapture ever new, unknown,
  Through the faint frame is thrilling:
Hark! the ſoft echo of our moan
  The hollow diſtance filling;
Whence the Beloved towards us bend,
Their breathings of deſire aſcend.

Down to the Bride, to CHRIST we go,
  The Bridegroom gone before us;
Be of good comfort, mourners; lo!
  Grey twilight deepens o'er us:
A dream diſſolves our chains unbleſt,
Our FATHER takes us to His Reſt.

Paradise.

From the Spanish of Luis de Leon.

REGION of Life and Light!
   Land of the Good whose earthly toils
      are o'er;
Nor frost nor heat may blight
   Thy vernal beauty; fertile shore
Yielding thy blessed Fruit for evermore!

There without Crook or Sling
   Walks the Good Shepherd; blossoms white and
      red
Round His meek Temples cling;
   And, to sweet pastures led,
   His own loved Flock beneath His Eye are fed.

He guides, and near Him they
   Follow delighted; for He makes them go
Where dwells eternal May,
   And Heavenly roses blow,
   Deathless, and gathered but again to grow.

He leads them to the height
   Named of the infinite and long-sought Good,
And Fountains of Delight;
   And where His Feet have stood
   Springs up, along the way, their tender food.

And when in the mid skies
  The climbing Sun has reached his highest bound,
Reposing as He lies,
  With all His Flock around
  He witches the still air with modulated sound.

From His sweet Lute flow forth
  Immortal harmonies, of power to still
All passions born of earth,
  And draw the ardent will
  Its destiny of Goodness to fulfil.

Might but a little part,
  A wandering breath of that high Melody
Descend into my heart,
  And change it till it be
  Transformed and swallowed up, O Love, in
    Thee!

Ah! then my Soul should know,
  Beloved! where Thou liest at noon of day;
And from this place of woe,
  Released, should take its way
  To mingle with Thy Flock and never stray!

The Incarnation.

TIME hath no brighter jewel on his brow
    Than this, all worlds, all ages, won-
        dering scan:
  Shall GOD in very deed Himself allow
Limit and bound, and dwell on earth with man?

The Incarnation.

I marvel not that some should misconceive—
I marvel one should easily believe;
    That when the Tale is told
    (Sole tale which ne'er grows old)
How Flesh and Blood the Invisible once did shrine,
Rather all hearts incredulous not combine
Such mightiest task of faith, unequal, to resign.

The fabled lore that lured the untutored ear
  Of the young world, ere fancy's vernal age
Had ripened into reason—then more dear
  Than all the time-schooled wisdom of the Sage—
The most unbounded flights e'er roved at will
By lawless dreams, or thoughts more lawless still,
    Lose all their wild and strange,
    To most experienced range
Brought meanly down, of credence easier far
Than that the WORD, He by Whom all things are,
Changed for His high Abode one poor inferior star.

Down from the Heavenly hills in Love descending,
  Far in the depths of night His Eye descried
The clusters of His Universe, one blending
  Of infinite Lights—stars in their courses, tied
By order firm and ne'er-infringèd law;
A world of worlds, whereof each one doth draw
    About the central bright
    Its duteous satellite;

Q

Yet chose He not His Palace in some sun,
By Heaven alone in native light outdone,
But this our darker Orb His radiant Presence won.

There was no lack of Sovereign seats and thrones
   Worthy of His possessing; large domains
Waited His Lordly bidding; populous plains,
   The wealth of Empires, all the mingled tones
Of queenliest Cities called Him—pomp and song
And loud applause of many a rapturous throng:
      But, such as these passed by,
      Beneath the Syrian sky
He sought the meanest state, the lowliest shed,
That, earth's most bitter lot most throughly read,
No heart might sink so low but He might lift it high.

And therefore did the greatness of His Scorn
   Vouchsafe the measure of His glorious Rise;
And they who here with Him that Shame have borne
   Shall share His Crown and Triumph in the skies:
He That descended is the same That rose
Above all Heavens, victorious o'er His foes,
      And evermore doth stand
      A Priest at GOD's Right Hand,
Till, in the fulness of the times, once more
He come with Might and Majesty, His floor
In Righteousness to purge, and all things to restore.

And thou and I (O wondrous thought and ſtrange !)
  May call Him Brother ; eat His Fleſh, and
      live ;
Drink of His Blood, that with all-quickening
    change
  Doth joy for grief, health for unſoundneſs give :
May love Him, though we ſee Him not ; may
    hear
His Voice behind us, feel His Footſtep near :
    Thou, Who doſt all things fill,
    Art with Thy Children ſtill,
Who here through ſighs and tears their voices
    raiſe,
Or round Thy Throne, with rapt adoring gaze,
Lift high the harmonious Anthem of perpetual
    praiſe.

I will exult, my evil days and few
  Spending where GOD hath ſojourned ; His dear
    Breath
Hath left a ſweetneſs in the air, a new
  Celeſtial fragrance, all the damps of death
Quite overmaſtering, filling with perfumes
The grave unlovely, and dark funeral rooms ;
    That each glad Soul may ſpring
    Upward from earth, and ſing,
Beholding in her tomb Heaven's opened door,
And hearing in her knell His Summons ring—
' Come up, dear Child, and dwell in Reſt for
    evermore.'

The Incarnation.

The Earth He trod is consecrated ground;
  One stone His Feet have touched hallows the
    whole,
Reclaimed for Heaven's just uses, from the round
  Of torrid heats, to either utmost pole:
Where He alighted burst a Spring, that flows
To every land, and ever widening goes,
    Sustained by what distils
    From the everlasting Hills,
And still shall swell, a River broad and deep,
Till its great flood, with all-compelling sweep,
The bars and gates of Hell triumphantly o'erleap.

Whoso receiveth this, doth all receive:
  His faith can soar no further; all the train
Of Signs and Wonders written, that doth leave
  A breach in Nature's statutes, to explain
By reason's rules he aims not, lest as wise
Himself professing, folly's meed he gain:
    But, in mute awe profound
    Upon that holy ground
Standing unshod He hears, amidst the cries
Of jarring doubts and creeds, the still small Voice
Speak to his immost heart, and trembling doth
    rejoice.

His the unfettered Faith to childhood given,
  That questions not how such a thing might be;
Whom large experience hinders not that Heaven
  Should mix with earth, but whose clear eye doth
    see

Jael.

In happy dreams the golden Ladder bending,
And Angel-feet for evermore descending:
    Thus human and Divine
    To childlike hearts combine,
Who from the world's Soul-deafening noise retreat,
And meekly sitting at the Master's Feet
Lift to His Heaven-brought Words in contemplation sweet.

Jael.

LONELY Woman's feeble hand—
    A mail-clad Warrior in his might—
At her tent-door behold her stand
    To greet the Captain of the fight.

Stern greeting hers! for from on high
    Unbidden comes the LORD's Behest,
And fires with wrath her gentle eye,
    And arms with fraud her guileless breast.

LORD, whence is this? what spell is cast?
    Whence this up-heaving flood within,
This lightning-blaze, this whirlwind-blast,
    Too calm for rage, too pure for sin?

It comes: it comes: she may not pause;
    Herself the hammer of Heaven's will,
She executes the unwritten Laws,
    Nor wists the word that bids her kill.

Jael.

One blow—and where is he whoſe head
    Gave ſtrength and guidance to an hoſt?
Low at a woman's feet and dead,
    Man's foe and GOD's lies ever loſt.

And who ſhall doubt—that in GOD's Book
    Hath ſcanned the Goſpel through the veil,
And learned beyond the Law to look—
    Whoſe is the hammer and the nail?

The Woman among women bleſt,
    Where but at Bethlehem is ſhe?
The victor vanquiſhed in his reſt,
    Where but on crimſon Calvary?

'Twas ſhe who, when the ſtrife ran high,
    Gave fleſh and birth to GOD's Own SON,
Gave to the Life the power to die,
    And raiſe by death a world undone.

O SON of Mary! cheat our foe,
    Down with him even to the ground;
In the grave's ſlumber lay Death low,
    And in the weak let ſtrength abound.

Funeral Hymn.

BROTHER! now thy toils are o'er,
    Fought the battle, won the Crown;
On Life's rough and barren ſhore
    Thou haſt laid thy burden down:
  Grant him, LORD, eternal Reſt
  With the Spirits of the Bleſt.

Through Death's valley dim and dark
    JESUS guide thee in the gloom,
Shew thee where His Footprints mark
    Tracks of Glory through the tomb:
  Grant him, LORD, eternal Reſt
  With the Spirits of the Bleſt.

Angels bear thee to the Land
    Where the towers of Sion riſe,
Safely lead thee by the hand
    To the fields of Paradiſe:
  Grant him, LORD, eternal Reſt
  With the Spirits of the Bleſt.

White-robed at the cryſtal gate
    Of the New Jeruſalem
May the Hoſt of Martyrs wait,
    Give thee part and lot with them:
  Grant him, LORD, eternal Reſt
  With the Spirits of the Bleſt.

Funeral Hymn.

Choirs of Angels over us
   Bear Christ's weak and trembling Lamb,
Give thee peace with Lazarus
   At the breaſt of Abraham:
     Grant him, Lord, eternal Reſt
     With the Spirits of the Bleſt.

Reſt in Peace: the gates of Hell
   Touch thee not, till He ſhall come
For the Souls He loves ſo well—
   Dear Lord of the Heavenly home:
     Grant him, Lord, eternal Reſt
     With the Spirits of the Bleſt.

Earth to earth, and duſt to duſt,
   Clay we give to kindred clay;
In the ſure and certain truſt
   Of the Reſurrection Day:
     Grant him, Lord, eternal Reſt
     With the Spirits of the Bleſt.

Christ the Sower ſows thee here:
   When the eternal Day ſhall dawn
He will gather in the ear
   On that Reſurrection morn:
     Grant him, Lord, eternal Reſt,
     Light and Life at Thy Beheſt,
     With the Spirits of the Bleſt.

The Story of the Cross.

The Question.

IN His own Raiment clad,
  With His Blood dyed,
Women walk sorrowing
    By His Side.

Heavy that Cross to Him,
 Weary the weight,
One who will help Him waits
    At the gate.

See! they are travelling
 On the same road—
Simon is sharing with
    Him, the LORD.

Oh whither wandering,
 Bear they that Tree?
He Who first carries it—
    Who is He?

The Answer.

FOLLOW to Calvary;
 Tread where He trod,
He Who for ever was
    SON of GOD.

You who would love Him, stand,
  Gaze at His Face,
Tarry awhile on thine
            Earthly race.

As the swift moments fly
  Through the blest week,
Read the great Story the
            Cross will teach.

Is there no beauty to
  ' You who pass by,'
In the lone Figure which
            Marks that sky?

The Story of the Cross.

ON the Cross lifted
  Thy Face I scan,
Bearing that Cross for me,
            SON of MAN;

Thorns form Thy Diadem,
  Rough Wood Thy Throne,
For us Thy Blood is shed—
            Us alone.

No pillow under Thee
  To rest Thy Head—
Only the splintered Cross
            Is Thy Bed.

Nails pierce Thy Hands and Feet,
　　Thy Side the ſpear;
No voice is nigh to ſay,
　　　　　　Help is near.

Shadows of midnight fall
　　Though it is day;
Thy Friends and Kinsfolk ſtand
　　　　　　Far away.

Loud is Thy bitter Cry;
　　Sunk on Thy Breaſt
Hangeth Thy Bleeding Head
　　　　　　Without reſt.

Loud ſcoffs the dying Thief,
　　Who mocks at Thee;
Can it, my SAVIOUR, be
　　　　　　All for me.

Gazing afar from Thee,
　　Silent and lone,
Stand thoſe few Weepers Thou
　　　　　　Call'ſt Thine Own.

I ſee Thy Title, LORD,
　　Inſcribed above—
'JESUS of Nazareth,'
　　　　　　King of Love!

What, O my SAVIOUR,
　　Here didſt Thou ſee,
Which made Thee ſuffer and
　　　　　　Die for me?

The Story of the Cross.

The Appeal.

CHILD of My Grief and Pain,
  Home of My Love,
I came to call thee to
        Realms above.

I ſaw thee wandering
  Far off from Me;
In Love I ſeek for thee—
        Do not flee.

For thee My Blood I ſhed,
  For thee alone—
I came to purchaſe thee
        For Mine Own.

Weep not for My Grief,
  Child of My Love;
Strive to be with Me in
        Heaven above.

The Reply.

OH, I will follow Thee,
  Star of my Soul,
Through the deep ſhades of life
        To the goal!

Yes, let Thy Croſs be borne
  Each day by me;
Mind not how heavy if
        But with Thee.

The Passion.

LORD, if Thou only wilt
  Make me Thine Own,
Give no companion save
        Thee alone.

Grant through each day of life
  To stand by Thee!
With Thee when morning breaks
        Ever to be!

The Passion.

Jesus dying.

OVER each tower and minaret,
  And where in channel dark as jet
  The streams of Kedron toil and fret,

Falls the inexplicable Veil,
The Sign when Nature's powers shall fail
Of universal woe and wail.

No light and shade, in interchange
Softening the dark horizon's range,
But sudden midnight stern and strange!

Rushed the uptreasured Darkness from
Its hidden, uncreated home
To witness GOD's own Martyrdom?

Or did the LORD Who hides His Face
In Shadows that betoken Grace,
And drapes in gloom His Dwelling-place,

Did He in His moſt awful Mood
Curtain around the Holy Rood
From man's unchaſtened neighbourhood?

Or came the Type and Form wherein
Wrong works, to watch the ſtrife within,
And learn the death of death and ſin?

Thou GOD That hideſt, who can tell,
Unleſs Thou teach us how to ſpell
And learn aright the Miracle?

It huſhes all things; not a ſound
Or far or near is heard around;
The guard ſeems rooted to the ground.

No word the Divine Sufferer ſaith;
Only is heard His heaving Breath
Fighting the duel fierce with death.

And breaking o'er His quivering Lips:
Only the Blood that as it drips
Throbs through the palpable eclipſe!

Oh, vanquiſhed Light return once more;
Oh, breaking Heart that we adore,
When ſhall this travail-pang be o'er?

When ſhall the day its fetters burſt,
And JESUS, from the Tree accurſt
Speak once, and own Himſelf athirſt?

Laſt act of His Humility
Better to witneſs, than to ſee
This ſtill and voiceleſs Agony.

SAVIOUR, and Suffering GOD! when I,
Knowing it is my time to die,
Upon my final croſs ſhall lie;

When Nature's deepening ſhadows fall
O'er Soul and ſenſe, and like a pall
Suit all things to the funeral;

In my eclipſe, oh, let me ſee
Thy Sorrows, borne in love for me,
Upon Thy Croſs, on Calvary—

Borne, that I might in dying reſt,
And lay, undarkened, undepreſſed
My head on Thy all-loving Breaſt.

Jeſus dead.

STAY the obſequious fingers!
   O ſpare the myrrh and balm!
From the depths of this pure ſilence
   This inexpreſſive calm;
From the lineleſs Lips where Slumber
   Sets her conſecrating ſeal,
Back on the world that wronged Him,
   He ſmiles His laſt Appeal.

Not like daylight's laſt effulgence,
    So tender yet ſo bright;
When reluctantly the glory
    Juſt flaſhes out of ſight:
But Sorrow and Forgiveneſs
    Are blended on His Cheek,
Like the gleam that fills the twilight
    As the dawn begins to break.

For Him is no more ſorrow,
    There is neither change nor loſs;
Life has no further torture,
    Nor Agony, nor Croſs:
The Counſels of the Ages,
    The Deſtiny of Time,
At laſt are conſummated
    In this Martyrdom ſublime.

He was weak, when in the Manger
    He drew an Infant's Breath;
He was weak, when in the Garden
    He ſorrowed unto Death;
Beneath the Croſs He fainted,
    On the Croſs He bowed His Head:
But here is more than weakneſs—
    All is finiſhed! He is Dead!

But the Love that is undying
    Lights His Features, like a Mind;
And His final Look is pleading,
    With the Heart of Humankind.

That owns, when it is hardeſt
  Death's power to control,
And conquer and o'ermaſter
  The paſſions of the Soul.

And thus His Look is pleading—
  No more your anger keep:
O My Brother, give thy pity!
  O My Siſter, turn and weep!
I was True, in Love unceaſing,
  Though My Labour was unprized;
And My Crown of ſorrows pierced Me
  When I ſaw that Love deſpiſed.

Ah, the world remains unheeding,
  And will not brook the ſight:
Quick! ſhade the Features, winding
  The CORSE of GOD in white:
Let the hands that Love has hallowed
  Cloſe faſt the holy Eyes;
Let the two familiar faces
  Look on Him where He lies.

There He lies! the wondrous Maſter
  Upon Whoſe Lips we hung;
Who had Might upon His Finger,
  And Life upon His Tongue:
Still and cold! that glorious Teacher
  Who had GODHEAD in His Eye!
Oh, cruel Heart within me,
  Wilt thou never break and die?

Thoughts from the Manual of S. Augustine.

He that dwelleth in Love, dwelleth in God, and *God in* him.

WHO neither loves, nor seeks for JESUS'
  Love,
 His Soul a barren desert shall remain;
  And life will prove
To him, whate'er its joys, but life in vain.

To live for Thee, O LORD, alone is Life;
To live without Thee, were at once to die,
  'Twere but the strife
Of aimless folly swiftly passing by.

Most Merciful! to Thee I give anew
The life and understanding which I owe;
  That Thou art true
And wilt that life restore, by Faith I know.

Believing, I will love Thee and adore,
With Whom I hope for ever to remain,
  Or, could I more,
In endless Rest and Blessedness to reign.

What Soul, unloving, seeks not after Thee,
The slave of sin and earthly love impure,
  His lot shall be
The helpless thrall which guilty men endure.

O may this bondage never, LORD, be mine,
But let my pilgrimage securely end
        Along the line
Of aspirations pure which Heavenward tend.

My Soul, in this her exile, longs for Rest;
Be that to her, O LORD, for which she longs,
        Softly expressed
In contemplation sweet, or grateful songs!

In sorrow, or in joy, when tumults swell,
Grant her the shelter of Thy guardian Wing;
        Do Thou compel
A calm, from whence soe'er the tempests spring.

O richest Master of the noblest Feast,
And bountiful Dispenser unto all,
        Even the least,
On whom the mercies of Thy Goodness fall!

Do Thou to weary Souls sweet Food afford;
Thy scattered Children safely gather in;
        O Loving LORD,
Set free the bound, restore the lost in sin!

Lo! at the door a wretched Wanderer stands
And knocks! O brightest Day-spring from on High,
        Brightening the lands
Of death and sin, in mercy hear his cry!

Open! and let this craving suppliant in,
That freely he may find his way to Thee,
        And rest from sin,
And with Thy Heavenly Food refreshèd be.

For Thou, of Life the Bread and Water art,
Of Light eternal the eternal Fount,
   The living Heart
Of righteous Men who climb the Heavenly Mount.

*There shall be no more Death, neither sorrow,
   nor crying.*

THRICE blessed Land of Heavenly gladness!
 Where life is Life in endless flow;
Where undisturbed by fear or sadness
 Greatness and Peace their sweets bestow;
Where Health is pure, unchecked by sickness,
 And 'laid up' Treasure never fails;
Where no more Death betrays its weakness,
 Nor Time its fleeting course bewails;
Where Happiness unyoked from sorrow
 Fills up its ample store with Love;
And face to Face, no more we borrow
 Figures to shadow GOD above.

There too, we know as we are known,
 The heights of Love Divine we scan,
And see the Light from out the Throne
 Enlightening ere the worlds began;
The unfailing Food of Life is there,
 Beholding Whom our Souls are fed;
Beholding, yet with longing care
 Still to behold—still upward led.

All quickening there, with beauteous Ray
  The Sun of Righteoufnefs is fet,
Illuming all the golden Way
  Where Citizens of Heaven are met.

Nor only fo! but the Redeemed
  Are there, one mighty World of Light,
As never Mortal could have dreamed
  Of fun or ftars, fo dazzling bright!
To God Immortal joined are they
  Who no corruption more fhall fee;
And now, O Jesu, day by day
  They claim that Pledge which fell from Thee—
Father, I will that where I dwell
  Whoe'er are Mine may dwell with Me,
As Thou and I, fo they, may tell
  The wondrous Blifs of Unity!

Childlike Holinefs.

EAUTIFUL is Noon!
  The glory and effulgence of the day;
  Bright zenith of the Sun's majeftic fway,
  Whofe fceptred light floods forth for
      Nature's boon.
Hufhed are all birds; the fhortened fhadows lie
Crouched'neath the trees. We feel a Prefence nigh,
    As from our fhady nook,
  On the clear outward glare we look,
    And reverence the Power
Who hath fet forth His Image in this hour.

Beautiful is Eve!
The ſtars are tangled in her deepening Veil;
On the great ſea grows dim the ſnowy ſail;
With twitterings low, the birds their concert leave;
The dewdrops form upon the thirſting blades,
And timid Peace ſteals from her ſilent glades.
    The village hum is ſtill;
  The ſheep are folded on the hill;
    And we our ſpirits yield
Unto the reſt that wraps ſky, wood and field.

    Yet, lovelier far
Than Noon-tide, or the infant ſteps of Night,
Is Morn! Rekindled Hope and new-born Might
Riſe up, and hail his weſtward-coming car.
And there is ſong in Heaven and ſong in earth;
And ocean dimples o'er with ſmiling Mirth;
    And the ſad evening heart,
    That thought not from its grief to part,
    Sees with aſtoniſhed eyes
Rays of unlooked-for joy mount up the ſkies.

   *   *   *

    Inſpiring is the ſight
Of Manhood's Piety! Amid the fight
  Of this world's haraſs, work and care,
  The weary day, the ſhortened night
  To mark his unforgotten prayer,
  His evening queſtioning of heart,
  His faith ſtill burning in its ſhrine;
Loyal to Heaven, in Senate, Feaſt or Mart,
Bringing to earthly labours Love Divine.

Childlike Holiness.

And beautiful is Age !
As worldly cares do lefs its heart engage,
  When, like the tranquil end of day,
  Its warmeſt feelings ceaſe to rage,
  And ſhed a clear but quiet ray,
  Shining as ſtars, benign and fair :
  And Youth grows reverent at the ſight ;
And Children gather round the well-loved chair
Of CHRIST's tired Pilgrim, bidding Earth ' Good-
    night !'

  But oh ! more ſweet than all,
Than Manhood's faith, or Life's calm autumn fall,
  Is holy Childhood ! 'Tis the dew
  That after-hours can not recall ;
  A joy which years can ne'er renew ;
  'Tis incenſe in a virgin fane ;
  'Tis new fallen ſnow from fields above ;
The white-bleached robe, awhile without a ſtain,
Drawing our gaze of mingled awe and love.

  No more the ſacred voice
Which interpoſed, and bade faint hearts rejoice
  Falls on our ears. But echoes tell
  That GOD, for neareſt Heaven, makes choice
  Of Infant hoſts. His Aſphodel
  For the young, ſpotleſs brow is twined ;
  And unveiled Viſion waits the eyes
Of childlike Purity, with Love enſhrined
In hearts, where'er they beat beneath the ſkies.

The Advent.

HOW by shining Forms attended,
    By what golden stair,
He, the SON of GOD, descended,
    Tell me, Earth and Air!
Hark! the Heaven itself is ringing,
    All the blue wide arch
Rolls a sound of Angels singing
    His triumphal March.

Not with iron steeped in slaughter,
    Nor with blood-red feet
Comes He! but like rills of water
    Where the dry suns beat:
Love with happy eyes before Him
    Melteth sin like snow;
All whom He hath made adore Him,
    Fount of Peace below.

Wise Men of the East unravel
    Wondrous Signs afar;
Forth to Judah's land they travel,
    Led by the new Star:
Thither, for their Soul divineth
    Some great Birth foretold,
Each his several Gift consigneth,
    Incense, Myrrh and Gold.

The Advent.

On the quiet hills, far sleeping
   In a silver light,
Shepherds lonely watch were keeping
   Mid their flocks by night,
When strange Harmonies above them
   Bursting, wave on wave,
Told of CHRIST come down to love them,
   CHRIST, Supreme to save.

Turn and look where feeble, tender,
   Helpless to behold,
Lies our King, bereft of splendour,
   Touched with heat and cold:
In a stable, in a manger,
   Heir to sorrows born,
Even He, a BABE, a Stranger,
   Naked and forlorn.

Tell me what Divine Affections
   Throng that Infant Brain!
Say what dreamy recollections
   Breathe, preluding pain!
Holy CHILD, Priest, Prince, and Prophet,
   That mysterious rest
Shadows, though men know not of it,
   Anguish in Thy Breast.

Read, O Man, that sacred story,
   How the GOD most High
Came down, emptied of His Glory,
   Here to mourn and die—

Canſt thou, ere the long nights darken
  O'er thine evil day,
Canſt thou hear it, and not hearken,
  Weep, repent, obey?

Yet, when thou art filled with ſadneſs
  At thy Saviour's Woe,
Peals an Angel-ſtrain of gladneſs
  And thy joys o'erflow:
By that All-ſufficing Spirit,
  Born to human Breath,
Souls Eternity inherit,
  And men vanquiſh Death.

Thus to hail Thine Advent hither,
  Grant, O Lord, to me
Large delight and griefs together
  May united be:
Here though bitterneſs hath found Thee
  For our guilt undone,
God's high Pæan ſails around thee
  For a conqueſt won.

Thus alternately to borrow
  Health from pain and loſs,
Joy's companionſhip with ſorrow
  Yield me from Thy Croſs;
Tears for Thy deep Tribulation
  And ſin's winepreſs trod,
Praiſe for uttermoſt Salvation
  And the Hymns of God.

Colloquies between the Disciple and the Divine Master.

Judge not, that ye be not judged.

TELL not abroad another's faults
   'Till thou haſt cured thine own;
Nor whiſper of thy neighbour's ſin
   'Till thou art perfect grown:
Then, when thy Soul is pure enough
   To bear My ſearching Eye
Unſhrinking, then may come the time
   Thy brother to decry."
      ' JESU, SAVIOUR, pitying be;
      Parce mihi, DOMINE!'

" Thine ears may hear, thine eyes may ſee
   The word or deed of ill,
But not the tears that flow to Me,
   Nor contrite ſighs, that thrill
Beyond the ſtars, and through the hoſts
   Of all Mine Angels bright;
Which that poor grieving heart pours out
   In ſilence of the night."
      ' JESU, LORD, O pardon me;
      Parce mihi, DOMINE!'

" And if not yet he own the fall,
   And unrepentant be,

Then pray for him as for thyſelf,
  Plead for his Soul with Me.
And if he wrong to thee have done,
  Still plead more earneſtly,
Till prayer of Faith becomes the prayer
  Of glowing Charity."
      'Lord of Love, O help Thou me ;
    Parce mihi, Domine!'

"And weary not! I watched for thee
  On mountains lone all night:
Athirſt, for love of thee, I toiled
  All through the hours of light.
In meekneſs and in lowlineſs,
  In wearineſs and pain,
I ſpent My Life, I died My Death
  Thy dead, loſt Soul to gain:
And on My Heart I bear thee ſtill,
  That thou with Me may'ſt reign."
      'Lord of Life, Who loveſt me,
    Parce mihi, Domine!'

The Complaint of a Pilgrim.

LORD, my God, the way is rough and
    long;
And I through wearineſs am faint and failing.'
"I am thy Staff, and I will ſtrengthen thee,
  Though earthly help is vain and unavailing."

'There is no water in this weary land,
While thirſt conſumes my parched and fainting
    Soul.'
" Come unto Me! of living Streams the Fount;
  I will refreſh thee; I will make thee whole."

' But, O my Lord! my heavy daily Croſs
    Doth well-nigh weigh me down. Lord, ſuccour
        me!'
" I bear it with thee, O faint-hearted One,
    Who a far heavier Croſs have borne for thee.

" Fold not the darkneſs fondly round thy heart,
    Think of My Mercy ſweet, and comfort thee,
My poor, unworthy Child; for Mine thou art,
    And ſin alone can ſnatch My Child from Me.

" I leave thee never; thou art not alone,
    And with thine own and thee Mine Angels
        dwell:
Poſſeſs thy Soul in patience; freely give
    Me love for Love, and all ſhall yet be well.

" The Time is ſhort. They that now weep, ere
        long
    Shall be as though they wept not: they that
        mourn
Be comforted, for I will comfort them:
    And ſweet ſhall be their glad thankſgiving
        Song."

In Domo Patris.

Of the various Mansions and Rewards of the Elect in the Heavenly Jerusalem.

IN My FATHER's House on high,
Where He reigns above the sky,
Many Mansions, passing fair,
I for Mine Elect prepare:
They alone shall enter in
Who in holy strife with sin
Fight till they the battle win.

Foremost there is Mary seen,
'Mid the Virgins Virgin-Queen:
Blest is she, supremely blest,
Thus preferred before the rest:
Close to Me she holds the seat
For My Best-belovéd meet,
With the Angels at her feet.

Glad is she with great delight,
Keeping **ever** in her sight
Me, her own Beloved SON,
Who alone the Victory won,
Seated **at the** FATHER's Side,
Ruling o'er creation wide,
King of all the Glorified.

In Domo Patris.

Joying with the Heavenly Choir,
Adam, man's primeval Sire,
Gladly renders thanks to Me;
Comforted to hear and ſee
How the fallen human race,
Loſt through his defection baſe,
Is by Me reſtored to Grace.

Lo! the Patriarchs with mirth
Leap for gladneſs at My Birth:
Promiſes they heard of old
Now accompliſhed they behold:
All the nations, Faith confeſſing
In My Name, receive the Bleſſing,
Endleſs Life through Me poſſeſſing.

Sweetly harping in My Praiſe
There the Prophets tune their lays;
Joyful they have found the Grace
Thus to ſee Me Face to face:
In the world, in days of old,
While they lived of Me they told;
True were all their ſayings bold.

David, Iſrael's Pſalmiſt ſweet,
John, who gave Me Baptiſm meet,
In the place of light Divine,
With eſpecial brightneſs ſhine:
Sent before, as I drew nigh,
Not ſo much to propheſy,
As to point and teſtify.

How illustrious appear,
Those My twelve Apostles dear!
In My Throne of Glory sharing,
Part with Me in Judgment bearing:
From themselves to Me they turned,
All their earthly treasures spurned;
With My Love their spirits burned.

Martyrs brave, of faith unfailing,
Who, ten thousand deaths assailing,
For My Name their witness bare,
Robes of gleaming crimson wear;
Shining clear, in splendour bright,
Glowing with a rosy white,
Raised to Honour's topmost height.

All who patiently endured
Glory have with Me secured,
Decked with fewer pearls or more,
As they heavier trials bore;
Now their groans and tearful sighing
Stores of gladness are supplying,
Source of pleasure never dying.

Free at length from earth's turmoils,
Each according to his toils,
Well Confessors are repaid,
In befitting robes arrayed;
Purple vestures are their due,
Blending tints of diverse hue,
Crimson red with azure blue.

Golden chains about their neck
Mine elected Teachers deck;
Doctors, by My ſpecial Love,
This Reward poſſeſs above;
By whoſe doctrine, clear and ſound,
Faith in Me, with Virtue crowned,
Spread to earth's remoteſt bound.

Monks, who kept the life Divine,
Drink their fill of My new Wine;
Feaſting with their Heavenly King
Songs of joy and praiſe they ſing:
All the labours which they wrought,
Diſcipline, with rigour fraught,
Sweeten now their every thought.

Anchorites, with Grace endued,
Hermits, from their ſolitude,
With bright beatific glance
View My beaming Countenance:
Thirſting ſore this Bliſs to taſte,
Long they ſojourned in the waſte,
And a ſtraitened life embraced.

They that brake a ſtubborn will
Strict obedience to fulfil
Now are My Companions made,
And in garments fair arrayed:
Now no ſelf-conſtraint they uſe,
No inviting pleaſure loſe,
Nothing ſhun which they would chooſe.

s

In Domo Patris.

Humble Souls, and poor in spirit,
Exaltation great inherit:
Once by men on earth abased,
Warmly now by Me embraced:
They for whom contempt was shewn,
To My Side are raised alone,
Seated on a lofty Throne.

Virgins, pure in life and heart,
Bear with Me a gladsome part;
Through the Halls of Heavenly song,
In the dance, they sweep along;
Perfume sweet they cast around,
With immortal garlands crowned;
All their Hymns My Praises sound.

Constant Widows, true and chaste,
My celestial Glory taste:
Great indeed is their reward
Who were faithful to their LORD:
Earthly nuptials they disdained;
In the Heavens a House they gained,
And My glad Embrace attained.

Well-beloved, with Me abide
Holy Souls in wedlock tied;
They, according to My Will,
Zion's holy City fill:
From their blessed children's store
Grows the band upon the Shore,
Saints in number more and more.

In Domo Patris.

Unto those whose continence
Triumphed o'er the joys of sense
Many crowns by Me are given,
For the times that they have striven;
Glittering with brighter sheen
As the struggles they have seen
Harder and more fierce have been.

Safe they kept their innocence,
Guiltless of the great offence,
Much they marvel, much rejoice,
At their Heavenly-guided choice;
How throughout they were defended
From the sin to which they tended,
Sin which with their birth descended.

Penitents, with equal joy,
Rest in Peace without alloy:
Now their Souls are cleansed within
From the stain of all their sin:
Hence their glory; hence their praise;
Hence to Me immortal lays
With exulting heart they raise.

Masters, Servants, bond and free,
Nursed in wealth or penury;
Every sex and every age,
Prince and peasant, fool and sage;
Each, according to his measure,
Holds a never-failing Treasure,
In the Realm of peace and pleasure.

All this Heavenly company
Live for evermore with Me :
Wondrous glad is their thanksgiving
In the **Man**ſion of the living :
Round **them they** behold diſplayed
More than all **for** which they prayed
While below, on earth, they ſtayed.

Earthly pleaſures therefore leave,
To the Heavenly **country cleave** :
Let thy labours know **no** bound,
That thou mayeſt be holy found,
So, when thou haſt bravely ſtriven,
Unto thee ſhall part be given
In the Happineſs of Heaven.

   *   *   *

Fount of Bleſſing, whence doth flow
Every good that **man can know** ;
Holy TRINITY, the ſum
Of the Saints' reward to come ;
Still Thy Majeſty tranſcends
All the praiſe which Thee attends,
To the age that never ends.

Grant that with Thy Saints above,
One **in** Faith and Hope and Love,
We, amid the ranſomed throng,
Join the everlaſting ſong :
Unto **Thee our** anthems pour,
Thee with glowing hearts adore,
Praiſing Thee for evermore.

Thoughts in Lent.

Confolation.

HARK! yon white-robed Angel-choir
Strike their tuneful golden lyre;
Hark! refponfive to their cry
Pure and faint-like Souls reply,
They whofe victory-crowned brow
Knows not fin nor fuffering now:
Hark! how floats that found along;
Lift! the notes of Heavenly fong—
Holy, Holy, Holy, LORD!
Burfts from each foft echoing chord,
Robed in Brightnefs o'er the Sun,
Thou, the High and Holy ONE!

LORD! what earthly voice can tell
Joys which minds Celeftial fwell?
Or can join with them to raife
Hymns of never-ending praife?
Yet wilt Thou Thyfelf impart
To the meek and contrite heart;
Nor wilt Thou, O GOD, defpife
A broken Spirit's facrifice.
He that trembleth at Thy Word
Need not fear Thy glittering Sword,
Reconciled through Thy Dear SON
To the High and Holy ONE.

Thoughts in Lent.

Though **Thou hear'ſt the** Seraphs cry,
To the humble Thou art nigh;
Though in Heaven Thy Dwelling-Place,
Thou haſt **yet a** Throne of Grace;
Thou haſt ſaid **that** Thou wilt be
With each Soul that ſeeketh Thee,
Him in Righteouſneſs array
Till the great and final Day,
Fit him by Thy SPIRIT's Power
For the peaceful parting hour:
In thoſe Heavenly regions high,
Paſt mortal thought or mortal eye,
Thou haſt ſaid that ſuch ſhall be
In thoſe glorious Realms with **Thee,**
By Thy SPIRIT, through Thy SON,
When life's toilſome courſe **is** done,
With the High **and** Holy ONE!

Humiliation.

FOUNT of all Mercies, lo, I come
   Again to ſeek my long-loſt Home,
And Thee the GOD of Comfort pray—
Turn not Thy Suppliant away.
Thou Who reſtrained Thine Anger's power
In Salem's penitential hour,
Thou Who waſt found, and found to bleſs
The Wanderer in the Wilderneſs,

Who hearest grief and suffering's cry
And washest out the purple dye,
Who sinful Nineveh didst spare,
Hear! oh, hear! my contrite prayer.

I ask not that Thou should'st restore
The earthly joys I loved before;
I ask not that my life's sad sun
Should in its former splendour run;
The Christian's hope, his first glad song
To fallen Souls no more belong;
That Robe so spotless once, so bright,
Is ever soiled in human sight:
I only ask Thee—nor deny
To hear Thy Suppliant's mournful cry;
I only ask, O God of Heaven,
To die in peace, to die forgiven!

Verses from the German.

Retirement.

AH, whither flee, or where abide?
Where is the lone sequestered spot,
Where outward things can reach me not
And from their turmoil I may hide?

Can no deep solitude be found
    Where prayer and praise might ceaseless be
    To Him Whose Grace had set me free
From each distracting sight and sound?

For desert wastes my spirit longs;
    Had she the pinions of a dove,
    There would she seek the Source of Love
Far from these restless noisy throngs;
She dare not longer make abode,
    She cannot keep her own Faith pure,
    Where men are caught in Folly's lure,
And strive but to forget their God.

Then forth my Soul! Escape amain
    From snares that long have held thee fast;
    Quit worldly schemes and friends at last,
That so thou may'st that rest attain,
Where voice nor touch nor sight can come
    To break thy commune deep and still
    With Him Who every want can fill,
Who is alone our proper Home.

There in some narrow quiet cell,
    My Paradise, my Promised Land,
    These wandering thoughts I might command,
And fixed in rapt devotion dwell,
No foe to thwart with blame or praise;
    My God alone should fill my Soul,
    As toward my peaceful death should roll
In changeless course my tranquil days.

* * *

Alas! poor Soul! hadst thou thy will,
  'Twere resting ere the field was won;
  How hopest thou all foes to shun
When blind self-will goes with thee still?
In outward things thou seekest rest,
  But thou wilt never find it so;
  Nought outward is so much thy foe
As what thou hast within thy breast.

Safe is Obedience, that alone;
  No loyal Soldier leaves his post,
  Though toil or pain or life it cost,
Until his Captain saith, ' Begone.'
And Faith knows not to pause or choose,
  And flees no strife however stern,
  Where in the struggle she my learn
How in GOD's Will her own to lose.

But if thy heart on Peace is bent,
  O'er fair false dreams no longer brood
  Of blest, congenial solitude,
They will but breed deep discontent;
No Paradise is left us here;
  Our Peace is in a will resigned;
  Then amid crowds thou yet may'st find
Thy Unseen LORD most surely near.

Midnight.

AT dead of night
Sleep took her flight;
I gazed abroad; no ſtar of all the crowds
That people Heaven, was ſmiling through the clouds
To cheer my ſight
That dreary night.

At dead of night
I ſcaled the height
Of giddy queſtion o'er our mortal lot,
My ſearchings found no anſwer, brought me not
One ray of light
In that deep night.

At dead of night
In ſtill affright
I turned, and liſtened to my throbbing heart;
One pulſe of pain alone, whoſe ancient ſmart
Had dimmed ſweet light,
Beat there that night.

At dead of night
I fought the fight,
Humanity, of all thy pain and woes;
My ſtrength could not decide it, and my foes
O'erwhelmed me quite
In that deep night.

Gethsemane.

> At dead of night
> All power and might
> I yielded, Lord of Life and Death, to Thee,
> And learnt Thou watchedst with me, and that we
> Are in Thy Sight
> In deepest night.

Gethsemane.

SIN hardens, all the heart with ice encrusting,
    And narrowing its current evermore;
Therefore, O Saviour, Loving, Pitying, Trusting,
  Thy Heart, the ice of sin ne'er crusted o'er,

Was tenderer to feel each pang that tried Thee
  Than any heart that ever broke or bled,
The timid Love that followed yet denied Thee,
  The selfish Fear that kept far off or fled.

      *   *   *

But sin must ever weaken while it hardens,
  Enfeebling to endure, or act, or dare,
Till nothing save the balms of Heavenly Pardons
  Can nerve the heart again to do or bear.

Then must Thy Heart be stronger far to suffer
  Than any sinful heart that ever beat;

And if **Thy** Path than any path be rougher,
   Yet haſt **Thou** Strength unſcathed its woes to
     meet.

What tide **of grief** then, Mightieſt, o'er Thee
   ruſhes
  Thus taſking e'en Thy Patience and Thy Truſt?
What **woe** beyond all woe Thy Spirit cruſhes,
   Bowing **Thee** Sinleſs, Spotleſs, **to** the duſt?

Martyrs for Thee have gone to meet their anguiſh
   Singing **glad** Hymns e'en with their dying breath,
Not all their tortures cauſing once **to** languiſh
   The hope that led them forth for Thee to death.

Thy **Stephen's** face ſhone like a holy Angel's,
   Uplifted midſt the **ſtones** towards Thy ſkies,
Beaming from radiant brows Thine own Evangels,
   And glowing with the welcome **in** Thine Eyes.

Yet **Thou,** LORD, lifteſt not Thy Face to Heaven,
   But boweſt proſtrate on the dewy ſod;
Thy Soul exceeding ſorrowful with death-pangs
   riven,
  Thy Sweat of anguiſh as great drops of Blood.

What ſtorm is this **in which Thou** all but ſinkeſt,
   Whoſe **Arm has borne** ſo many through the flood?
What bitter Cup is this from which Thou ſhrinkeſt,
   Strength of all Martyrs, Patient LAMB of GOD?

The sin of all the world, whose throne Thou claimest,
    Hadst made so fair, so fallen, loved and sought!
The sin of all Thine Own, to whom Thou camest,
    Thou camest, and Thine Own received Thee not!

The sin of all the Saved, that dying blessed Thee,
    Who from the sting of Death hadst set them free;
The sin of all Thy Martyrs who confessed Thee,
    And died rejoicing that they went to Thee.

This is the weight of Agony unspoken
    Which Thee, O Highest, thus so low hath laid?
The curse of all the law mankind had broken,
    The sin of all the world which Thou hadst made.

Earth's serried woe and crime in one compressing,
    Thou buriest all within Thy single Breast,
And changest thus our every curse to Blessing,
    Giving us Life through death, in labour Rest.

Old Testament Hymns.

David and Barzillai.

IN Blessing parted from the King
    By Jordan's brimming wave,
Yet shalt thou hear the City sing
    With him beyond the grave.

Thy Monarch's home should yet be thine,
　　Jerusalem the blest,
Though Gilead's balms in all their calms
　　Have steeped that aged breast.

O birthday crown of fourscore years,
　　Which some with strength attain!
Vain conquest, to survive with tears
　　And more than manhood's pain!

The King that eye shall yet descry
　　In all His Beauty rare;
To Angel's lute no voice is mute,
　　No ear is listless there.

Rizpah, the Daughter of Aiah.

BEFORE those bones unshrouded,
　　On Gibeah's deathful hill,
Beneath the skies unclouded,
　　Beside the gasping rill,
Watch! lonely Mourner, keeping,
　　With all thy sackcloth spread,
The raindrops of thy weeping,
　　The harvest of thy dead.

Those gracious tears are winning
　　The Blessing from above,
The Sacrifice for sinning,
　　Bathed with a sinner's love;

Not yet upon the mountains
  Falls there the promised dew;
Break, Heart, thy sorrow's fountains,
  Baptizing them anew.

Lift! lift His Cross, Wood-hewer,
  Draw! draw that water's tears—
The latter and the newer,
  The purer rain appears;
There droops a Sinless BROTHER
  His sweet atoning Brow;
There breaks the Virgin Mother
  A spotless heart below.

Is it well with the Child?

AS rippled, by the sickle prest,
  The cornfield's crested wave,
He sank upon the Reaper's breast
  Whose garner is the grave.

O well is it, sweet Child, with thee,
  Soft lies thy drooping head,
Death's pillow is thy Mother's knee,
  Thy bier the Prophet's bed!

'Tis not new Moon, nor Sabbath soon,
  No grief the Prophet knows;
No new Moon now of hope hast thou,
  No Sabbath of repose.

Hold! Mother, hold the **Man** of GOD,
  Lay there thy sorrow's loss;
He wakes not to the Prophet's rod
  Who sleeps beneath the Cross.

O full are they of healing sweet,
  His Saints, ere CHRIST appears,
Ere mourners hold those blessed Feet,
  Or wash them with their tears!

Elijah and Elisha.

STERN Remembrancer **of error**
  With the lightning of thine eye,
Locking with the key of terror
  All **the** portals **of the** sky,
Calling, while the blessing lingers,
  Laving flames on Carmel's steep,
Ere the cloud with dewy fingers
  Scoops the vapours of the deep:
    Man of GOD, no CHRIST I see—
    What have I to do with thee?

Earth with fire and blood baptizing,
  Mingling with the gracious rain,
Then on wheels of flame uprising,—
  Shine upon the mount again;
There with wrathful Moses standing,
  Smiting with the vengeful rod,

Fire from Heaven and earth commanding,
  Make thee like the Son of God:
    Darkeſt of the Clouded Three—
    We will build no houſe for thee!

Caſt thy mantle on another,
  Who ſhall all thy terrors quell—
Kiſſing Father, kiſſing Mother,
  Ere he bids the world farewell;
Like thee only once in curſing,
  When the ſcoffing ſons rebel,
As the Spirit gently nurſing,
  Save when Ananias fell:
    There the Son of God I ſee—
    Prophet, let me cleave to thee!

Thine the ſtill ſmall Voice remaining,
  Chiding Horeb's ſtormy blaſt,
Huſhing all the world's complaining,
  When the flaming Law is paſt;
Bidding with the Minſtrel's ſoothing
  All our angry paſſions ceaſe,
Softened by the Spirit's Smoothing
  All to Gentleneſs and Peace,
    Perfect Love, without a fear—
    Son of God, I ſee Thee near!

T

An Allegory.

I STOOD in the ſhade of a ſtately Tree,
    The Foreſt Monarch; far and wide
    It ſpread its branches on every ſide;
  Fruit alone there was none to ſee
On the wide-ſpread boughs of that ſtately Tree.

A ſtern dark Man, from whoſe gloomy brow
    Paſſed never a fearful frown,
    Rode through the Foreſt up and down;
His ſteed was pale as the driven ſnow,
And he carried an Axe at his ſaddle-bow.

Wherever that pale white horſe did tread,
    Some ſapling tall or gnarlèd oak
    Fell by the ſtern Man's ruthleſs ſtroke,
Or ſome the faireſt of flowers lay dead,
Like graſs on the houſe-top witherèd.

Yet all unchanged was the ſylvan ſcene,
    For ſtill as he journeyed from place to place,
    He left of his preſence no laſting trace,
But the Foreſt grew on as thick and green,
As through it the pale horſe had never been.

While I muſed on this, forth from the glade
    That ſame pale horſe and its Rider ſtern,
    With fixed fell purpoſe, ſeemed to turn,
Till where the tall Tree caſt its ſhade,
Horror of horrors! their courſe was ſtayed.

An Allegory.

Oh, what fear! oh, what dismay!
  I would have fled from the doomèd spot,
  But my spell-bound limbs suffered me not;
I would have opened my mouth to pray,
But the words unuttered died away.

Thrice he brandished his Axe in the air!
  Thrice the Hand of ONE unseen
  Came the Axe and the Tree between,
And I heard a Voice—Depart! forbear!
Let it alone another year.

Reluctant the stern Man obeyed,
  And slow withdrew; but ere he passed,
  Forth his Axe from his hand he cast,
And the keen edge of the glittering blade
At the root of the stately Tree was laid.

And One, 'bright as the Morning Star,'
  Yea, 'bright as the Sun' when he rides at noon
  Through the cloudless sky, 'fair as the Moon,'
Awful as serried armies are,
Bearing their 'banners' aloft for war,

Stood and cried—Repent! repent!
  Now the Axe lies at the root
  Of every Tree not bearing fruit;
Ere thy Day of Grace be spent,
Child of Adam, repent! repent!

Then as far as my ſight could pierce the wood,
  I ſaw that Axes all around,
    At the root of the Trees, covered the ground;
And the Trees were no longer Trees, but I ſtood
In the midſt of a Human Multitude!

Aged Sires with hoary hair,
  Tender Infants, Children young,
    Women and Men, fair and ſtrong:
But at the foot of each one there
Lay an Axe, ſharp and bare.

And then a lurid darkneſs ſeemed
  To cover the whole, and forth there broke
    Gnaſhings, wailings, fire, ſmoke;
Awful Words not to be named—
God be praiſed, I had but dreamed!

The Burial.

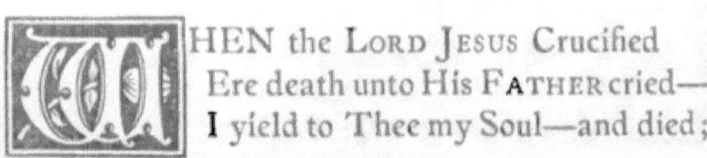HEN the Lord Jesus Crucified
Ere death unto His Father cried—
I yield to Thee my Soul—and died;

  When the Centurion ſtanding nigh
  With mighty ſtirrings heard that Cry
  And God in Christ did glorify;

The Burial.

When they who gathered round as one
The things to witneſs which were done
Had wildly beat their breaſts and gone;

Joſeph the rich man then waxed brave
The Body of the LORD to crave
That he might lay It in the Grave.

When Pilate bade it ſo to be
There came a little company
And ſadly gathered round the Tree.

From Hands and Feet the nails they wrenched,
Weeping that they ſo late had blenched,
And came not till the Light was quenched.

From His dear Head they took the Crown,
Half thinking He might know His Own,
And ſadly then they took Him down.

Upon the earth its Maker lies;
They gently cloſe His All-pure Eyes,
They feel His late-felt Agonies.

Each gracious Arm, which ſtretching wide
To claſp the world for which He died,
So long was parted from the Side,

Each Arm, ſo kind to things ſo baſe,
Now ſeeks Its natural reſting-place,
Yet ceaſes not from that embrace;

But for the Blood which left each Vein
They need not wash That sacred Stain,
To wash all else It doth remain.

Where is the Linen Joseph bought?
The Spices Nicodemus brought,
Aloes and Myrrh? Be wanting nought.

The snowy Cerements wrap Him well,
The Spices Him yet sweeter tell,
We add our hearts with Him to dwell.

Slowly they lift Him from the sod,
With holy fear the path is trod,
As men should walk who bear their GOD.

In reverent order sad and slow
From the dark place of Death they go,
Or weeping wild or sobbing low;

And yet they tend to happy bowers,
Alone among the garden-flowers
They go to lay their GOD and ours.

Now to the hard Rock He is borne;
Sweet Rock by after-pilgrims worn,
Sweet Field of the dead Wheaten Corn.

A little while their Trust they keep,
A little while they pray and weep,
And then they lay Him down to sleep.

The Burial.

They cloſe the Tomb and go away
To keep that awful Sabbath-day,
But with the LORD in heart they ſtay.

How may a ſoon-forgotten rhyme
Thus faintly ſhadowing things ſublime
Bear fruit to live in after-time?

Look back, O Brother, on the Hill,
Where late the Enemy had his will,
Where eve is falling calm and ſtill.

What crowns its ſummit now? declare;
Thou ſay'ſt a Croſs alone is there;
A Croſs alone? O would it were.

O blind with error! pray for eyes,
Still on the Croſs the Victim dies,
Still ſin the Sinleſs crucifies.

More ruthleſſly the ploughers plough,
More ſharp the thorns about His Brow,
More cruel nails transfix Him now.

Daily by ſins of Chriſtian men
In buſy ſtreet and peaceful glen
The LORD is crucified again.

Daily by ſins of me and you
The LORD is crucified anew;
What, Men and Brethren, ſhall we do?

The Burial.

We, His true murderers heretofore
Will bear the Burden Joseph bore,
Will take Him from the Cross once more.

The broken contrite-hearted wail
May lift the thorns, may wrench the nail,
May all the sad past countervail.

So, ere our life's sun reach the west,
We will take down the Only-Blest,
And lay Him in the Grave to rest;

Lay Him to rest, and cast within,
Through His dear Dying, all our sin,
Then wait and weep and strive to win.

The Cross stands out against the sky;
The LORD has left it. Ye and I
Must hasten where He died to die;

Be ours awhile the nails and thorn,
So never ours the shame and scorn
In the great Resurrection-Morn.

So never be to us addressed—
Depart, ye cursèd, to unrest;
But—Come ye, of My FATHER blest.

The Power of Contrition.

An Ode from the Italian.

POWER irresistible
  In lowly prayer contained!
  There's nothing but unfeigned
Repentance may procure.
Ascend, my Soul, to Golgotha,
  And see the Cross displaying
  A proof beyond gainsaying
That all this hope is sure.

Remember, in Thy Majesty
  In Heaven when Thou art seated—
  The contrite Thief entreated—
Remember me, O Lord,
Of sinners me the wofullest.
  The zeal of his confession
  Had under death's oppression
A thrill of warmth restored.

And Jesus to the suppliant
  Inclined His Ear to pardon;
  Said—Thou in Heavenly Garden
This day shalt be with Me.
His Father's Realm of Blessedness
  He brought him to inherit,
  When He resigned His Spirit
Upon the painful Tree.

The Power of Contrition.

Before the Apostles' Fellowship
  This penitent Transgressor
  Was made by Grace possessor
Of Heavenly Riches sure.
O Power irresistible
  In lowly prayer contained!
  There's nothing but unfeigned
Repentance may procure.

O Tear beyond all valuing
  Which penitence expresses:
  No pearl the East possesses
Can be compared with thee.
In Heaven the very profligate
  Becomes admitted by thee,
  And let but God descry thee,
No Rigour more hath He.

Thou Tear, that Mary Magdalen's
  Face trembling rannest over,
  Thy glistening to discover
Made all the Angels glad.
'Gainst forfeitures innumerous
  An instant compensation,
  An earnest of Salvation
In thy great worth she had.

And when upon the countenance
  Of Peter thou didst trickle,
  From eyelid unto fickle
Lips that untruth had stained,

Thou cleared'ſt all his perfidy:
Such is thy worth excelling,
And ſinful Souls paſt telling
Have cleanneſs thus regained.

O would this gem paſt valuing
Were granted me to cheriſh!
May Grace before I periſh
This boon confer on me!
For, where the tear ſpontaneouſly
The contrite Soul expreſſes,
No pearl the Eaſt poſſeſſes
Compared with it can be.

Lux advenit veneranda.

A Sequence for the Feaſt of the Purification.

AY of bright illumination,
Day of choral jubilation;
Kindling hearts have caught the blaze;
Joyful light which brings another
Feaſtday of GOD's Virgin Mother,
Sacred Day of ſolemn praiſe.

Let melodious voices ſounding,
Hearts with deep emotion bounding,
Part in glad thankſgiving bear:

Praise to God's supreme Perfections!
In our glowing recollections
   Let His noble Mother share.

Glorious in her exaltation,
Tender in commiseration,
   Named from penitential Love:
Crowned with Dignity Maternal,
With Virginity eternal,
   Shining in the Heaven above.

As the Bush with fire was glowing,
Yet the flames, their power foregoing,
   Scathèd not the tenderest rod;
So she whom the Spirit graces,
Free from conjugal embraces,
   Maid and Mother bare her God.

Sealèd Fount of waters rising,
Garden shut, yet fertilizing
   With the seeds of Virtues, she:
She was that mysterious Portal
Closèd by the King immortal,
   Ne'er for man unclosed to be;

Gideon's Fleece with dewdrops streaming,
Field with scented odours steaming,
   Fragrant to the bounds of earth;
Aaron's Rod in secret growing,
Earth with Righteousness o'erflowing
   For the faithful in that Birth.

Types of her, the myſtic Fountain,
Were the Caſtle, Temple, Mountain,
   Palace, Chamber, City fair:
And whatever names of glory
Mark the Saints in ſacred ſtory,
   Let her alſo in them ſhare.

Bleſt was ſhe, with Grace endued;
By her name is joy renewed,
Lilies to her fragrance yield,
Honey by the ſweetneſs ſealed
   In her lips is far outdone:
Richer than the wine's red glow,
Whiter than the gleaming ſnow,
Softer than the dewy roſe,
Brighter than the moon ſhe ſhews
   In the Light of the True SUN.

Thou, O King of Hoſts ſupernal,
Vanquiſher of powers infernal,
Way which muſt to Heaven be taken,
Nor by conſtant hope forſaken;
Gather to Thyſelf the erring,
Call them back, their ſpirits ſtirring
   By the faithfulneſs of Thine:
SON of Mary, true Phyſician,
Grant us our devout petition;
Look not on ſin's aggravations,
But behold our ſupplications;
Guilty Souls in fear abiding,
Only in Thy Love confiding,
   Take into the Life Divine.

Verselets.

Master, say on!

THOU art gone Home, Thine earthly Work complete:
   Yet from the calm height of Thy Heavenly Seat,
By Thine own Messenger, the PARACLETE,
         Master, say on!

Those many things that Thou hadst yet to say
We fain would hear, and be they what they may,
Would bear them for Thy sake and in Thy way;
         Master, say on!

We have heard Thy loved Voice, and followed Thee
All through Thy Life, through all Thy Ministry
From Bethlehem to glorious Bethany;
         Master, say on!

Friends freshly parted soothe their yearning pain
With written words that make them one again:
Link us to Thee by Thy sweet Comfort's chain;
         Master, say on!

Dear are glad tidings from a distant strand;
But dearer are the traces of Thy Hand,
The greetings from Thy far-off Holy Land;
         Master, say on!

Until Life's weary Summer heat be paſt,
And joys and griefs, like Autumn leaves, fade faſt,
We liſten ſtill, then till Thine Advent blaſt,
            Maſter, ſay on!

Eaſter-Day.

THE Graves grow thicker, and life's ways more bare
    As years on years go by:
Nay! Thou haſt more green gardens in thy care,
    And more ſtars in thy ſky!

Behind, hopes turned to griefs, and joys to memories
    Are fading out of ſight:
Before, pains changed to peace, and dreams to certainties
    Are glowing in GOD's Light.

Hither come backſlidings, defeats, diſtreſſes,
    Vexing this mortal ſtrife:
Thither go progreſs, victories, ſucceſſes,
    Crowning immortal Life.

No jubilees, few gladſome feſtive hours
    Form landmarks for my way:
But Heaven, and earth, and Saints, and friends, and flowers
    Are keeping Eaſter-Day!

The Lord's Largess.

TWO Days, by contrast linked together,
Sharing the wealth of spring-tide weather,
The buoyant cloud, the breezy calm,
The budding growth of flower and palm,
Each with a holy history
Fraught with a hidden Mystery:
To that, the depth of shame and sadness;
To this, the height of glorious Gladness.
That, darkest hour of sorrow's night,
Is brightened by the coming Light;
This, to enhance her joy, would fain
Glance backward to that shade again.
Lo! for each pent-up pang of trouble
The promised Peace is rendered double;
No claim receives its due discharge,
But more—the LORD hath heard at large:
He bids the sinful throng depart,
Whose watch weighed down each stony heart;
Then sends those hearts so cold and hard
The Blessing of an Angel-guard.
The Earth's drear curse of brier and thorn
On the bleak hill of Calvary borne,
Returns from Paradisal bowers
An Easter boon of buds and flowers.

Ad perennis Uitae Fontem.

A Hymn of S. Peter Damiani on the Joys of Paradise.

FOR the Fount of Life eternal is my thirsting Spirit fain,
And my prisoned Soul would gladly burst her fleshly bars in twain,
While the exile strives and struggles on to win her home again.

As she groans beneath the troubles which with weary weight oppress,
She is thinking on the Glory which she lost through wickedness,
And the thought of joy departed but increaseth her distress.

Who can tell the perfect gladness of the Peace within the skies,
Where, of living pearls upbuilded, Mansions for the Blessèd rise,
Where the golden halls and rooftrees shine and glow with radiant dyes?

Framed alone of precious jewels stately Dwellings there appear,
And the highways of the City, paved with gold, as crystal clear;
Mire is far, and filth is banished, nought that may pollute is near.

Ad perennis Uitae Fontem.

Winters snowing, summers glowing, never thither
    pain may bring,
There the gorgeous roses flower in the calm of
    endless spring,
Balms exude, and crocus blushes, lilies fair are
    blossoming.

Meads are sheening, fields are greening, honey
    drops from combs of bees,
Liquid odours, fragrant spices, shed their perfume
    on the breeze,
Never falling fruits are hanging from the ever
    leafy trees.

There no moon through phases passes, sun and
    stars bestow no light,
But the LAMB on His glad City, Light unsetting,
    shineth bright;
There the day is everlasting, gone for aye are
    time and night.

For the Saints, now crowned in triumph, like the
    sun in radiance glow,
Greet each other in that gladness which the Saints
    alone can know,
While, secure, they count their battles with their
    subjugated foe.

Fleshly wars they know no longer, since with
    blemish stained is none,

For the spiritual body and the Soul at last are
  one ;
Dwell they now in Peace eternal, with all stumbling
  they have done.

To their first estate return they, freed from every
  mortal sore,
And the Truth, for ever present, ever lovely, they
  adore,
Drawing from that living Fountain living sweetness
  evermore.

And they drink in changeless being as they taste
  those waters clear ;
Bright are they, and swift, and gladsome, no more
  perils need they fear ;
There the youth can know no ageing, never cometh
  sicknes near.

Thence they draw their life unending, passingness
  hath passed away,
Thence they grow, and bloom, and flourish, freed
  for ever from decay,
And deathlessness hath swallowed up the might of
  death for aye.

They know Him Who knoweth all things, nothing
  from their ken may flee,
And the thoughts of one another in the inmost
  heart they see ;
One in choosing and refusing, one are they in
  unity.

And though each for divers merits there hath won
    a various throne,
Yet their love for one another maketh what each
    loves his own,
Every prize to all is common, yet belongs to each
    alone.

Where the Body is, together in their flight the
    eagles ſpeed,
There the Saints and there the Angels ſeek
    refreſhment in their need,
And the Sons of Earth and Heaven on that One
    Bread ever feed.

Ever full, yet ever craving, they deſire, and yet
    poſſeſs,
But their fulneſs brings no loathing, and their
    hunger no diſtreſs,
Eagerly they eat for ever, ever eat in joyfulneſs.

In new harmonies unceaſing they with voice me-
    lodious ſing,
While their liſtening ears are gladdened with the
    harps' exulting ring,
And for He hath made them victors, praiſes chant
    they to their King.

Where the King of Heaven is preſent, happy is
    the gazing Soul,

She is not dead, but sleepeth.

And ſhe ſees the double framework of the globe
    beneath her roll,
Sees the ſun and moon and planets and the ſtars
    that ſtud the pole.

Jesu, Palm of all Thy Soldiers, who in Thee
    alone confide,
Bring me to that Holy City when my belt is laid
    aſide,
Grant that I may ſhare the portion of the Saints
    who there abide.

While the war is yet unended, give me vigour for
    the fray,
Give me, when the fight is over, Peace that paſſeth
    not away,
Give Thyſelf to me, O Jesu, as my one Reward
    for aye.

She is not dead, but sleepeth.

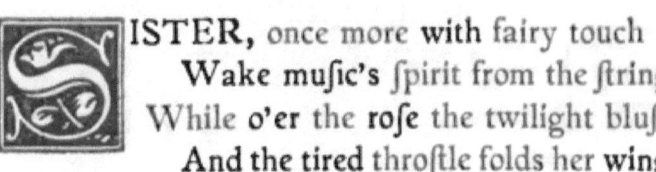

SISTER, once more with fairy touch
    Wake muſic's ſpirit from the ſtrings,
While o'er the roſe the twilight bluſh
    And the tired throſtle folds her wings.

My body lies within this room
    Worn by the ſtrife of buſy day—
But far beyond the deepening gloom
    My Soul hath fled, far, far away.

She is not dead, but sleepeth.

Beyond yon mountain in the clouds,
    Whose white peak faintly flushes still,
I steal 'mid Angel-glist'ning crowds
    That slowly float adown the hill.

What seems to thee a wild blue plain
    Among cloud headlands, is a lake,
On whose clear ripple rests no stain,
    While Angel-voices o'er it break.

Their long robes glistening as they pass
    Oaring on gently with soft flight,
Cloud-shadows noiseless o'er the grass—
    Are these the Children of the Light?

Seven Angels coronalled with gold
    And lilies, lift above each head
Their white arms, in whose tender fold
    A little Sister lieth dead.

A Baby-angel, on whose face
    God's holy Dew is shining yet,
Who nestles in her resting place,
    Her lips with tearful kisses wet.

O'er the blue lake their footsteps sail,
    While myriad echoes haunt the sky,
Around that tiny form so pale,
    Around that sleeping stirless eye.

Just where the fringe of deathless flowers
    Is kissed by every dimpled wave,

She is not dead, but sleepeth.

They lay her in the careless bowers
   Of Paradise beyond the grave.

Yet one Boy-Angel stoops to kiss
   The silver Cross upon her brow—
In the lap of Eternal Bliss
   The Baby is no Baby now.

Higher and higher soar the wings—
   I cannot see their azure eyes;
Yet one clear voice upsoaring sings—
   In me its music never dies.

In silence of the wakeful night,
   Beside the hurry of Life's stream,
I listen with a strange delight,
   I wander in a stranger dream.

I dream that men may cark and moil,
   And yet their labour be in vain;
Their knowledge but a mocking toil
   Which lands them on the shores of pain.

But that dead Baby seeth now
   What our dim eyes aye fail to see—
The glories of that radiant bow
   That links Time to Eternity.

I dream God's Angels stand around
   To watch the Baby's waking smile,
As couchèd on the holy ground
   Where nought may enter to defile.

She reads with knowledge, clear and ſtrong,
  The Truths from Angels eyes concealed,
And bears upon a flood of ſong
  Love's fuller, brighter Creed revealed;

Is fondled by the LORD's Redeemed,
  Is kiſſed, and paſſed from hand to hand,
As one upon whoſe face had gleamed
  The love light of the old home land.

And o'er the lake, and through the clouds,
  Gazing they yearn to hear once more,
From out ſin's miſt that overſhrouds
  The ſurges of earth's troublous ſhore;

Once to hear how their loved ones fare;
  Once to breathe—We are happy here,
Where is no ſin or ſtrife or care,
  Where childlike Love hath loſt all fear.

'Tis o'er—the muſic Melts away—
  Death's voices tremble on its tide.
Oh, in my Soul, through life's brief day
  The wiſe grief of that ſong abide!

The Holy Sacrifice.

EHOLD! all things await
    Thy Coming, Lord, in state.
  The Altar-Vessels gleam, the Tapers
    burn:
  O must not <u>we</u> prepare
  Our hearts Thy Light to share,
And should not all our Souls with longing yearn?

    O Childhood, dear to Him
    Who sways the Cherubim,
O Manhood, with the careworn brow so pale,
    That into Truth can'st look,
    And wilt not shadows brook,
Come! at His Shrine the Incarnate Lamb to hail.

    And thou, true Woman's heart,
    That knew'st not to depart
When thy Lord lay deserted in the Tomb,
    Rejoice! The greatest now
    Before Him bend the brow.
Come! earth's remotest Nations, there is room.

    Once, Saviour! once alone
    Upon Thine Altar-Throne,
Dear Calvary's Cross, didst Thou for sinners die;
    But in Thine own Abode
    Thou art the Lamb of God,
And blendest earth and Heaven in spousals high.

As victims slain of yore
  Beside the open door,
Within the veil by fire Heaven's Gifts became,
  Love infinite, Divine,
  On Heaven's translucent Shrine
Consumes, and yet consumes not, in its flame.

  Sweet Lamb of God, once slain,
  Who alway dost remain
The Undying Lamb on Heaven's vast Throne
    above,
  At this most wondrous Feast
  Each Christian Soul is Priest,
And yields Thyself, the Sacrifice of Love.

  Lo! over earth's expanse,
  Beneath Heaven's countenance,
A myriad Altars wait the Incarnate Guest,
  Who stoops, whilst time and space
  Lie in His Arms' embrace,
To be the Inmate of the faithful breast.

  As from the source of day
  A myriad sunbeams play
Upon earth's vales, and fill each chaliced flower,
  So He, Who guards Heaven's Throne,
  Still makes His Presence known
Through earth's wide courts, and comes in Love
    and Power.

  Not in all gems of Inde
  Couldst Thou be fitly shrined,
Most gracious Presence, Heavenly, yet most True;

The Holy Sacrifice.

  Our earthly accents fail,
  Nor Heaven may speak the tale,
But hearts may yield the fervent homage due.

  Descend, O Lord! And we
  Will supplicate, through Thee,
For all we love in earth or Spirit-sphere,
  And for Thy costly sake
  We know that God will take
Our feeble prayers, as flowers of love and fear,

  And bind them in a wreath
  To circle Hell and Death
And draw the universe to His great Throne.
  This is our service due;
  Come! Children, aid may you,
For Christ is here, and Children are His Own.

  And all the sacred throng
  Shall join in our glad song;
Angels, Archangels, Thrones and Hierarchies,
  And she, that Virgin Blest,
  Who cradled on her breast
The Lord of all, and kissed His sleeping Eyes.

  With her each Patriarch great,
  All Souls that conquered hate,
Prophets, Apostles, Martyrs, all as one,
  Swell high the blissful Song
  Which, ages vast along,
High Heaven shall carol to the Father's Son.

God's Acre.

 O Holy Ghost, come! fire
 Our hearts, and joy infpire
Worthy His Prefence Who defcends this morn.
 Peace, Mortals: fong nor fpeech
 Can this great Myftery reach;
Into a world of finners God is born.

God's Acre.

UN was fhining bright and fair,
 Wind was hufhed, and calm was there,
 Calm, and Peace beyond compare
   In God's Acre.

 Flowerets blooming, rare and gay,
 Decked the Grave-plats on that day,
 And each Chaplet feemed to fay—
   We fade and bloom.

 Thought I then with joy and woe
 Of dear Friends I once did know,
 Sleeping now long years ago
   In God's Acre.

 Thought I then with throbbing brain,
 Heart was beating—not with pain,
 For I heard a glorious Strain
   From God's Acre.

"We—the Voices seemed to say—
Far from pain and grief away,
Ever, for thee, lone One, pray,
   Watches keeping.

" Thine awhile must be the strife,
Thine the battle-field of life,
Thine the day with sorrow rife,
   Yet be hopeful.

" Wear thine armour, Soldier brave,
Sailor, breast the swelling wave,
One there is all strong to save,
   Then be faithful.

" Wipe the tear-drop from thine eye,
And repress the rising sigh :
We unseen, yet ever nigh,
   Will cheer thee on.

" Ye who toil, and we that wait
By the bright and golden Gate,
Till we reach the highest state,
   In CHRIST are one."

Sun was shining bright and fair ;
Blest Spirit-voices filled the air ;
With thankful heart I said my prayer
   In GOD'S ACRE.

The Five smooth Stones of David.

READY for battle's grim array
Encamped two hostile armies lay—
   Now trumpet sounds and drum;
But still from yonder mountain's side,
Though signs there are of martial **pride**,
   None armed for combat come.
A mighty Champion's standing here,
And all his form gigantic fear:
Fierce is his look, his Challenge loud;
Pale terror haunts the fainting crowd.

His height six cubits and a span,
By half he passes mortal man:
   Who can his stature reach?
The very love God gives of life
To turn from such unequal strife
   Would all but madmen teach.
Thus argue still the worldly wise,
For ever seeing mountains rise,
And trembling lest a little breath
Should swell into the storm of Death.

A brazen helmet on his head
Nods terrible, and plates are spread
   Of polished brass around;

Of ſtature vaſt he treads the earth
Like offſpring of ſome monſtrous birth.
    And ſhakes the ſolid ground.
Impregnable appears the ſhield
One bears before him on the field;
His hands, like hazel wand, uprear
Of dreadful length his iron ſpear.

Methinks I trace in him again
The great Arch-enemy of men,
    In verſe immortal told:
He, when his fury fierceſt burned,
From armoury celeſtial turned—
    And why art thou leſs bold?
'Twas Angels and an Arm Divine
Repulſed him then: ſuch arms are thine:
The Soldiers of a Heavenly King
To combat Heavenly weapons bring.

Thou who in youth haſt often read,
" Salvation ſure ſhall fence the head,
    True Peace the feet defend,
Strong Faith, reſiſting every dart
With ample Shield, fence every part,
    And round thy ſteps deſcend"—
His ſimple Word to thee is " Stand!
Girt round with Truth, and in thy hand
Tight graſp, to ſerve for ſpear and ſword,
The two-edged falchion of His Word."

There's but one secret in the fight—
The trusting to Another's Might;
   For, strange as it may seem,
Whoe'er shall to the lists descend,
Though armed in proof, without this Friend,
   Will find his strength a dream.
We wrestle not with things of earth,
But subtle Foes of airy birth:
Who combats in that shadowy field
Must more than mortal weapons wield.

He who this Champion vast withstood
Thought not e'en royal armour good
   Whose temper was unknown;
But mindful of a former strife,
Trusted Who then preserved his life
   Would still with triumph crown.
Now first, ere join we in the fray,
A moment each in earnest pray;
Together turn we then and look
For five smooth Pebbles in the Brook.

Inquire you where that River flows?
On Sinai first the Fountain rose,
   Then Judah's valleys laves,
Till, mixing with the waters free,
From one small Well in Galilee
   It swelled to mightiest waves:
And still with never-ceasing song
It rolls majestical along,

The Five smooth Stones of David.

Fountain of Peace in every land,
Or Zembla's ice, or Afric's sand.

One Stone resplendent o'er the rest,
Fit Jewel for an Angel's breast,
  Shines bright in cold or heat;
And not in all yon Eastern train,
'Mid mines of gold where Sultans reign,
  May such your vision meet:
No larger than the mustard's seed,
From it such lustrous rays proceed,
Where'er Faith's lucid sparkles shine,
They make whate'er they touch Divine.

Fragment of some unshaken Rock
This seems, whose force may bear the shock
  Of tempest and of tide;
And though, perchance, of rougher face,
It stands with more enduring grace
  Than smoother works of pride:
If placed beside the waters' brink,
Who treads on it shall never sink;
Wild though the waves of sorrow roll,
They may not whelm the Patient Soul.

In the clear depths another lies
Of which secure a Shaft may rise
  Ascending day by day;
Upright and pure, the busy morn
Shines on it from the early dawn
  Till gleams the evening ray:

Contented with the rules of old,
It seeks no adventitious gold
Of man's device.   Thus spake the Lord!
Obedience asks no further word.

Goodly thy structure : clouds will form
And shroud it with the coming storm;
   Perchance thy heart may quail—
The Pillar of Obedience rock
Unsteady 'neath the thunder shock,
   Well-nigh the basement fail;
Faith's Jewel will its light supply
More radiant through its bright ally :
Who could with earthly sorrow cope
Unlighted by the Gleams of Hope?

Now all seems polished, fixed, secure,
Rock, Pillar, Jewel, to endure
   And shine through years to come;
Yet somewhat still deficient seems,
A warmer glow to shed its beams
   On neighbour and on home :
It shines with such diffusive ray,
Ne'er on one spot its glories stay;
Base, column, capital above,
All sparkle with the Rays of Love.

O might I such a Temple rise,
Compact with what the Lord supplies,
   The Unction of His Grace!

O might my life henceforward be
Pure, ſtraight, from worldly follies free,
   Stedfaſt in its own place!
Patient myſelf, with active Zeal,
True Love that can for others feel,
With Hope ſtill cheerful in my breaſt,
And Faith in an Eternal Reſt.

Hymns for Whitſuntide: from the Latin.

Jam Chriſtus aſtra aſcenderat.

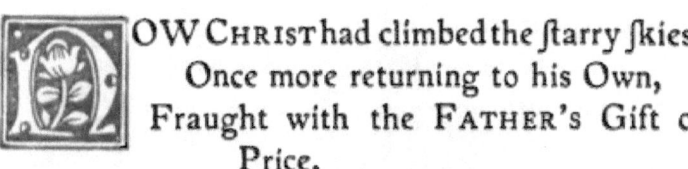OW Christ had climbed the ſtarry ſkies,
   Once more returning to his Own,
Fraught with the FATHER's Gift of Price,
   To ſend the HOLY SPIRIT down.

Onward the Solemn Feaſt-day rolled,
   Upon its ſeven-fold circle borne;
The myſtic week of weeks, that told
   The coming of that bleſſed morn.

It comes, the third Hour of the day,
   While thunder ſhakes the world's wide dome,
And, as the bleſt Apoſtles pray,
   Heralds aloud that GOD doth come.

Forth from the Everlasting Sire
 The Flame Divine falls manifest,
With the True Word's enkindling Fire
 To fill each faithful Christian breast.

The Holy Spirit breathes abroad,
 And while their freshened hearts rejoice,
They speak the mighty Works of God
 With varying tongue, but one true Voice.

To men from every Nation called,
 Barbarian, Latin, Jew, and Greek,
Wondering alike, alike appalled,
 With tongue of each the Preachers speak.

False Jewry then, with heart untrue,
 And spirit stern and evil-willed,
Dares madly taunt Christ's faithful few—
 ' Yea, with new wine these Men are filled !'

But with high deed and sign of might
 Peter confronts the crowd, and shews
By proof, on Joel built aright,
 That falsely speak those faithless Jews.

Beata nobis gaudia.

ROUND roll the weeks our hearts to greet,
 With blissful joys returning;
For lo! the Holy Paraclete
 On twelve bright brows sits burning.

With quivering Flame He lights on each,
In fashion like a Tongue, to teach
That eloquent they are of speech,
   Their hearts with true Love yearning.

While with all tongues they speak to all,
   The nations deem them maddened;
And drunk with wine the Prophets call,
   Whom GOD's Good SPIRIT gladdened;
A marvel this, in Mystery done,
The Holy Paschal-tide out-run,
The duly numbered days have won
   Remission for the saddened.

O GOD most Holy, Thee we pray
   With reverent brow low bending,
Grant us the SPIRIT's Gifts to-day,
   The Gifts from Heaven descending:
And since Thy Grace hath deigned to bide
Within our breasts, once sanctified,
Deign, LORD, to cast our sins aside,
   Henceforth calm seasons sending.

Inter sulphurei fulgura turbinis.

AMID the whirlwind and the thunder cloud,
   Amid the lightning fires that flash abroad;
With blast of trumpet sounding long and loud,
   On Sinai's Mount of awe,
Unto Thine ancient Race their ancient Law
   Thou givest forth, O GOD:

By terror thus Thou triest their faithless hearts;
   Dost sin forbid? Or as the price of sin
Dost death assign? But what avail these smarts;
    Can dark and dismal threat
  In them obedience or true Love beget,
    Can dread their homage win?

Lo! at the foot of that still smoking Hill
   The People, heedless of their plighted troth,
The loved, the faithless People, faithless still,
    A molten Image make,
  And for an Idol their True GOD forsake,
    The GOD of Sabaoth.

Oh! without Thee, our Souls' far better part,
   What can our poor weak minds avail, O LORD?
Pour light upon our spirits; from our heart
    Its iron hardness draw,
  And make us, for Thou canst, obey Thy Law,
    And doers of Thy Word.

Quo vos Magistri Gloria, quo Salus.

GO where your Master's Glory
    Invites your band abroad;
Go forth for man's Salvation
   And bear the Word of GOD;
Go where the Virgin harvest of all lands—
Go where a Brother's Soul your loving care demands.

Go! sacred Band: behold ye,
  Even now the fields are white;
For Brethren thrice a thousand
  Have caught the Words of Light;
Matured whereby, and ripened like a field
That GOD hath blessed, their fruit a thousand fold
    they yield.

Pricked to their inmost hearts'-core
  They weep with bitter tears;
And in the hallowed laver
  Their stains of by-gone years
Fain would they wash away—they burn, they
    burn,
For that blest Stream whose waves all stains to
    freshness turn.

But not to Judah's border
  Shall that bright sunshine cling,
The Sun, where through all regions
  He runs his golden ring,
Lights up fresh fields of triumph for your feet,
And warms all hearts with glee your gladsome call
    to greet.

A thousand fanes are falling;
  Proud wisdom vails its front;
The courtly tyrant trembles;
  The murdering sword is blunt:
Wild though the torturer's wrath—his furies
    cease,
And conquered vengeance quails before the Men
    of Peace.

The Church.

Come! All-creating Spirit,
   Thou a new world didſt frame;
On us Thy Power out-pouring,
   Our Souls with Love enflame;
Almighty God, All-gracious, All-benign,
Us with Thy Grace renew, and make us wholly
   Thine.

The Church.

THOUGH thou art lowly now,
   Pale and diſcrowned,
Laying thy holy brow
   Faint on the ground,
Traitors deceiving thee,
   Scorners ſurrounding,
Falſe teachers grieving thee,
   Cruel hands wounding;
Though the ſtorm hover
   Frowning and dark;
Though the wave cover
   The walls of thine Ark,
And Hope's ſweet Dove for thee
   Bring not one leaf,
Mother, our love for thee
   Grows with thy grief!

What if her word may be
   Void of command!

The Church.

What if the ſword we ſee
   Drop from her hand!
Shall we not fear her?
   Dare we forget her?
Cling we the nearer!
   Love we the better!
Let our thoughts only paint
   What ſhe has been;
Meek as a lonely Saint!
   Crowned as a Queen!
When ſhe lies dumbly
Gather we humbly
   Kneeling and ſay—
Powerleſs and lonely!
Speak, whiſper only,
   We will obey!

No idle ſigh for her!
Ye who would die for her,
Nerve ye to live for her;
Suffer and ſtrive for her;
Pray for her tearfully;
Hope for her fearfully;
Let your tears rain on her,
Till each foul ſtain on her
   Paſs from the ſight,
And there remains on her
   Robes of pure white!

By the dews of thy morning,
   Holy and ſoft,

By words of sweet warning
   Uttered so oft,
By accents adorning
   Daily which rise,
Where spires upsoaring
   Pierce the deep skies,
By Him Whose Mission
   Gave, not in vain,
The awful Commission—
   Remit and Retain!
By the Life which thou livest
   E'en now in thy shame,
By the Food which thou givest
   We dare not to name,
By the Gifts that are in thee,
   Power, Faith, and Purity
Seek we to win thee
   From sloth and obscurity.
Answer our loyalty
   Waiting and weeping!
Put on thy royalty!
   Rise from thy sleeping!

Take thine own place again
   Where stars are bright,
And from God's Face again
   Drink deathless Light!
Rise and subdue to thee
   All, as of old,
Those that were true to thee,
   Those that were cold;

Children who pained thee,
  Rebels who took thee,
Foes who difdained thee,
  Friends who forfook thee!
Yes, all fhall gaze on thee,
Showering their praife on thee,
As thofe pure rays on thee
  Vifibly fhine;
Earth, now no home for thee,
Then fhall become for thee
  One mighty Shrine,
One vaft Community,
Known by its Unity
  Truly Divine!

Call ye this vanity,
  Work never done,
Which poor Humanity
  Mars, ere begun?
Nay, no defpair for us!
Think on CHRIST's Prayer for us—
  Let them be One!
Ear to the thunder dull,
  Senfe-blinded eye,
GOD ftill is wonderful,
  CHRIST yet is nigh!

The Salutation of the Greek Church on Easter Day.

SPRINGTIDE birds are finging, finging,
    For the daybreak in the Eaſt,
Silver bells are ringing, ringing,
    For the Church's glorious Feaſt.
CHRIST is riſen! CHRIST is riſen!
  Sin's long triumph now is o'er.
CHRIST is riſen! Death's dark priſon
  Now can hold His Saints no more.
    CHRIST is riſen! riſen, Brother!
    Brother, CHRIST is riſen indeed!

Holy Women ſought Him weeping,
    Weeping at the break of dawn,
Sought their LORD where He lay ſleeping,
    In the love of hearts forlorn,
Life for death on death's throne meeting
    Joy for ſorrow, faith for fear,
For their tears the Angel's greeting—
    CHRIST is riſen! He is not here.
    CHRIST is riſen! riſen, Brother!
    Brother, CHRIST is riſen indeed!

Loved Apoſtles, ſcarce believing
    In His Triumph o'er the grave,
Hear the tale amid their grieving,
    Haſten eager to the Cave,

Find the folded grave Clothes lying,
　　Death's unloosed and shattered chain,
Find Him gone, Death's power defying,
　　From the Cavern sealed in vain.
　　　　Christ is risen! risen, Brother!
　　　　Brother, Christ is risen indeed!

Mary comes, a refuge seeking
　　For her mourning and her shame,
Lo! a well-known voice is speaking,
　　Lo! the Master calls her name—
First, the life o'er sin victorious,
　　She who wept for sin adored,
For her tears the mission glorious
　　To announce the Risen Lord.
　　　　Christ is risen! risen, Brother!
　　　　Brother, Christ is risen indeed!

For her tears, O glad reversing
　　Of the Woman's work of old,
Glorious Tidings now rehearsing;
　　For the tale in Eden told,
Woman's voice that tale supplying,
　　Brought in death by Satan's lie;
Woman's voice is now replying—
　　Christ is risen! we shall not die.
　　　　Christ is risen! risen, Brother!
　　　　Brother, Christ is risen indeed!

Where the noontide rays are falling
　　On the rugged mountain side,

Salutation of the Greek Church.

Brethren journey, ſad recalling
    How He loved, and how He died.
He is with them! He is hearing
    How their truſt and hope had fled,
To their loving faith appearing
    In the Bleſſing of the Bread.
        Christ is riſen! riſen, Brother!
        Brother, Christ is riſen indeed!

Flaſhing back the ſunſet glory
    Burns a caſement high and dim,
There the Ten, on all His Story
    Sadly dwelling, ſpeak of Him.
He is there! the Light that never
    Into twilight fades away,
Day-ſtar of the Dawn that ever
    Breaks into the perfect Day!
        Christ is riſen! riſen, Brother!
        Brother, Christ is riſen indeed!

Saints! your Croſs in patience bearing,
    Mourners! ſtained with many a tear,
Penitents! in ſorrow wearing
    Darkeſt weeds of ſhame and fear,
Christ is riſen! loſe your ſadneſs
    Joying with the joyous throng,
Faithful hearts will find their gladneſs
    Joining in the Eaſter ſong.
        Christ is riſen! riſen, Brother!
        Brother, Christ is riſen indeed!

De Laudibus S. Scripturae.

CHRIST is riſen! CHRIST the Living,
   All His mourners' tears to ſtay,
CHRIST is riſen! CHRIST forgiving
   Wipes the ſtain of ſin away.
CHRIST is riſen! CHRIST is riſen!
   Sin's long triumph now is o'er;
CHRIST is riſen! Death's dark priſon
   Holds His Faithful never more.
     CHRIST is riſen! riſen, Brother!
     Brother, CHRIST is riſen indeed!

De Laudibus S. Scripturae.

An ancient Latin Poem.

TO cull the gems of ſuch a theme for praiſe,
   Though in a feeble ſong is gracious toil;
This is the houſehold grain for famine days
   That Hebrew Pilgrims drew from Coptic ſoil.
The palatable Manna from the ſky
   Flavoured with every ſweet to every lip;
Briefly in price it doth the gold outvie,
   In ſheen the Sun, in taſte what bees do ſip.
What day brings earth, it doth to mankind bring;
   Day lights the fields: this lights the Soul within;

A garden-brook, a fathomleſs waterſpring
   Nurturing all thoughts, all hearts o'erparched
      with ſin ;
God's Paſture and Christ's Wine-ſtore : Heavens
      that glow
   With ſtars for every myſtery they hide ;
This the quick writer's pen, and this the bow
   Whoſe medicinal ſhafts each heart divide.
The in-wheeling wheels that like to Ocean's flow
   Are full of wonder, all are here again ;
Four forms, one kind, that mount or ſtand or go
   As the indwelling energies ordain.
The Roll upon the Lamb's Right Hand, writ
      through,
   Within the myſtic, and the plain outſide ;
Here Moſes' face is hidden from the view ;
   Here Christ's own Glory draws the veil aſide.
This which in figure Moſes, Christ in deed
   Sprinkled with Blood, both form and matter
      holds ;
The old, the form, the new Law for our need
   More large ; what that would cover this unfolds.
While laſts the type that teſtifieth, Deep
   Calls unto Deep.   Fit title for the twain :
A ſlender bolt doth thoſe abyſſes keep,
   But to embrace them were an effort vain.
Here evermore to muſe, to ſearch, and know
   Is to enjoy Heaven's light, and Heavenly ſtore ;
No better lot has man, than ſtudying ſo,
   To root his life where Life is evermore.

Happy, who thirſting, in this ſpring can find
  Elixir to embalm his life each day;
Elſe doth the man ſeem taſteleſs to my mind
  Who fails, to learn by heart this Heavenly lay.
Who ſtudies it for wealth or human praiſe
  He is not wiſe nor yet to Wiſdom near;
She for herſelf muſt courted be always,
  And oh what boons ſhe gives her lover! Hear:—
More chaſte the love becomes; the ſenſe more
    bright,
  From temporal preſſures is the mind more free;
The text breeds virtues ever, renders light
  The Soul, and bids all mortal failings flee!

S. Patrick's Coat of Mail.

RM me to-day, in this awful hour,
    My prayer to the All-Holy TRINITY,
  My faith in Him Who reigneth in
      Power,
The GOD of the Elements, FATHER, and SON,
And PARACLETE-SPIRIT, Which THREE are
    The ONE,
  The Incomprehenſible DEITY.

Arm me to-day, my Prayer to the LORD,
  To CHRIST the Eternal WORD,
Who came to redeem from ſin and death

Our fallen race;
And I would place
The Virtue that compaſſeth
His Incarnation lowly,
His Baptiſm pure and holy,
His Life of toil and tears and affliction,
His dolorous Death, His Crucifixion,
His Burial ſacred and ſad and lone,
His Reſurrection to life again,
His glorious Aſcenſion to Heaven's high Throne,
And laſtly His Coming dread—
His terrible Coming to judge all men,
Both the living and the dead.

Arm me, and keep me, in this dark place,
With Virtue that dwells in the Seraphim's love;
The Virtue and the Grace
That are in the obedience
And unſhaken allegiance
Of all the Archangels and Angels above:
And in the hope of the Reſurrection
To everlaſting Reward and Election;
And in the Prayers of the Fathers of old;
And in the Truths which the Prophets foretold;
And in the Apoſtles' manifold Preaching;
And in the Confeſſors' faith and teaching:
And in the purity ever dwelling
Within unſullied virgin's breaſt;
And in the actions bright and excelling
Of all good Men who the Lord confeſſed.

S. Patrick's Coat of Mail.

Arm me to-day, in this fateful hour,
The Heaven above with all its power,
And the ſun with its brightneſs,
And the ſnow with its whiteneſs,
And fire with all the ſtrength it hath,
And lightning, with its rapid wrath,
And the winds with their ſwiftneſs along their path,
And the ſea with its deepneſs,
And the rocks with their ſteepneſs,
And the earth with its coldneſs—
      All theſe I place
      By God's good Grace
Between myſelf and the Devil's boldneſs.

      Arm me to-day,
      O God, my ſtay;
May the Strength of God now nerve me!
May the Power of God preſerve me!
May God the Almighty be near me!
May God the Almighty cheer me!
May God the Almighty hear me!
  May God give me eloquent ſpeech!
May the Arm of God protect me!
May the Wiſdom of God direct me!
  May God give me power to teach and to preach!
May the Shield of God defend me!
May the Hoſt of God attend me,
      And ward me,
      And guard me,

Againſt the wiles of Demons and Devils,
Againſt temptations of vice and evils,
Againſt bad paſſions and wrathful will
  Of the reckleſs mind and the wicked heart;
Againſt every man that deſigns me ill,
  Whether leagued with others or plotting apart.

    In this hour of hours
    I place all theſe Powers
Between myſelf and every foe
    Who threats body or Soul
    With danger or dole;
To protect me againſt the evils that flow,
From lying Soothſayers' incantations;
From the gloomy laws of Gentile Nations;
From Hereſy's hateful innovations:
    Be all theſe my defenders,
      My guards againſt every ban,
Againſt ſpell of Druid and Witch and Magician;
    Againſt knowledge that renders
    Thick night the condition
      Of ſpirit and Soul of man.

    May CHRIST, I pray,
    Protect me to-day
  Againſt poiſon and fire,
Againſt drowning and wounding,
That ſo, in His Grace abounding,
  I may earn the Preacher's hire.

CHRIST, as a Light,
  Illumine and guide me!
CHRIST, as a Shield, o'erſhadow and cover me!
CHRIST be under me! CHRIST be over me!
  CHRIST be beſide me,
  On left hand and right!
CHRIST be before me, behind me, about me!
CHRIST be this day within and without me!

CHRIST, the Humble, the Lowly, the Meek,
  CHRIST, the All-powerful, be
In the heart of each to whom I ſpeak,
  In the mouth of all who ſpeak to me,
    In all who draw near me,
    Or ſee me, or hear me.

Arm me to-day in this awful hour,
  My Prayer to the Holy TRINITY!
Glory to Him Who reigneth in Power,
The GOD of the Elements, FATHER, and SON,
And PARACLETE-SPIRIT, which THREE are
    The ONE,
  The Everlaſting DIVINITY.

Salvation dwells with the LORD,
With CHRIST the Omnipotent WORD;
From generation to generation,
Grant us, O LORD, Thy Grace and Salvation!

Dies est laetitiae.

Hymn on the Nativity of our Lord Jesus Christ.

IN this festal Day we sing
   Joyful tidings hearing,
For this **Day** our Heavenly King
   On our earth appearing
Comes a Sweet and Lovely CHILD,
Born for us of aspect mild,
   Made for **us a** Creature;
He Who reigns in boundless space,
GOD, **Who** has no form, nor face,
   Takes our human feature.

Mother **here a** Daughter **see!**
   Here the FATHER SON **is!**
What more wondrous things could be?
   GOD and MAN here One is;
Servant is, and Master too,
Whom, though here, we cannot **view,**
   Nor can apprehend Him;
Present here, yet distant far:
Lost in deepest mist we **are,**
   None can comprehend **Him.**

Nature **at** this **Wonder** done
   Lost in mute surprise is,
When a Rose, GOD'S Only SON,
   From a Lily rises;

When a Virgin gives Him birth,
Him, Who made the Heavens and earth,
   Him, our GOD Eternal;
And her sacred Virgin Breast
Feeds Him, and affords Him rest,
   In her love Maternal.

Lo! an Angel bright appears
   In deep night descending,
Calms the humble Shepherds' fears,
   Who their flocks are tending;
Joyful Tidings brings to earth
Of the King and SAVIOUR's Birth,
   Infant feebly crying,
He Who is the Angels' LORD,
By all Heaven and earth adored,
   In a Manger lying.

Crystal pure will still remain
   Sunbeams through it shining,
So the Virgin knows no stain,
   No high gifts resigning;
Spotless after, as before,
Her blest Womb for mortals bore
   GOD to earth descended;
Blessèd is that Virgin Breast;
Blest those hands, which first and best
   CHRIST, an INFANT, tended.

Night in darkness shrouds His Birth,
   Who the Sun gives splendour,

Dies est laetitiae.

In a stable lies on earth
    Earth's Prince and Defender.
That right Hand so closely bound
Fixed the brilliant stars around,
    And the Heavens extended;
He is heard in infant Cries
Who with thunder rends the skies,
    With dread lightnings blended.

Lo! the Virgin humbly goes,
    In her chaste Womb bearing
GOD'S OWN SON, to rank with those,
    Who in crowds repairing,
Are in Bethlehem enrolled:
O may we our names behold
    On Heaven's glorious portals,
With those Angels, who in love
Glory sung to GOD above,
    Peace proclaimed to mortals.

Now with prayer be homage done,
    Hearts and voices raising,
Worshipping the Infant SON,
    And the Mother praising:
Here a Wondrous CHILD is found,
Publish then His Name around:
    Thee our LORD imploring,
We proclaim our GOD most High,
Thee our JESUS ever nigh,
    With all earth adoring.

Go, and come.

CHRIST, Who with Almighty Hands
    This our being gave us,
When we broke His high Commands
    Would be born to ſave us;
To Him now devoutly pray—
LORD forgive our ſins this day,
    Do Thou never leave us,
Let us not at death be loſt,
But to join Thy Heavenly Hoſt
    In that hour receive us.

Go, and come.

THOU ſayeſt to us, "Go!
    And work while it is called to-day;
    the Sun
    Is high in heaven, the harveſt but begun;
Can hands oft raiſed in prayer, can hearts that
    know
The beat of Mine through love and pain be ſlow
To ſoothe and ſtrengthen?" Still Thou ſayeſt
    "Go!
Lift up your eyes and ſee where now the Line
Of GOD hath fallen for you, one with Mine
Your Lot and Portion. Go! where none relieves,
Where no one pities; thruſt the ſickle in
And reap and bind, where toil and want and ſin
Are ſtanding white, for here My Harveſts grow:

Go ! glean for Me 'mid wasted frames outworn,
'Mid Souls uncheered, uncared for; hearts forlorn,
With care and grief acquainted long, unknown
To earthly friend, of Heaven unmindful grown;
In homes where no one loves, where none believes,
For here I gather in My goodly Sheaves."
    Thou sayest to us, " Go !"

    Thou sayest to us, " Go !
To conflict and to death." While friends are few
And foes are many, what hast Thou to do
With peace, Thou Son of Peace ? A Man of war
Art Thou from Youth ! when Thou dost girded
  ride,
Two stern Instructors, Truth and Mercy, guide
Thy Hand to things of terror ; friends and foes
Thine Arrows feel ; a Sword before Thee goes,
And after Thee a Fire, confusion stirred
Among the nations even by the Word
Of Meekness and of Right. " Yea, take and eat
Of these My Words," Thou sayest, " they are
  sweet
As honey; yet this roll that now I press
Upon your lips will turn to bitterness
When ye shall speak its message ; lo ! a cry
Of wrath and madness, ere the ancient Lie
That wraps the roots of earth will quit its hold,
A shriek, a wrench abhorred ; and yet be bold,
O ye My Servants ! take My Rod and stand
Before the King, nor fear if in your hand

It seem unto a serpent's form to grow;
Rise up, My Priests! My mighty Men, with sound
Of solemn Trumpet, walk this City round,
A Blast will come from GOD, His Word and Will
Through hail and storm and ruin to fulfil;
Then shall ye see the Towers roll down, the Wall
Built up with blood and tears and tortures fall,
And from the living Grave the living Dead
Will rise, as from their sleep, disquieted;
O Earth, this Baptism of thine is slow!
Not dews from morning's womb, not gentle rains
That drop all night can wash away thy stains.
The Fire must fall from Heaven; the blood must flow
All round the Altar."—Still Thou sayest, "Go!"

And that Thou sayest, "Go!"
Our hearts are glad; for he is still Thy Friend
And best beloved of all whom Thou dost send
The furthest from Thee; this Thy Servants know;
Oh, send by whom Thou wilt, for they are blest
Who go Thine Errands! Not upon Thy Breast
We learn Thy Secrets! Long beside Thy Tomb
We wept, and lingered in the Garden's gloom;
And oft we sought Thee in Thy House of Prayer,
And in the Desert, yet Thou wert not there.
But as we journeyed sadly through a place
Obscure and mean, we lighted on the trace
Of Thy fresh Footprints, and a whisper clear
Fell on our spirits—Thou Thyself wert near;

And from Thy Servants' hearts Thy Name adored
Brake forth in fire ; we said, " It is the Lord."
Our eyes were no more holden ; on Thy Face
We looked, and it was comely ; full of Grace,
And fair Thy Lips ; we held Thee by the Feet ;
We listened to Thy Voice, and it was sweet ;
And sweet the silence of our Spirits ; dumb
All other voices in the world that be
The while Thou saidest, " Come ye unto Me !"
The while Thou saidest " Come !"

     We said to Thee, " Abide
With us ! the Night draws on apace ; but, lo !
The Cloud received Thee, parted from our side,
In Blessing parted from us ! Even so
The Heaven of Heavens must still receive
    Thee ! dark
And moonless skies bend o'er us as we row.
No stars appear, and sore against our bark
The current sets ; yet nearer grows the Shore
Where we shall see Thee standing, never more
To bid us leave Thee ! though Thy Realm is wide,
And Mansions many, never from Thy Side
Thou sendest us again ; by springs serene
Thou guidest us, and now to battle keen
We follow Thee, yet still, in peace or war,
Thou leadest us. Oh, not to sun or star
Thou sendest us, but sayest, " Come to Me !
And where I am, there shall My Servants be."
Thou sayest to us, " Come !"

The Three Comings.

The First Coming.

TEN thousand stars were burning bright
    To charm the lonely Shepherd's eye,
But not a watcher turned that night
    To count the gems in Bethlehem's sky,
All Heaven was up and chanting still—
Glory to GOD, to Man good will!

How eager then that listening throng
    Pressed to the lowly Manger gate
To greet their Infant GOD with song,
    And at His Feet with homage wait
Till e'en the walls with rapture thrill—
Glory to GOD, to Man good will!

Blest BABE! on this Thy holy Day
    From gaudy suns of earth we turn,
To where with soft and spotless ray
    The Star of Bethlehem loves to burn:
Hark! LORD, our songs the Manger fill—
Glory to GOD, to Man good will!

Thus at Thy Cradle while we kneel,
    And from Thy Lips a Blessing seek,
Bid o'er our hearts Thy Image steal,
    Humble like Thee and good and meek:
Thy Birth-day Promise thus fulfill—
Glory to GOD, to Man good will!

The Second Coming.

THE Univerſe is ſhaking
 Big with ſtupendous ſong,
Skies into voice are waking
 With chorus loud and long;
The Morning Stars are ſinging
 With a ſublime accord,
And all Heaven's courts are ringing—
 Thy Kingdom come, O Lord!

With a profound emotion
 Earth hears the lofty ſtrain,
And burſts into devotion
 Mountain and rock and plain:
Ocean glad homage paying
 With all her waves is heard,
O Foreſts! ye are praying—
 Thy Kingdom come, O Lord!

And now of rapt creation
 Time's kindreds catch the ſound,
And each ſucceſſive nation
 Rolls the great Anthem round;
Till at the Throne of Glory
 Breaks in one mighty chord,
The univerſal Story—
 Thy Kingdom come, O·Lord!

In wondering expectation,
 Lord! ſhall we ever wait?

Great Monarch of Salvation,
  Aſſume Thy royal State:
Angels and Saints implore Thee,
  Gird on Thy conquering Sword,
And bow all hearts before Thee—
  Thy Kingdom come, O LORD!

The Third Coming.

IN my laſt long ſlumbers lying
    I ſhall hear, O Trump, thy ſound;
Time itſelf and Nature dying,
    Say, and where ſhall I be found?
Sun and Moon grow pale with wonder,
    Stars appalled with horror flee,
Seas and Earth are rent aſunder,
    JESUS, LORD, remember me!

Hark! again that Trump reſounding,
    Heaven's diſſolving pillars nod;
'Riſe, O Man!' the Voice is ſounding,
    'Riſe to meet Thy Coming GOD!'
On the Clouds of Empire riding,
    SON of MAN, Thy Form I ſee;
Mid Thy radiant Hoſts preſiding,
    JESUS, King, remember me!

Yet again, again 'tis pealing;
    Sinners! mourn in helpleſs woe;

Righteous! hail the morn revealing
   All Redemption can beſtow;
Earth! draw nigh and hear the ſtory,
   Yonder bar is raiſed for thee;
Mid the lightnings of Thy Glory,
   Jesus, Judge, remember me!

Once upon a darkened mountain
   I that Form in Blood eſpied;
I approached the crimſon Fountain
   And was cleanſed beneath the tide;
At Thy Croſs for Mercy ſighing
   Peace I found and Pardon free:
To Thy Throne for refuge flying,
   Jesus, God, remember me!

The Old-Year's Bleſſing.

AM fading from you,
   But one draweth near,
Called the Angel-guardian
   Of the coming Year.
If my Gifts and Graces
   Coldly you forget,
Let the New-Year's Angel
   Bleſs and crown them yet.
For we work together;
   He and I are one:

The Old-Year's Blessing.

Let him end and perfect
   All I leave undone.
I brought good Desires,
   Though as yet but seeds;
Let the New-Year make them
   Blossom into Deeds.
I brought Joy to brighten
   Many happy days;
Let the New-Year's Angel
   Turn it into Praise.
If I gave you Sickness,
   If I brought you Care,
Let him make one Patience,
   And the other Prayer.
Where I brought you Sorrow,
   Through his care at length
It may rise triumphant
   Into future Strength.
If I brought you Plenty,
   All wealth's bounteous charms,
Shall not the New Angel
   Turn them into Alms?
I gave Health and Leisure,
   Skill to dream and plan,
Let him make them nobler—
   Work for God and Man.
If I broke your Idols,
   Showed you they were dust,
Let him turn the Knowledge
   Into Heavenly Trust.

If I brought Temptation,
 Let ſin die away
Into boundleſs Pity
 For all hearts that ſtray.
If your liſt of Errors
 Dark and long appears,
Let this New-born Monarch
 Melt them into Tears.
May you hold this Angel
 Dearer than the laſt—
So I bleſs his Future,
 While he crowns my Paſt!

Verſes.

God did ſend Me before you.

OD hath ſent a MAN before thee!
 Faint not, fear not, Chriſtian Soul;
One hath run the race thou runneſt,
 One hath won for thee the goal.

GOD hath ſent a MAN before us!
 Whatſoever griefs oppreſs,
He hath known them in the fulneſs
 Of extremeſt bitterneſs.

GOD hath ſent a MAN before us,
 Tried and tempted e'en as we,
Who hath fought our every battle
 Who hath won the victory.

God hath sent a Man before us,
   Not along Life's bright highway
'Mid the beauty and the fragrance
   And the pleasant light of day;

But in lonely paths and rocky,
   Where we only trace the Road
By the drops of Blood which tell us
   Where the Man of Sorrows trode.

Yea! He sent His Christ before us
   Unto Pain and Agony;
Nor from Death's dark hour withheld Him,
   Willing for our sakes to die.

He within the Veil is entered,
   Where He offers still on high,
Priest and Victim, for our cleansing,
   Sacrifice unceasingly!

The Lord shewed him a Tree.

The Disciple.

SHEW me a Tree, my Gracious Lord,
   For o'er my troubled Soul
The bitter waters of despair
   In whelming torrents roll:
Thou Who of old by Marah's tide
The healing Wood didst swift provide,
Oh! hither speed in Love and Power,
And shed Thy Light on this dark hour.

The Divine Master.

There was a Tree in Eden set
   The day that Adam fell,
A Tree, whose sweetness mortal words
   May not essay to tell:
Though 'neath its weight thy weakness sink,
To those dark Waters' cheerless brink
Bear it, and cast it boldly in—
It hath Divinest Medicine!
The MAN of Sorrows' royal Throne—
That Word all grief, all woe hath known.
Dost thou despair? oh! haste to take
The Cross where I, in anguish spake—
Wherefore My GOD, dost Thou forsake!

The Disciple.

Seeking as erst a sweet'ning Tree,
   To Thee, O LORD, I haste,
For heavy on my fainting Soul
   The hand of grief is prest.
'Mid bitter foes, 'mid friends grown cold
Alone I stand: oh! now behold,
And deign in love the Wood to show
That can to sweetness change sad woe.

The Divine Master.

O hard of heart! hast thou not yet
   Found hidden in My Cross

Virtue for all that bitterest seems,
    All gain for every loss?
On Calvary from the scornful Tree
The Words were spoken e'en for thee,
For thee, that thou mayest speak and live—
They know not what they do, Forgive!

The Disciple.

I stand upon the awful brink
    Of Jordan's bitter Stream;
Cold flow its waves,—O LORD, my LORD
    Whose Pity did redeem,
Thou Who in every trial-hour
Hast succoured me with saving Power,
Cast in the Tree, the sweet'ning Tree,
Lest I be borne away from Thee
And sink and perish utterly!

The Divine Master.

My Child, in passing through that Stream
    No evil need'st thou fear;
My Rod and Staff, the Holy Cross,
    Sheds sweetness ever here:
Take to thee then My Words as shield—
FATHER, to Thee My Soul I yield!
Stoop to the waves, My Cross shall bear thee o'er,
Calmly and safely bear to Canaan's shore.

Laetabundi jubilemus.

A Prose for the Transfiguration.

RISE and sing a joyful Lay,
  O Bride! to Him thou lovest well;
 On this most solemn Holy-day
  Be it thy joy to tell
(So He but aid thee) how the Light
Of GODHEAD gleamed on Tabor's height.

O He was ever what He then
 Appeared, Death's Conqueror strong and true,
Giver of Life to dying men—
 But He had hid from view
All that bespoke Him GOD until,
As on this Day, He sought the Hill.

And O! while He was kneeling there
 His Face became a Sun for Light,
The Garb which girt the Only Fair
 With utter whiteness white,
Foreshowing how with Beams Divine
The Just should one day rise and shine.

And when the CHRIST, the Power of GOD,
 To Peter and the Brothers blest
That Excellence of Glory showed,
 Two Prophets left their rest,
This Truth to witness from the dead—
To talk with GOD how dear, how dread!

And then a cloud o'erſhadowed all,
   And thence the Everlaſting ONE
Crowned with His Voice our Feſtival,
    Saying—This is My SON—
Since there Omnipotence is rife,
O hear, O heed that WORD of Life.

O clad in Brightneſs paſſing bright
   Behold the univerſal King,
The Light of Saints, the cloudleſs Light
    Which lightens everything,
The HOLY ONE of GOD, the CHRIST
For earth's Salvation ſacrificed.

O now there ſhould be rage in Hell,
   For now is loſt for evermore
The bitter claim the Serpent fell
    Had on our race before;
The FATHER'S WORD in Fleſh revealed
The mortal wound of Fleſh hath healed.

He died for us, He roſe again
   That Heaven and Earth at one might be,
And ended evermore the reign
    Of the laſt Enemy;
And now, Transfigured, He it is
Whom the Great FATHER owns for His.

But troubled by thoſe Accents dread
   Upon the earth thoſe Fathers three
Lay till another Word was ſaid—
    Ariſe, nor fearful be—

And then they looked on CHRIST alone
In the poor guiſe they firſt had known.

And till the LORD ſhould riſe again
   He willed to none the Sight were told,
But now the SPIRIT leads the ſtrain,
     And Voices manifold
Come after. On this marvellous Day
Be cords of Death all caſt away.

Paradiſe.

The Land that is afar off.

WHERE is the Land he ſaw in glorious
   Viſion,
     The lone old Prophet in the Sea-
     girt Iſle,
True antitype of all the dreams Elyſian,
   Faſhioned by Hope earth's ſorrows to beguile?

Call them not idle, all the tales they fabled
   Of Happy Iſles in far Heſperian Seas,
Whoſe ſtraining ſight no torch of Truth enabled
   To pierce by faith the unſeen Myſteries.

Call it not vain, the rude untutored longing
   For higher life each meaneſt mind that moves,
That murmurs ſtill, when baſe affection wronging
   Our nobler part too oft victorious proves.

Paradise.

Where is that Land? above, beneath, around us?
   Lost in all space, or to a star confined?
O for one hour to pass the shores that bound us,
   And fathom all the future of the mind!

Ye who have left our side to join the chorus
   Of holy Minstrels in that distant clime,
Waft some faint echoes of your harpstrings o'er us,
   To chase the mystery from your homes sublime.

They send no sound! Sweet Patience singeth only,
   "Strive to the end, and struggle to the goal!"
Then, for earth's hours of anguish, dark and lonely,
   Bright dawns eternal sunshine on the Soul.

Then they who mourn for earth's frail joys departed,
   Oblivion sweet of all their woes shall gain;
The heavy-laden and the broken-hearted,
   Balm for their wounds, and solace from their pain.

O Mourner, weeping long thy loved ones taken,
   They tread the shining paths by Angels trod!
O thou by trusted hearts in need forsaken,
   Love shall not fail thee in the Land of GOD!

There, Soul with Soul in converse sweet confiding,
   Nor shy mistrust, nor selfish aim shall know;
Pure as the crystal Stream beside them gliding,
   All wish, all thought, in unison shall flow.

Brave heart, hold on! in dauntless strength of duty
   Work out thy lot, nor murmur at thy star!
So shall thou soon, in glory and in beauty,
   Behold the King in that bright Land afar.

The Land of Beulah.

THEY trod not now the perilous ground enchanted,
   They breathed no more the thick and slumbrous air;
But a delightsome Land by Angels haunted
   Appeared, Heaven's portal fair.

Straight lay the road through this bright Country leading,
   Balmy the air, and sweet each breath they drew:
On corn and wine and all abundance feeding,
   Their Souls rich solace knew.

Here evermore they saw the flowers upspringing;
   The Sun shone o'er them always, night and day:
Ever they heard the birds in gladness singing,
   The turtle's voice alway.

Far, far behind Death's shadowy Vale was lying;
   They spied not hence the towers of grim Despair:
But lo! before, in golden lustre dyeing
   The azure depths of air,

Shone forth the Walls of pearl, the Gates of glory,
   End of their hope, their hearts' defire and fong;
For this they marched, through all its changeful
    ftory,
   Their pilgrim path along.

And from that Light Celeftial radiance bringing,
   Fair fhining Creatures met them as they trod,
Walking amid that Paradife, or winging
   Their bright way home to GOD.

And from that City came the found of voices
   Many and loud, that fang with folemn glee—
Even as the Bridegroom o'er the Bride rejoices,
   Lo! joys thy GOD o'er thee.

Heaven.

  HEARD the voice of Harpers, harping
    fweetly
   On harps of gold:
I faw a cryftal River—calmly, widely
   Its waters rolled.

I caught the flafh of turrets, wrapt in fplendour
   Of funlefs light,
Like to a ftar moft luftrous, fhedding glory
   Out of the night.

I dreamed of Lands Elyfian, emerald Iflands
   In fhining feas,
Soft perfumes wafted by fweet-whifpering breezes
   From fadelefs trees.

The Disciple whom Jesus loved.

I saw the ranks of Angels, silver-pinioned,
   And golden-crowned,
Swift radiant Forms, that like a sunbeam passing
   Touched the bright ground.

I saw the ancient Worthies, Heroes saintly
   Resting in calm,
Clad in white robes, out of great tribulation
   Bearing the palm.

I saw a King in beauty, cloud-encircled,
   Shrouded in light,
The likeness of a Throne, a Sea of glory
   Dazzling all sight.

A Voice as of great waters—Myriads falling
   Low on the sod:
A Silence: Harps struck louder; Seraphs singing
   " Glory to God!"

The Disciple whom Jesus loved.

BLANCHED in the blaze of light, all
   still and bare,
  The Fishers gaze upon Gennesaret.
  The sunset comes. Behind the Roman
   town
The dark boat's circled topsails swell and shift,
The tuniced boatmen dip their nets an hour,
And the sun goeth down on Jezreel.
The flickering furnace of the dust is quenched,

The mountain branded as with red gold rust.
But ere the cresset lights are in the vault
Where nothing trembles, suffers, wars or weeps,
To the Twelve comes ONE Purer than the stars:
And as a man just wakened in a room
Fronting the ocean, scarcely knows at first,
A little whiteness dawning on the pane,
A little line insufferably bright
Edging the ripple that orbs out anon,
Until he recognize the sun itself,
So hour by hour their knowledge grew of Him.

And as a mighty City far-off kenned,
Stretches with its immeasurable streets,
And though the same from every different height
Looks different to the merchantmen who wend
Towards its guarded gate, driving the ass
And camel, bearing spicery and balm,
Figs and all manner of fruits, tinct like the flower,
Half a blue week in summer ere it blows;
Not otherwise, before those simple men,
That wondrous Nature grew from year to year,
Till to S. John it seemed to orb away
Into the Infinite Majesty of GOD.

Three years Love-sheltered from the outer world
His Spirit grew, as grows a delicate child
Brought over seas from foggy Northern lands,
And far a-forest lodged 'mid Southern pines,
Where all day long the needles of the light
  Dart through green plumes upon the dropping
      stems.

Three years, three wondrous years, three silent
     years,
Silent that he might hear the SAVIOUR speak
Of Light and Love, and the Baptismal Dew,
Water of Life, and Sacramental Bread—
Until at last he stood beside the Cross,
And heard the sweet Bequest that gently gave
The Virgin-Mother to the virgin Soul—
Two Heavenly Gems in the small coronet
Of one poor home—and much he talked with her,
The pale and passionate Magdalene, who stood
Love-blinded in the garden by the veil,
Whose silver lines were woven of her tears,
That morn when first the sunlight touched the
     Grave,
And for the first time Angels dressed in white.

In Sapientia disponens omnia Aeterna Deitas.

A Sequence on the Circumcision.

OD, Who in Wisdom sweetly ordereth
     all,
     Grieving for man long held in direst
         thrall,
An Angel sent, taught in His Purpose well,
The FATHER's Promise of the SON to tell.

He hails the Virgin—GOD and Man, faith he,
SAVIOUR, First-fource of all, shall spring from thee.

Not long the Promife halts; He speaks, 'tis done,
By Grace conceiving, Mary bears a SON.

Light of the faithful, earth He comes to blefs,
Shining on all, the Sun of Righteoufnefs.

A Heavenly fight the fimple Shepherds fee;
Not for earth's great ones may that vifion be.

Look! in the Manger ONE is lying low,
Whofe Might Divine no earthly bound may know.

The Bright and Morning Star is fhining clear,
On Jeffe's Rod the Flowers of Grace appear.

See, the Three Kings their duteous Offerings bring,
Gold, Incenfe, Myrrh, to the GOD-MAN their King.

He, Who for us affumed this mortal life,
Muft now endure the Sacrificial knife:

In Jordan's ftream a milder Rite He gives;
There man his fins doth wafh, and wafhing lives.

The Virgin to the Temple brings her SON,
That all the legal Rites be duly done.

There thankful Simeon in his arms doth hold
The SAVIOUR long in facred lore foretold.

At Cana's Feaft CHRIST'S Glory firft doth fhine,
When the pure water blufhes into wine.

He makes the blind to see, to walk the lame,
And tongues long dumb His matchless Power
    proclaim.

He That is born for man is God's Dear Son,
The King of Heaven, and other Lord is none.

Let all the Heavenly Host His Praises tell,
And all His Saints the chorus join to swell.

The Living Death.

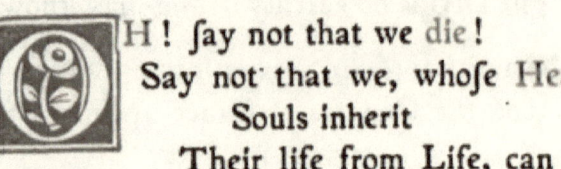

OH! say not that we die!
   Say not that we, whose Heaven-born
    Souls inherit
     Their life from Life, can ever pass
    away;
That we, whose source is the Eternal Spirit,
  Can yield what is from God to slow decay.

   Say! say! is it to die—
To give this weary body unto sleeping?
  To lay down sorrow's crushing cumbrous load?
To rest where we can hear no sounds of weeping,
  Far, far away from life's tear-tracen road?

   Oh! say is it to die—
To burst from out this tottering mortal dwelling,
  A Spirit unembodied, unconfined?
To view the wide expanse of Glory swelling,
  And earth and all its anguish left behind?

The Living Death.

    Oh! say is it to die—
To pass from life's rough channel to the ocean?
    To enter on the solemn after-life?
To feel our being pass with Spirit's motion
    Free from the conflict and the mortal strife?

    Say! say! is it to die—
To cease to drink the cup of earthly sorrow?
    To cease to tread the narrow vale of tears?
To waken to that day that knows no morrow,
    Where time is not, nor flowing, ebbing years!

    Oh! say is it to die—
When Angels o'er the parting Spirit linger
    Just as it passes to its GOD on high;
And point with beaming smile and beckoning finger
    To far-off Mansions in the happy sky?

    Say! say! is it to die—
To lay aside a body daily wasting
    With toil outworn, with weight of care opprest?
And spring away with eager faith, foretasting
    The peace, the quiet of the promised Rest?

    Oh! say is it to die—
To wear the SAVIOUR's radiant Form of brightness?
    To see Him as He is, with Glory crowned?
To stand in robes of pure unsullied whiteness,
    Joining the Songs of happy Saints around?

The Living Death.

    Oh! this is not to die—
To leave a world of changes and of ſeeming,
  Where amid fleeting phantaſies we dwell;
And wing away, as from a ſtate of dreaming,
  To waking and to Bliſs unchangeable.

    Oh! this is not to die—
Is it not rather into Life expanding,
  Breaking the trial-ſtate to live indeed?
Safe from the tempeſt in the haven landing,
  From ſtorms, from toils, from rocking billows freed?

    No! no! we cannot die—
In Death's unrobing room, we ſtrip from round us
  The garments of mortality and earth;
And breaking from the embryo ſtate which bound us,
  Our day of dying is our day of birth!

    And yet to earth we die—
Born to new Life with all its weight of Bleſſing,
  Born to a world where ills can never preſs;
Exalted, pure, Angelic joys poſſeſſing,
  If this be Death, then Death is Happineſs!

Thoughts in Verse.

The true Light.

I SEE the sun go down behind the wood,
　　I watch his glories as they die away,
My spirit yearns to float adown that flood
　　Of light to endless Day.

For while I stand and gaze the shadows fall;
　　What was so bright and warm grows dull and cold:
No longer plays the light upon the wall,
　　No longer on the wold.

The only light is in the western sky,
　　A single streak of crimson and of gold:
All things beside within the shadows lie
　　Of evening's sable fold.

So, too, when our short day is almost done,
　　And Death casts shadows on the joys of earth,
The Light of our dim path will be but One,
　　And He of Heavenly birth.

All round, the shadows of dark thoughts may fall,
　　And all around may tempt the Soul despair:
O! Burning Light of Love, no fears appal
　　If only Thou be there!

Cœlestis Urbs Jerusalem.

CLEARLY he sang, as only Angels sing—
  "Turn thou, beloved of GOD,
Look on the City of our Heavenly King
  Which He along hath trod.

"Founded she is upon the holy Hills:
  Four ways her buildings face,
Her firmament the Light of Heaven fills
  Reflexed from crown to base.

"In number as the Tribes of Israel,
  Of Pearls her portals are:
Twelve Angels here their hymns of glory swell
  To Him Who reigns afar.

"Her walls are Crystal, and her streets of Gold;
  And her foundations laid
On Sapphire, Amethyst and Emerald,
  Whose colours never fade.

"Nor sun by day, nor paler moon by night
  In this blest City burn:
Ever from out GOD's Throne eternal Light
  Shines full where'er ye turn.

"Within those walls, unstained of mortal strife,
  Fresh streams of Wisdom spring,
And here the Branches of the Tree of Life
  Their goodly shadows fling.

" Thoſe Gates are open, and that River flows
   For Souls redeemed of ſin,
Who with the Bridegroom and His Heavenly
      Spouſe
   For ever enter in."

Boyhood's Home.

WE named our flower-crowned Veſſel, 'Home,'
   Ere ſhe ſet ſail for worlds to come,
  And all on board were young and fair:
Full many a happy boat we paſſed;
In ſunny bays we anchor caſt
  Off iſlands rich in fragrance rare.

Ah me! that thoſe bright days are gone;
We left our Veſſel one by one:
  Now ſome on ſtranger barks are ſailing;
And ſome there are whoſe Spirits bleſt
On peaceful ſhores for ever reſt,
  Far off from wind and ocean's wailing.

The Deſcent of the Spirit.

A Hymn for Whitſun-Day.

SILENCE reigned at Eventide,
   On the day when JESUS died;
   Shaken earth, in Sabbath reſt,
    Folded Him within her breaſt:
  Silent on the Eaſter-morn
  Roſe to Life the Virgin-born.

Silent, through the Forty Days,
Bowed the Church with humble gaze;
While the LORD in order told
To the Shepherds of His Fold
How He willed that they ſhould keep
Watch and ward around the Sheep.

Hark! a ruſhing mighty ſound
Of the reſtleſs winds unbound;
In the Heaven of Heavens above
Spreads His Wings the Holy DOVE:
At their waft the kindling choir
Wakes to ſong with Tongues of Fire.

Now the HOLY GHOST doth brood
O'er the ſurface of the flood,
And the quickened ſtreams are rife
With the progeny of Life;
On the Font deſcendeth He,
LORD of Life, abundantly.

On the waters' face doth move
To and fro the Heavenly DOVE,
From the depths of death and ſin,
Olive-branch of peace to win;
Reſting-place He findeth none
But the Ark of CHRIST alone.

LORD of Life, to Mary's Womb
Fraught with GODHEAD did He come:
Lord of Life, at Whitſuntide
Comes He down upon the Bride,

The Descent of the Spirit.

Bearing through the scented air
Presence of the Bridegroom there.

On the Altar dimly shown,
Flesh of flesh, and Bone of bone,
She shall win Him from above
In the Sacrament of Love,
That her children may be fed
From their Life-blood's Fountain-head.

Range the choir the Bride around
On the holy Chancel ground;
She is drest is bright array
For this festal Whitsun Day;
Ten long nights she watched in vain;
Now He comes to her again.

Lily for her Virgin-hand,
At her feet the Aloe wand,
Frankincense before her fling
For the Daughter of the King,
And at length the Crown of thorn
Roses for her brow has borne.

The Spirit and the Bride say—Come!
Fruit of Blessed Mary's Womb,
Come to hallow! Come to bless!
Comfort of the comfortless:
As to her Thou cam'st below,
Come, Lord Jesu, even so.

The Palimpsest: an Allegory.

IN the Abbot's oaken Chamber
    Long the Parchment hidden lay,
Given o'er to dust and spider,
    Buried from the light of day,
Written o'er with Monkish story
    On each old and crumbling page,
Written o'er with Legends hoary
    Of the dim forgotten age;
Till the Traveller's glance alighted
    Where the Parchment long had lain,
And all mildewed, stained and blighted
    Drew it to the light again;
And his loving care bestowing,
    Day by day its treasures bared,
Till he traced in beauty glowing,
    Olden lines which time had spared;
Traced the glory underlying,
    Traced the azure and the gold,
Traced, in letters still undying,
    Treasures which it bare of old;
Till the Words of Truth confessing,
    Words of Prophet and of Seer,
Words of Love and Truth and Blessing,
    Stood in all their beauty clear;
And the old immortal Story
    Shone upon its pages plain,

Gleaming with their olden glory,
  Speaking with God's Word again.

          *   *   *

Brother! gaze with look as earneſt,
  If earth's leſſons thou wouldſt trace;
Gaze in faith till thou diſcerneſt
  What is written on its face:
Dark thick duſt is on it lying—
  Duſt of dead and buried times,
Every age its duſt ſupplying,
  Charged with records of its crimes:
And the preſence in the Writing
  Firſt that meets the caſual eye
Is of Satan, ſtill inditing
  Records of his victory:
Poor men's groans and rich men's weeping,
  Pinching want and grinding cares,
Wars and famines o'er it ſweeping—
  Such the records that it bears.
Brother! gaze upon its teaching,
  As men gaze through the thick night,
Till thine eye, its ſecret reaching,
  Read its hidden Legend right:
Faith ſhall pierce this dark adorning,
  Grief and ſorrow, ſin and ſhame,
Show thee where, in earth's glad morning,
  God hath written His own Name;
Show thee, how that Name remaining,
  Turns its darkneſs into light,

All its tangled courſe explaining,
  Ruling all its wrong to right;
Till, beneath Sin's ſad inditing,
  Tales of woe and tears and blood,
Thou ſhalt trace the old handwriting—
  It is GOD's, and it is Good;
And the old immortal Story
  Shines upon its pages plain,
Gleaming with the olden glory,
  Speaking with GOD's Word again.

Via Sanctae Crucis.

NE bleſſed noon in Autumn's ſweeteſt
    weather,
  I wandered forth a pilgrim by the
    way,
Where GOD's good Providence ſhould lead to
  ſtray,
Muſing how Truth and Mercy met together.

Now by the rough road-ſide, now o'er the meadows,
  Through the green paſtures, by the waters ſtill,
  Where the gleam-tinted trees beneath the hill
Caſt round my path their Vale-of-death-like
    ſhadows.

Bleſſed be GOD! I had an open Viſion—
  Good Angels were abroad in earth and ſky,

Revealing Heavenly Forms to Faith's purged
    eye,
Of Peace and Beauty, as in fields Elyſian.

All was an Emblem in me and around me,
    Betokening Gifts more real than appear;
    High thoughts, myſterious feelings, love and fear
Of wondrous ſpiritual depth and fulneſs bound me.

Sudden, as ſent from GOD, a mightier Token
    Than yet my marvelling Spirit had wrought
      upon,
    The Sign adorable of His Dear SON,
On which His Blood was ſhed, His Body broken!

In the dim diſtance, by the old flood riven,
    The purple hill roſe, looming through the miſt,
    Which, gilded by the noonday, crowned its
      creſt
With Saint-like halo, blending earth and Heaven.

And like an Angel's cinĉture, white and ſhining,
    A ſilver thread belting the upland's girth
    Led, as by Heavenward ſtair, from this low earth
To brighter vales on the Eaſtern ſide declining.

Here ghoſtly pale the mighty Croſs ſuſpended
    As 'twere mid air, backed by the hill's bare ſide,
    Was graved by unknown hands in ancient-tide
Where, circling round its baſe, the path aſcended.

Via Sanctae Crucis.

Whether to mark the scene of battle holy,
   Through victory of the Saints on this fair spot;
   Or Hermit, here embowered in hill-side grot,
Emblemed lone Peace and Soul-sweet Melancholy;

Or, likelier yet, blest Austin's hooded Sages
   Led the procession from yon sainted tower,
   And raised the image here of JESUS' Power,
To point the way of future pilgrimages.

The only way to Life and Peace internal,
   Way of the Holy Cross, though steep, most sure!
   Seek where thou wilt, none other so secure
Leads to the untravelled realms of Bliss Supernal.

Who dares to climb, though way-worn, faint and weary,
   Braced by Heaven's freshening gales, gains strength anew,
   Sees sights to eyes below ne'er brought to view,
Peopling with glorious shapes plains waste and dreary.

Blest be the hour which led my footsteps thither,
   On that sweet Festival of earth and sky!
   Chance thoughts so sown, bear fruit in destiny
For good or evil, which shall never wither!

Jerusalem, du hochgebaute Stadt.

A German Hymn of the XVII. *Century.*

JERUSALEM! thou City towering high,
  Would GOD I were in thee!
My longing Soul doth ever pant and sigh
  Within thy walls to be:
By faith from earth it sallies,
  And far o'er stretching plains,
Far over hills and valleys,
  Soars, till thy gate it gains.

O joyful day, and O thrice joyful hour,
  When will thy dawn appear,
When I with heart released from sin's dread power,
  And joy unmixed with fear,
My parting Soul commending
  To GOD's Own faithful Hand,
Shall at my journey's ending
  Reach that blest Fatherland?

Then in a moment shall my Spirit quit
  This lower element;
In silent mystery high-soaring, flit
  To Heaven's bright firmament
Elijah's chariot mounting,
  Borne on sustaining Hands,
That baffle powers of counting,
  Of joyful Angel-bands.

Jerusalem, du hochgebaute Stadt.

Hail! glorious City: O that thou would'ſt ope
   Thy gates of mercy wide,
To enter which with ſtill deferred hope
   I long have groaned and ſighed;
While here my weary Spirit,
   In this wrong world of ſin,
The Kingdom I inherit
   Has thirſted ſore to win.

Who are theſe Myriads bright, whoſe glorious band
   In countleſs throng appears,
By JESUS ſent to meet me on the ſtrand
   Of this dark land of tears?
Of endleſs Life the winners,
   Theſe are His Joy and Crown,
Whom from this world of ſinners
   He choſe to be His Own.

Prophets and Patriarchs there, and Chriſtians all,
   Who have in every age
Endured the Croſs, or at their Maſter's call
   Braved perſecution's rage,
Now, amid Joy unbounded,
   From earthly ſorrow free,
With cloudleſs day ſurrounded,
   A dazzling Hoſt I ſee.

When GOD to His bleſt Paradiſe of Joy
   My Soul at length ſhall raiſe,
Pleaſures ſhall fill my mind which never cloy,
   My mouth glad notes of praiſe:

Voices in concord vying
  There Alleluia sing;
Unwearied still replying
  There loud Hosannas ring.

From choir to choir, before the LAMB's bright
  The sound is borne along,   [Throne,
Till Joy's bright Temple to the wondrous tone
  Vibrates in choral song:
In notes of exultation
  Unnumbered voices rise,
E'en since the first creation
  Thus echoing through the skies.

I am the Rose of Sharon and the Lily of the Valleys.

A WILDERNESS of barren sand,
  With scorching sun-glare, hot and red,
  Where whitened bones of men long
    dead—
A level broad deserted land.

Storms swept across it, and the sky
  Deepened its red to blackest gloom;
  It seemed a buried nation's tomb,
So desolate below, on high.

Years passed, years slowly passed again:
  A long pale line of eastern light
  Broke at the murkiest hour of night,
To herald sounds of summer rain.

Then on that lone and ſandy flat
   A Lily grows, with milk-white bloom,
   The wilderneſs no more a tomb—
The deſert beautiful for that.

And ſoon another flower expands,
   The Roſe of Sharon for the dew
   And ſilver morning light ſo new;
Tranſplanted then to other lands:

But leaving many a Bleſſing there,
   Odours of beauty and of Grace,
   Leaves for the healing of a race,
Rich Gifts forgotten, new and rare.

A barren wilderneſs no more;
   Athwart, a way to yonder Fold,
   Beyond thoſe ſeas of green and gold,
A peaceful bright and ſunny ſhore.

Jeſus Chriſt, the Same yeſterday, to-day, and for ever.

THE Same: hear all that ſpurn!
   We wane and alter, but Thou changeſt
      not;
   Ever the ſame kind Heart, the ſame
      ſad lot—
To love without return.

Bone of our bone indeed!
Moſt human Heart, more loving than the beſt,
For ever wounded—aye, ye know the reſt,
 And oft have made It bleed!

Mere image call ye this?
Not ſo: the tendereſt nature ſtill muſt be
Moſt ſenſitive, and Tender, Friends! is He,
 Not wrapped in ſhadowy Bliſs.

His Will, with GOD at one,
Accepts all ſorrow, and foreruns the end.
Round Him all Heaven-born melodies aſcend
 In glorious uniſon.

An inner joy is His
Thought may not fathom, Holineſs intenſe,
Rapture tranſcending mortal ſight or ſenſe,
 What ſhall be, and What is.

Yet ſtill His Heart remains
Touched with our anguiſh; beating at each throb
In ſympathy with this poor Orphan's ſob,
 With that faint Widow's pains.

O Wonderful and Sweet!
Still like a beggar ſueſt Thou for each heart
That bids Thee unbeloved and cold depart,
 And thruſts Thee to the ſtreet.

O Myſtery profound!
The Greateſt thus beneath the leaſt deſcends,

And vainly asks to call His Creatures 'Friends:'
    Who such abyss can sound?

    Here, here is Love.   O stay!
The All-Creator, with a human Heart,
He seeks thee, though He knows thee what thou
    art;
    Thou look'st another way.

    Great is the Power that cast
Yon myriad stars to ring the rolling spheres;
Greater the Love that through the inconstant years
    Seeks thee, and wins at last.

    The LAMB of GOD, That takes,
Each living hour, a world's red guilt away,
Undying Victim! must His Angels say—
    ' Man scorns, and earth forsakes?'

    O Heart, too fickle, know,
' Thou art the Man:' thou wound'st thy Master
    still.
He waits, thy LORD, a Vassal on thy will.
    O, must it aye be so?

    Wilt thou not wake at last
And sigh—O Thou That seek'st to be beloved,
I dare not look upon Thy Tears unmoved:
    Canst Thou forgive the past?

    Ah, with Thy tenderest Heart
Mine keeps not pace; 'tis base, 'tis mean, O LORD,

And thrice unworthy of Thy Love adored;
  But Thou art what Thou art,

And lov'ſt for Love's ſake ſtill.
Sunſhine can flood the deepeſt deep with light;
Thou art All-Splendour, if my heart be night:
  Have Thine All-gracious Will!

En Dies eſt Dominica.

A Hymn for the Lord's Day.

THIS Day, which JESUS calls His Own,
    Muſt our devout obſervance gain;
  On it His ſacred Power was ſhown,
    By riſing from the Grave's domain.

This Fact is now, while life endures,
  Our weekly celebration made;
That the great things its truth enſures
  May never from our memory fade.

O'er this dark world it poured a ray
  Of living hope beyond the tomb
From realms of everlaſting day,
  So long concealed in trembling gloom.

And thus a pledge our Souls receive
  Of ſure advancement to the ſkies;
For all who in His Name believe
  Shall with their Riſen LORD ariſe.

In Him we find a boundlefs ftore
  Of Wealth to make us rich indeed;
Without referve He makes it o'er,
  Our common fund in times of need.

Hence Glory, Life without decay,
  Immortal Bleffednefs above;
With Peace and Joy while on our way
  To claim thefe Bleffings of His Love.

The cheering memory of thefe things,
  Revived with Sunday's dawning ray,
To pious hearts the reafon brings
  Why this is called ' the LORD's own Day.'

O'er death triumphant He arofe
  On this great Day, and lived anew;
A glorious Fact in Him, which fhows
  What is in us in figure true.

Our finful paffions being quelled,
  We rife above them from the duft,
Left the free Spirit fhould be held
  In bonds by any cherifhed luft.

Our pious Souls muft now review
  The Decalogue which GOD has given,
And humbly our belief renew
  In Articles of Faith from Heaven.

The Holy Sacrament muft fhare
  The loving memories of the Day,

And other things, which claim our care,
   To speed us on our faithful way.

With earnestness the mind must shun
   The tongue's pollution, taking heed
Lest greater wickedness be done
   By thoughtless word than manual deed.

With greater vigour we must press
   In duty onwards in GOD's Ways,
By thoughts and acts of Righteousness,
   By meditation, prayer, and praise.

And chiefly now our Souls must aim,
   Through Grace which lifts us from the fall,
To rest with conscience free from blame
   In sight of GOD, Who is our All.

The mighty Love of GOD afresh
   Must seize us as its rightful lot;
That midst the allurements of the flesh
   Our Souls, as dead, may feel them not.

And let us ask—Whence we have come?
   And what and where we are? and why
We live? and where will be our home?—
   And seek a practical reply.

Oh! into misery from GOD,
   And into darkness out of light,
Came GOD's Similitude abroad,
   At first so happy and so bright.

Now must our sinful wanderings cease;
  To God we must retrace our way;
Then holy Joy and Heavenly Peace
  Will turn our darkness into day.

The Glory of our primal birth
  We must for ever keep in view,
Lest we become the slaves of earth,
  And its vile vanities pursue.

Of spiritual essence free,
  Divine in his primordial state,
Man was designed by God to be
  The Angels' fit associate.

The native grandeur of his race
  The stature of his body proves;
He walks erect, with upward face;
  And like a God below he moves.

Stamped on his visage here we find
  The Light of God's own Countenance;
And the bright image of his mind
  Shines out in living splendour thence.

Internal Wisdom sheds its light,
  In glowing thoughts, on things around,
The outward witness in our sight
  Of what within his mind is found.

And then, O Mystery Divine!
  Impressed on his anointed brow,

En Dies est Dominica.

The Cross, the Spirit's quickening Sign,
   Has made him Christ's own Servant now.

To-day, as Christ's, let this be done—
   The present with the past compare;
And think what progress has been won,
   And what the failures—how and where?

Deep hatred of all evil seek;
   Of what is good take special care;
And looking towards the coming week,
   For new and vigorous war prepare.

Within let grateful joy have place
   That time on earth has yet been given,
To grow in Knowledge and in Grace,
   And meetness for a glorious Heaven.

In holy thoughts and acts like these,
   When earthly works are put away,
Our lowly minds the Lord should please,
   On this His own most blessed Day.

To Thee great Author of our days,
   True Rest of every faithful Soul,
Be given all Honour, Glory, Praise,
   While everlasting ages roll.

Tria Dona Reges ferunt.

An Epiphany Sequence of Adam of S. Victor.

KINGS, with triple Gifts provided,
 Seek their King, and on are guided
 By a Star, whose rays betided
  Light from high for ever brought;
Gold, His Regal state implying,
Incense, GODHEAD signifying,
Myrrh, that shadows forth His Dying,
 Bring they, by the SPIRIT taught.

They from far Sabæan Nation,
On this day of jubilation,
Serving Him with adoration
 Win the joyful boon of Peace;
Faint the Hebrew race is growing,
Knowing much, but GOD not knowing,
CHRIST, His Face to Gentiles showing,
 Biddeth them in Faith increase.

Synagogue, thou once elected,
Once in holy Faith perfected,
Now for unbelief rejected,
 Knowest not the Kingly CHILD;
And CHRIST's Field, once sparely planted,
Once in fruit and culture scanted,
Now in Light which He hath granted,
 Sees the World's Redeemer mild.

Sarah's Race new might is gaining,
Thou, blind Synagogue, art plaining
For the bondſlave's race, remaining
   Underneath its load of ſin;
Thou doſt mourn and ſorely grieveſt,
Sarah laughs while ſobs thou heaveſt,
For ſhe knows thou diſbelieveſt
   Him Who comes to ſave His Kin.

By his father conſecrated,
Jacob's joy with fear is mated,
Thou with dews of heaven art ſated,
   And with earth's rich fatneſs bleſt:
All thy joys from earth thou gleaneſt
From things vaineſt and obſceneſt,
Jacob's thoughts on things ſereneſt
   And on JESUS' Sweetneſs reſt.

Where His Nard the air perfumeth
Haſte the Saints whom Love conſumeth,
For with wondrous Flower bloometh
   JESUS' Pardon newly won:
She whom ſin but late was chaining,
Now her ſpouſal Gifts obtaining,
New-made Bride, in joy is reigning,
   And a golden Crown hath on.

Next the King in exaltation
In her thankful adoration
Stands the Bride, and keeps her ſtation
   In a golden Veſture clad:

From the thorns within that bower
Springs a Rofe, in bud or flower
Thinking aye on JESUS' Power,
  In His royal Bounty glad.

She, the myftic Bride, can never
From her plighted Bridegroom fever,
May that Bridegroom guard us ever
  From the fhocks of flefhly vice :
May He cleanfe us from pollution,
Grant us perfect reftitution,
Save from final retribution,
  Bring us unto Paradife.

Have mercy on me, O Lord, Thou Son of David.

WITHIN the cool Quadrangle's wel-
        come fhade,
    Beneath the linen awning, JESUS
        fought
A moment's quiet, while the fountain played
  Her pleafant interlude to weary thought.

Through the porch gleamed the rofe-red funfet
    fnows
  Of the wild crags of northern Galilee :
What awful Life is in the GOD-Repofe,
  That with the Paft and Prefent welds Futurity!

Thou Son of David.

Up the benched gateway thrills a Woman's cry,
  As if the swollen torrent of deep care
Had torn down silence in its agony
  To fling Grief's secret on the trembling air!

The loneliness of one unuttered woe,
  The silent tears when every Hope had fled,
The sacred Love, which Mothers best may know,
  When sickness glooms around a first-born's bed.

The weary hours beside her little Child,
  The patient sadness of her darling's eye,
As with unselfish love she feebly smiled
  All, all, came sobbing on that bitter cry—

O Lord, Thou Son of David, pity me!
  So 'mid the wreck, bareheaded, 'gainst the spray,
A drowning Man might shriek across the sea,
  When hope of human help had past away.

O Lord, Thou Son of David, pity me!
  While ghastly doubt stung her sin-laden breast,
If for the guilt, done by her secretly,
  God's Curse had fallen on what she loved the best.

He did not answer her one single word,
  Yet Love was speaking in His ev'ry Look:
When earth is silent then may Heaven be heard,
  In sorrow's gloom Faith best reads God's own Book.

Think'st thou He hears not, when for many a day
  Thy knees are worn with fasting and with prayer?
Think'st thou He turns from any love away,
  Because thou seest no Angel on the air?

Tempter, away! each throb of pain He knows;
  I will kneel on, and wait His blessed Time;
Up the steep staircase of Life's darksome woes
  I'll climb and sing, till overhead God's Chime

Break with one roar of an eternal Sea;
  And lo! if I have prayed He giveth more;
I stagger down, half-blind with victory,
  Whispering the Chant from out the opening
    Door.

A Song which none but the Redeemed can sing.

E came not in with broad
    Full canvass swelling to a steady
      breeze,
      With pennons flying fair, with
        coffers stored;
For long against the wind, 'mid heavy seas,
With cordage strained and splintered masts we
  drave,
And o'er our decks had dashed the bitter wave,
And lightening oft our lading, life to save,
Our costly ventures to the Deep were given:

Yea, some of us were caught and homewards
    driven
Upon the storm-wind's wings; and some rock-riven
Among the treacherous reefs at anchor flung,
Felt the good ship break under them, and clung
Still to some plank or fragment of its frame
Amid the roaring breakers—yet, we came!

    We came not in with proud,
Firm, martial footstep, in a measured tread,
Slow pacing to the crash of music loud;
No gorgeous trophies went before; no crowd
Of captives followed us with drooping head;
No shining laurel sceptred us, nor crowned,
Nor with its leaf our glittering lances bound;
'This looks not like a Triumph,' then, they said;
With faces darkened in the battle flame,
With banners faded from their early pride,
Through wind and sun and showers of bleaching
    rain,
Yet red in all our garments, doubly dyed,
With many a wound upon us, many a stain,
We came with steps that faltered—yet, we came!

    Through water and through fire
We came to Thee, and not through these alone;
We came to Thee by blood! Thou didst require
One only Sacrifice, and like Thine Own.
The Life Thou gavest us Thou didst desire
And all was ready for us: Lo! the knife

And cloven wood were waiting; bound or free
We too were ready! In the battle ſtrife,
Or by the lonely Altar unto Thee
We offered love for Love, and life for Life.
And as we came to Thee a ſound of war
Ran after us from diſtant fields; the jar
Of ſhield and ſword and battle bow; a cry
Confuſed and harſh, that rolled to 'Victory'
And ſeemed upon the darkening heavens to ceaſe;
For as we neared Thy City morning broke,
And all along its lofty ramparts woke
One word of greeting, flooding all the ear
And all the heart with ſolemn muſic, clear
As of a Trumpet talking with us—Peace!

De Parente Summo natum.

A Sequence for the Feaſt of the Transfiguration.

OF the Higheſt generated,
 And not by His SIRE created,
  From before all time the WORD
 One GOD with the FATHER reigned,
By the Right to Him pertained,
 And by Gift of none conferred.

Guilty man from death redeeming,
GOD the WORD in outward ſeeming
 Was an humble Servant made;

Thus becoming a new Creature,
He restored our human nature,
   Nor aside His GODHEAD laid.

In Himself, both Weak and Worthy
He united; but the Earthy
   Clad, not crippled, the Divine:
Neither did the strong Superior
Swallow up the frail Inferior,
   But by suffering made it shine.

Each in its own Nature single,
Not as wines with water mingle
   Were they in debasement linked;
But that most mysterious Union
Which had placed them in communion,
   Kept them perfectly distinct.

Symbol of that high relation
Was the WORD'S Transfiguration,
   To the eye of faith designed:
Wherein is to us revealed
That which was before concealed
   By the Veil of human kind.

Like the candid snow for whiteness,
Like the splendid Sun for brightness,
   Lo! the Flesh which sin atoned
Is beforehand rendered glorious,
Over shame and death victorious,
   And the WORD in Light enthroned.

Hark! the confirmation given,
Not from earth but out of Heaven,
 Vouching CHRIST the SON of GOD;
Thus His DEITY aſſuring,
Though, beneath a ſhade obſcuring,
 Earth in Form of MAN He trod.

Gaze upon the Viſion beauteous;
Him confeſs, with homage duteous,
 GOD, and yet the Virgin's SON;
In a ſingle Perſon ſhining,
Yet two Natures ſo combining
 That they ſeverally were one.

See, the Stone by Jews rejected,
But by Choice Divine elected,
 To the Corner-head is raiſed;
He on Whom in Godlike Splendour,
Erſt in raiment mean and ſlender,
 Now the rapt Diſciples gazed.

Theme of Prophets' proclamation,
Him they knew in transformation
 'Twixt the two attendant Seers;
Shining in thoſe Robes of Glory
Pictured in prophetic ſtory,
 As from Bozrah He appears.

Grant us, JESU, to adore Thee,
And lay down our crowns before Thee,
 In the rapturous Viſion loſt;

Nor as heirs of Heaven ignore us,
Who in type didſt go before us
  When o'er Jordan Joſhua croſt.

Song of the early Chriſtian Confeſſors.

H, no! we may not whiſper now
  The Name by Hoſts adored,
No more we chaunt in choral vow
  Our dear Redeeming LORD.

They drag us ſlow with bleeding feet
  To many an Idol ſhrine;
They bid us taſte the offered Meat,
  Or quaff the offered Wine.

They ſtrive with ſlow reluctant fires
  Our conſtant Souls to break;
They ſpread the charms the world admires,
  But oh, 'tis death to take—

For neither bright Apollo's bow,
  Nor Daphne's laurel grove,
Nor ſounds of joy, nor ſights of woe,
  Can bend our loyal love.

Yet, if perchance by ſorrow tried
  Some ſighs our boſoms heave,
They bid us leave the Crucified—
  But we will never leave!

Oh, no! the quivering limb may throb,
  May ſtart the torture tear,

For crown of steel and fiery robe
    Are hard for flesh to bear.

But heavier was the Robe of scorn
    The MAN of Sorrows bore;
And sharper, sharper was the Thorn
    On bleeding Brows He wore:

And He can cool the torrent wave,
    Can stop the oppressor's joy;
For stronger is His Arm to save,
    Than theirs is to destroy.

They tell us He is buried now,
    And all our hopes are gone;
They saw not how in vest of snow
    He mounted to His Throne.

And chains may bind, and prisons dim
    Our fettered limbs control;
Our Souls, like eagles, fly to Him—
    They cannot bind the Soul.

The waves that wash our prison wall,
    The winds that hurry by,
The sweet, the gall, are records all
    Of Love that cannot die.

What if our Spirits tortures bow,
    Our limbs if fetters fret?
We see not now His radiant Brow—
    But how can we forget?

Being in an Agony, He prayed more earnestly.

WHAT are these Sighs, these low deep yearning Prayers
 Stealing o'er the silence of the midnight hour
From yon embowering Grove—the chill damp airs
 Rising around, while shivering night-winds cower?

Nay! draw not nigh—'tis awful, holy Ground.
 There, since the fall of eve, through hours of darkness drear,
Our LORD in prayer hath knelt, while slumber sound
 Enwraps that world for which He pleadeth prostrate near.

Nor will that wearied Form from prayer arise
 Till the faint-hearted dawn hath gathered strength to brave
The shades of night: the day may not suffice
 For His deep Love which yearns a darkling world to save.

That burning, wondrous Love! O how shall these
 Low grovelling hearts e'er comprehend its depth and height,

Its breadth and length? enfolding earth and
    ſeas,
    Heaven, yea, the Heaven of Heavens, in Mercy
        infinite?

Words fail to ſpeak aright; methinks on earth
    The ſilent adoration of o'erflowing hearts
In kindly deeds outpoured beſt owns its worth;
    Each little rill which from that loving Fountain
        ſtarts,

Bearing ſome portion of its Waters ſweet
    Along her lowly courſe, freſhening and glad-
        dening all
Where'er ſhe turns; yet loving beſt to greet
    Yon Streamlet broad, and hidden yield her
        tribute ſmall;

For ſmall, as lowlieſt drop, what here we deem
    The nobleſt Sacrifice—the keeneſt grief we
        know,
The love and labour of earth's ſhort-lived dream,
    Compared with the deep Ocean of Thy Love
        and Woe!

Here we may fearleſs plunge, and find our Life;
    Suſtained upon theſe Waters, as they riſe and
        fall,
Onward, while leſs and leſs of earth's rude ſtrife
    Shall reach our ears, abſorbed in Thee, our All
        in All!

Thou, Who ſtill pleadeſt in the Holy Mount
　For ſlumbering Souls enthralled in ſhades of
　　night below,
Plead on for us! that Thine, Celeſtial Fount!
　May be the only Source of Light and Love we
　　know.

The open Viſion.

WHY lies the darkneſs on the deep
　　Now that the world is old?
　Why do the ſigns from Heaven wax
　　faint,
　And Altar-fires wax cold?
The while men's Souls wait for the LORD
　By promiſe and by warning,
And wait and watch, yea, more than they
　That watch unto the morning.

Why echo ſtill earth's tempeſt-moans,
　Without Heaven's ' Peace, be ſtill?'
Why cry we yet, ' LORD, if Thou wilt;'
　Nor hear His calm ' I will?'
Why caſt we all our anchors out
　And wiſh the day were nearer;
While yet the far horizon ſhows
　No cloſer and no clearer?

Nay! aſk, if with us in the Ship
　We prayed our Maſter come?

Aſk, while we yet could ſee the ſhore,
　　Set we our ſails towards Home?
Aſk, if as in the ancient days
　　The Word of GOD is precious,
Have we the childlike hearts to know
　　The Voice that would refreſh us?

Aſk rather of the choſen Three
　　Neareſt to CHRIST allowed,
Why, ere they ſaw their Glorious SUN
　　They paſſed beneath His Cloud?
Why, as they marked His Meſſengers
　　Adore that bleſt unveiling,
They heard ſtrange preſages of ſcorn,
　　And buffeting, and railing?

Aye! others, like thoſe favoured Ones
　　Are drawn with Him apart,
The glory of His Woe to ſee
　　With ſad and troubled heart:
By ſome unearthly ſympathy
　　They know that this their trial
Accompliſhes His Agony,
　　Deſertion, and Denial.

The Cloud of myſtery draws on
　　And gathers over all,
While fearfully they enter in
　　Beneath its ſolemn pall;
But to the truſtful gaze, ſome gleam
　　Seems all its depth to brighten,
For verily the LORD their GOD
　　Shall all their darkneſs lighten.

'This is My Well-Belovèd Son!'
  The Father's Voice is past;
They waken from their awful trance,
  And know the Truth at last:
The darkness is not terrible,
  The silence is not lonely,
When they see no man any more—
  Themselves and Jesus only.

O Vision of reality,
  Faith's crowning diadem!
Themselves with Jesus found alone
  And He alone with them,
And never are His Cares so sweet,
  Never His Tones so tender,
As when He comforteth His Own
  After their Souls' surrender.

He turns their sorrow into Joy,
  Gives Peace instead of dread,
He stays their zeal's too eager haste,
  Urges their doubt's dull tread;
Till songs of love and praise burst forth
  From lips these themes embolden,
While that dear Presence is the Light
  Of eyes no longer holden.

Many are those once restless Souls
  To whom it has sufficed
To scale the Mount, endure the Cloud,
  And be alone with Christ:
Not heeding all earth's happiness,
  Nor all the world's derision;

Only not diſobedient found
  Unto the Heavenly Viſion.

For us, the veil but hides our pain
  Till perfect Peace be won,
Till man's enfeebled hand be ſtayed,
  And God's good Will be done:
Our Souls in patience we poſſeſs,
  God's Word cannot be broken,
' This is My Son '—He ſaith, and we
  Believe what He hath ſpoken.

We dare not deem that Heaven is dark,
  Though Heaven's light ſeem dim;
Our Maſter looks upon us ſtill
  Although we ſee not Him;
He leads us onward in His Love,
  He bears us in His Pity
To where the open Viſion ſhines
  In the Eternal City.

The Music of Heaven.

THE Muſic of Heaven is attuned to a meaſure
    Our Spirit's deep thirſt ever longs for in vain;
For the muſic of earth, though it thrills us with pleaſure,
  Gives pleaſure not wholly unmingled with pain.

And though for a moment the ear may be captured
  By notes that from Paradise seem to have birth,
By sounds to which Angels might listen enraptured,
  The dream is dispelled by the voices of earth.

Some weariness, pain, or some passing vexations
  The half-entranced soul from its bliss will recall;
Or the heart is unstrung, and the sweet modulations
  On earth-enchained senses untunefully fall.

When resoundeth God's Praise in the courts of His Dwelling,
  False jarrings of earth will too often begin;
And the higher and clearer the anthem is swelling,
  The more are we conscious of discord within.

But it will not be thus when to Heavenly regions,
  Released from its thraldom, our Spirit takes wing,
And uniting in concert with glorified legions,
  Shall learn that ' new Song' which none other can sing.

For ear hath not heard, nor the senses of mortals
  E'er caught the ineffable Music below
Of those Harmonies full which through Heaven's bright portals,
  With tide ever rising, unceasingly flow.

There voices Seraphic in concord are vying,
  And golden the strings of each well-tunèd Lyre;
Heart vibrates to heart, as for ever replying,
  Unwearied they chaunt in antiphonal Choir.

And ſhall we then hang the ſad harp on the willows,
　　As exiles ſhut out from the Land of our reſt,
Till we croſs the dark ocean of Death, and its billows
　　Have wafted us ſafe to the ſhores of the Bleſt?

No! whenever GOD's Praiſe in His Temple aſcendeth,
　　The theme and the melody kindle our hearts,
And conſtrain us, as richly the ſymphony blendeth,
　　To 'wake up our glory' and join in our parts.

And at length, when with Children of Zion admitted
　　Hoſannas to ſing by the Throne of the LORD,
Shall all hearts be new ſtrung, and each voice better fitted
　　With Angels' and Archangels' notes to accord.

Holy Childhood.

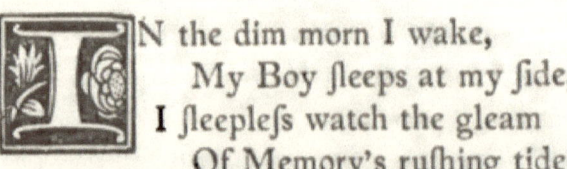N the dim morn I wake,
　　My Boy ſleeps at my ſide,
　I ſleepleſs watch the gleam
　　Of Memory's ruſhing tide.

From the Paſt's ſolemn woods
　　Stately the River came,
The ripple, and the breeze
　　Spake but one word—my name!

Calling me ever back,
  Till on the ſilent ſhore
I ſee a ſhadowy form,
  Myſelf—a Child once more!

With an unearthly hope
  I claſp the long-loſt hand,
And ſo from Time we wander,
  From Memory's ſhifting ſand,

Till through the gates of Morning
  We mark a roſy Dawn,
And the Child kneels in wonder
  On the Celeſtial lawn!

The lips ſmile adoration,
  I ſinful may not hear;
When lo! my Boy's young dreams
  Fall on my longing ear;

In ſleep he prays, 'Our FATHER!'
  In ſleep with his LORD's Prayer,
He fills my heart and conſcience,
  He fills the haunted air.

O LORD, make me a Child,
  Teach me fair Childhood's prayer,
Print on my Soul Thy Childhood,
  Waſh away Manhood's care!

Make me a little Child, O LORD,
  O fill my dreams with Thee,

Then, then, dark Memory's River!
  Carry them out to sea,

Out to the far-off surges
  That gird the sands of life,
Bear broken plan, and withered hope,
  Man's passion, and man's strife;

Bear them far, bitter River!
  I take the CHILD's pierced Hand;
And over moor, through forest,
  I seek the Blessed Land!

The CHILD in Priestly radiance,
  Before the golden Door,
Absolves; I enter, worship,
  GOD's Child for evermore!

Stanzas.

The End of Man.

LOVED the beauty of the earth,
  The brightness of the skies,
Life wooed me with its careless mirth,
  My birthright and my prize.

I loved in smooth self-chosen ways
  To guide my wayward feet,
I courted men's unmeaning praise,
  Their smile was all too sweet.

Stanzas.

The light of Heaven shone pale and dim
    Upon my earth-bound sight,
The echo of the Seraph's hymn
    For me had no delight.

My life and treasure they were here,
    My throbbing pulse beat high,
My step was free, my glance was clear
    With youth's gay buoyancy.

But youth was short, and life was frail,
    And human praise untrue,
Created beauty but a veil
    To hide Thee from my view.

'Twas not for these Thou madest me,
    But for Thyself, O Lord;
Thou bad'st me rest alone in Thee,
    My Prize and my Reward.

All earthly joy shall fail at last,
    All earthly love grow cold,
Save loves by that one Love made fast
    To Jesus and His Fold.

This earth is but a trial place
    To train the Souls of men,
Till Nature is transformed to Grace,
    We know not how nor when.

All earthly aims shall have an end,
    All earthly hopes expire,

All faiths that are not Faith, but tend
    To the eternal fire.

One Aim there is of endless worth,
    One sole sufficient Love,
To do Thy Will, my GOD, on earth,
    And reign with Thee above.

Who have in life that one true Aim,
    That one true Hope in death,
Shall pass unscathed the trial-flame
    And earn the amarant wreath.

From joys that failed my Soul to fill,
    From hopes that all beguiled,
To changeless Rest in Thy dear Will,
    O JESUS! call Thy Child.

In tempore Vesperi erit Lux.

OF old, O LORD, Thy Word was plight,
    'At evening time there shall be Light;'
Now darkly lowers the coming night—
        'JESU, mercy.'

Chill wintry gusts are sweeping by,
All faintly gleams the shrouded sky,
The stars are fading from on high—
        'Exaudi me.'

We see each Woe Thy Seers reveal,
Each Vial of Thy Wrath we feel,
Almost we hear the Trumpet peal—
        'Cum Angelis.'

Stanzas.

The Glories of Thine ancient Home
Serve but to show the gathering gloom,
The Sabbath of the world is come.

Where is the faith our martyr Sires
Owned in the canonizing fires,
The burning love, the high desires?

Cold is the Saints' unshrinking Faith,
The hope that cheered the Martyr's death—
Love freezes at the worldling's breath.

Yet most Thy promised Light display,
Left wandering from the ancient way,
Self-trusting still, we fondly stray.

Scarce with faint earth-dimmed glimmerings shine
The tapers set to guard the shrine,
To Faith's keen eye no certain sign.

Thou only Good, Thou only True,
When faith is weak and friends are few,
Do Thou that promised Light renew.

Beside the Altars of our land,
'Mid prayers untrue and rites profaned,
We wait, O Lord, Thy guiding Hand.

O be one gleam in mercy sent,
Ere by the Judgment-cry is rent
A flame-encompassed firmament—
     ' Cum Angelis.'

Ere yet that laſt, all-ſearching light
Breaks but to eternize the night,
The dawning of the infinite—
      'Exaudi me.'

So, when the dead, earth's countleſs race,
Are ranged before Thine awful Face,
May we among the Sheep have place—
      'Jesu, mercy.'

Requiem Æternam.

TO die and be at reſt
 Beneath the Churchyard ſod,
The Corpſe in ſere-clothes dreſt,
 The Spirit with its God!

To die and be at reſt
 Beyond the world's annoy,
No cares to vex the breaſt,
 No tears to trouble joy.

To die and be at reſt
 Where ſlander's tongue is ſtill,
Where praiſe nor mars our beſt,
 Nor conſecrates our ill.

To die and be at reſt
 Where earthly tumults ceaſe,
Where ſtorms may ne'er infeſt
 The Haven of our peace.

Stanzas.

To die and be at rest
   With them that part no more,
Rocked gently on the breast
   Of loved ones gone before.

To die and be at rest
   Beyond the power of sin,
Love an abiding guest
   The ransomed Soul within.

To die and be at rest—
   For this our natures crave,
The last home of the Blest,
   The World beyond the grave.

To die and be at rest—
   'Tis Childhood's earliest dream,
In terror unexprest
   Shrinking from life's dark stream.

To die and be at rest—
   'Tis Manhood's bitter cry,
With thankless toil opprest
   Of wasted energy.

To die and be at rest—
   Old age with feeble moan
Echoes the long request,
   To lay its burden down.

To die and be at rest—
   It is a Christian prayer,
For Death is GOD's Behest,
   CHRIST and His Saints are there.

Sequence on the Holy Spirit.

After Adam of S. Victor.

HEALTH of the helpless, Crown of Consolation,
 Giver of Life, sweet Hope of man's Salvation,
  Come with Thy Grace, O come,
Sun of the Soul, and let Thy Sunlight shine,
And warm with Love's soft glow the hearts of
  Thine;
And o'er the freshening field of Christendom
  Drop fatness, Dew Divine;
 Till day by day, and hour by hour,
 Fed with the fulness of Thy Power,
 Every woodland, every bower,
 Burst into leaf and fruit and flower,
  Filled with true Life's best food,
From Thee, the Fountain of all good.

 One in Substance, GODHEAD One;
 River, That from Both dost run,
 Spring, from Either sundered never,
 Bound to Both, and bonded ever
  In a mighty unison,
 With a bond that nought can sever;
 League of power, that none may part,
 Everlasting—as Thou art.

Sequence on the Holy Spirit.

Dew of Each, of Both in One,
Rich Vapour rising from the eternal River;
 May the Father and the Son
That Gift vouchsafe Whereof Thou art the Giver,
 Giver and Gift, Thyself on us bestow,
 Thyself—the Well Whose waters ever flow.

Thou hearest the Dew fall on earth, where it lies,
From the River thou hearest the Vapour arise,
And the scent of sweet Odour thou knowest,
  whereby
Thy faith can the Presence of Godhead descry:
 Dew, that from the Godhead bursts,
Whereof who deepest drinks the more he thirsts;
  Thirsting ever with a glow,
  Quenchless, as the Spirit's flow,
  Flowing alway, alway blessing;
  Thirst that knoweth no repressing.

 By Him the Wave is consecrate,
 Where for new Birth the holy people wait,
  The water on whose face was borne
  God's Spirit at Creation's morn.
  Fount, of all Holiness the spring
   Whence flows true Love abroad,
  Clear Fount that cleanseth from all sin,
   Fount from the Font of God;
  Great Fount, all fountains hallowing,
  Without all Blessing and all God within.

Fire of flint, with nought of wood,
Faring forth in myſtic Flood,
Kid conſuming, Fire of Heaven,
Feeding on the dread Unleaven,
Fire, all earthly fire unlike,
   On the Altar of our heart
Strike the ſpark of light, O ſtrike
The flame there ſtill to burn and never thence
   depart.

Shadow of the maidens ſeven,
   Seven that compaſſed the One;
Type of the very Truth of Heaven
   That through all things doſt run;
All-quickener, That with life the world doſt
   warm,
   O SPIRIT Septiform:
In ſeveral ſhape out-lined,
Yet varying not in kind,
Forefend it ever, that we ſay
   Of Thee, the Almighty Mind,
That Thou doſt form obey,
   To form and ſhape confined.

Fire of Life, Life-giving Spring,
   Cleanſe our hearts, and thither bring
Thy Gifts of Grace, to enrich them and to bleſs;
   That, kindled by the flame of Charity,
   Meet offering we become to Thee
      Of Love and Holineſs.

reath of the FATHER and the SON, Thou beſt
 Leech of the ſinful, Solace of the ſad,
 ſtrength of the weak, the worn wayfarer's Reſt,
 Health of the ſick, make Thou the mourner glad.
     Holy Love, like virgin's, chaſte,
         Fire of Soul, yet maiden-pure,
     Thoſe whom evil paſſions waſte
         May Thine hallowed Unction cure.

Voice of voices manifold,
Subtile Voice, by ſound untold,
In the ear, and in the breaſt,
Voice to each That whiſpereſt :
Voice enbreathed into the Bleſt,
Stilly Voice and ſecret—Voice
Making Men of Peace rejoice,
Voice of ſweetneſs, Voice of bliſs,
Voice of voices, ours be This
Sounding through our inmoſt heart :

Light, That bidſt all lies depart,
Light, That falſehood's router art,
Light, That draweſt unto Thee
Faith and Truth and Verity ;
Light, vouchſafe to us, to all,
Life and health and wealth, that we,
Lit with light perennial,
Live in ſunſhine, that ſhall be
Brightening everlaſtingly.

Of the Gifts of God.

From the Latin.

THOUGH for me the tongues of Angels
    With the tongues of men were blent,
Duly ſhould I ne'er be able,
    Giver of things excellent,
To return Thee praiſe, O Greateſt
    FATHER of Enlightenment.

For with Might Thou didſt create me
    For Thyſelf of nothingneſs,
And to bear Thy Likeneſs ſhape me
    By Thy Wiſdom fathomleſs,
And with Angels equal make me
    In my reaſon's nobleneſs.

Thus with faculties controlling,
    Faculties ſubordinate,
Like the pattern of Thy Glory,
    I ſurpaſſed the brutal ſtate,
Standing pure, enlightened, holy,
    Righteous and inviolate.

Yet had all been left imperfect,
    Having wrought me wondrouſly,
If as thankleſs, proud tranſgreſſor,
    Thou wouldſt doom me rigidly;
If deluded, loſt and wretched,
    Thou wouldſt not deliver me.

No! where I was lately fallen
  Underneath my hellish Foe,
Thou'st to hope for pardon brought me
  In Thy Grace, and laid him low:
To Thy Pasture hast Thou called me;
  Time for Grace Thou dost bestow.

Stumbling hast Thou me supported
  With enduring Patience;
Straying hast Thou me withholden
  With severe Beneficence;
Me delinquent hast absolved,
  And hast blotted mine offence.

Thou on every side dost wash me
  And dost heal me wounded sore,
And when washed and healed, upon me
  Thou dost Oil of Gladness pour;
Gleams of wondrous Hope surround me,
  When the painful stound is o'er.

Now withdrawing me from danger,
  Unto good Thou stablishest;
Now supporting mine endeavours,
  Gifts on me Thou lavishest;
Where Thou givest, where Thou takest
  Still my weal Thou compassest.

Thou providest for my table
  Daily food abundantly;
Thou dost bounteously for raiment
  Things beseeming me supply;

Care of me Thou takeſt ever
  Like the apple of Thine Eye.

Herein likewiſe muſt I glory,
  That to me Thou ſhouldſt confide
To bear tribulation for Thee
  From without and from inſide,
Since beloved Sons Thou always
  Haſt in ſuch encounters tried.

By the ſervice of Thy Creatures
  I am largely profited,
For their uſes, like their figures,
  Witneſs Thee their Fountain-head:
Still by Nature, ſtill by Scripture,
  Are we to Thy Traces led.

Yet beyond all theſe Thy Creatures
  Thou Thyſelf exaltedſt me
By aſſuming Man's condition
  In Thy wondrous Clemency,
And in Thy Paternal Wiſdom
  To Thyſelf redeeming me.

O what boundleſs depths of Pity
  Thy Paternal Grace diſplays!
O the Bounty that we witneſs
  In the Filial GODHEAD's Ways!
Therefore ſhall there be no period
  Of Thy Worſhip, Splendour, Praiſe!

Urbs beata Hirusalem.

BLESSED City, holy Salem,
 Home of peace, by Seers descried,
Rising in the courts of Heaven,
 Built of living stones and tried,
By Angelic hands adornèd,
 As her fellows deck a Bride.

Coming newly formed from Heaven,
 Ready for the nuptial bower,
Wedded to the LAMB for ever,
 As a bride in blissful hour;
All her streets have golden pavement,
 Golden ramparts round her tower.

Bright her gates of pearl are gleaming,
 Open are her chambers fair;
And by virtue of His Merits
 Every Soul shall enter there
Who, in this world, pain or sorrow
 For the Name of CHRIST shall bear.

Hewn with blows, and worn by pressure,
 Polished stones from every land,
All are in their places fitted
 By the Builder's matchless hand,
Firmly set, to rest unshaken,
 While the Heavenly mansions stand.

Corner-ſtone in her foundation,
  CHRIST the Rock is ſurely laid;
Who, in both the walls compacted,
  Hath of twain one Temple made;
Holy Sion Him accepted,
  All her hope on Him is ſtayed.

Sacred is that glorious City,
  Dear to GOD the mighty King,
Mingling with her tuneful praiſes
  Joyous burſts of triumph ring;
THREE and ONE their GOD proclaiming,
  All in welcome Anthems ſing.

The Church, Militant and Triumphant.

The Church Militant.

HOW ſtrong are her foundations! the opening
  How glorious of her portals! Yet within,
    What Babel-ſounds of ſtrife! Without, what din
Of malice and of wrath! Thoſe choirs which ſing
Eternal Alleluias to their King,
How muſt they wondering view the power of ſin,
Which, round her ſacred boundary who muſt win
And fold GOD'S Flock, ſuch direful ſpell could fling,

Marring her holy work—our Sion's height
O'ershadowing with gloom, where once shone clear
Heaven's purest radiance! O for a light,
Glimmering albeit afar! 'Dispel thy fear,'
A Voice exclaims, 'My Church's mourning night
Is well nigh spent; her Dayspring draweth near!'

The Church Triumphant.

WHO is it clad in garments radiant white,
Love on her breastplate graven, on her brow
Salvation diademed? Above, below,
Ten thousand thousand Spirits wing their flight,
A shining company. With glory bright
The army of Martyrs circle, which through woe
And peril, pain and death, dared face the foe,
Bearing their palms, with victor-chaplets dight.
In mild but awful majesty, to meet
The Bride comes forth the Bridegroom, in the skies
Enthroning on her everlasting seat.
From myriad Voices shouts of triumph rise:
' Her warfare is accomplished; at her feet
Fallen is the captive's chain—the conqueror pros-
    trate lies!'

Voices from the American Church.

Heart's Song.

IN the silent midnight watches,
    Lift thy bosom door,
  How it knocketh, knocketh, knocketh,
    Knocketh evermore!
Say not 'tis thy pulse's beating,
    Or thy heart of sin;
'Tis thy SAVIOUR stands entreating,
    'Rise! and let Me in.'

Death comes down with reckless footstep,
    To the hall and hut;
Think you Death will tarry, knocking
    Where the door is shut?
JESUS waiteth, waiteth, waiteth,
    But the door is fast;
Grieved, at length away He turneth;
    Death breaks in at last.

Then 'tis thine to stand entreating
    CHRIST to let thee in;
At the gate of Heaven beating,
    Wailing for thy sin.
Nay! alas, thou foolish Virgin!
    Hast thou then forgot?
JESUS waited long to know thee—
    Now, He knows thee not.

Song of Faith.

THE lilied fields behold!
    What King in his array
Of purple pall and cloth of gold
    Shines gorgeously as they?

Their pomp, however gay,
    Is brief, alas! as bright;
It lives but for a summer's day,
    And withers in a night.

If GOD so clothe the soil
    And glorify the dust,
Why should the slave of daily toil
    His Providence distrust?

Will He, Whose Love has nursed
    The sparrow's brood, do less
For those who seek His Kingdom first,
    And with it Righteousness?

The birds fly forth at will;
    They neither plough nor sow;
Yet theirs the sheaves that crown the hill,
    Or glad the vale below.

While through the realms of air
    He guides their trackless way,
Will man in faithlessness despair?
    Is he worth less than they?

As thy day, so shall thy strength be.

WHEN adverse winds and waves arise
 And in my heart despondence sighs,
When life her throng of cares reveals
And weakness o'er my spirit steals,
Grateful I hear the kind Decree
That ' As my day, my strength shall be.'

When with sad footstep memory roves
O'er smitten joys and buried loves,
When like a mourner low I bend,
Without a comforter or friend,
Then to Thy Promise, LORD, I flee,
Still ' As thy day, thy strength shall be.'

One trial more must yet be past,
One pang, the keenest and the last;
And when, convulsed with mortal pain,
Struggling I seek for ease in vain,
Then wilt Thou give my Soul to see
That ' As her day, her strength shall be.'

The fashion of this world passeth away.

IN careless Childhood's sunny hours
 When all we love is nigh,
No thorn amid life's opening flowers,
No cloud in all its sky,

We fear no ill, nor dream of care,
   But deem each following day
Shall light us on to fairer scenes,
   And beam with brighter ray.

And Childhood's vernal season past,
   And shunned Youth's thousand snares,
When Manhood's autumn comes at last
   With sorrows, fears and cares,
Still, autumn-like its skies are bright,
   And still the world seems young,
And still we love its mellow light,
   Its boughs with fruitage hung.

But Autumn's golden skies must fade,
   And Autumn's fruits decay,
And soon, mid snows and storms, must come
   Old-age's wintry day;
A wintry day at best—as short,
   As gloomy and as cold,
Till the worn body yields at last,
   And life lets go its hold.

And when its earthly hold is gone,
   The world's brief fashion past,
Are there no hopes that shall survive,
   No pleasures that shall last?
Yes! Christian, it is thine to know
   Life's but a weary way,
A short, though painful pilgrimage
   To realms of endless Day;

Where **Faith** her crown of life shall wear,
  And **Hope** be lost in joy,
And meek-eyed **Love** be paid with bliss
  That **time** can ne'er destroy:
For thither **has** the Lamb gone up
  Who suffered, and was slain,
That risen with Him, His Followers might
  With Him for ever reign!

The Glory reserved.

SINCE o'er Thy Footstool here below
  Such radiant **gems** are strewn,
O **what** magnificence must glow,
  My God, about Thy Throne!
So brilliant **here** those drops of light,
Where the full Ocean rolls, how bright!

If night's blue curtain **of the** sky,
  With thousand stars inwrought,
Hung like **a** royal canopy
  With glittering diamonds fraught,
Be, Lord, Thy Temple's outer veil,
  What splendour **at** the Shrine must dwell!

The dazzling sun, **at** noontide hour,
  Forth from his golden vase,
Flinging o'er earth the golden shower
  Till vale and mountain blaze,
But shows, O Lord! one beam of Thine,
What, then, the Day where Thou dost shine!

Ah! how ſhall theſe dim eyes endure
    That noon of living rays?
Or how my Spirit, ſo impure,
    Upon Thy Glory gaze?
Anoint, O LORD, anoint my ſight,
And robe me for that World of light.

The Prodigal's Return.

ALMIGHTY FATHER, LORD of all,
    Unworthy as Thy Sons to call,
    As ſervants at Thy Feet we fall.

By all the Love which Thou haſt ſhown
For wanderers from Fold and Throne,
Have mercy while our ſin we own.

As hirèd ſervants, can it be
That we muſt ſerve, who once were free?
O bring us to ourſelves and Thee.

While ſtill a great way off, we yearn
Thoſe tender words of Love to learn
Which greet the Prodigal's return.

The Ring ſhall on our hand be placed,
With Love's beſt Robe ſhall we be graced,
We who our own had ſo debaſed.

Ah! hateful now the wretched paſt
By turns with ſwine and harlots caſt;
We rioted—then ſtarved at laſt.

Thy Welcome, LORD, will purge away
The ſting of each rebellious day,
And Love will pardon All, for Aye,

Rejoicing Thou wilt give for pain,
For ſighs, a part in Heaven's glad ſtrain,
When all the Loſt are found again.

Home.

RISE! Mother, riſe! thy Infant is away;
 See, on the verge of yon ſharp cliff he ſtands,
 Aiding his tottering ſteps with clinging hands,
Wandering in fearleſs play.

Stay! Mother, ſtay! move not—nay! not one call;
 Stay, or thy voice will make the truant ſtart;
 Thruſt down that cry within thy burſting heart,
Or ſee thy Infant fall.

Oh! inſtinct wonderful of Mother's love,
 See! ſilent, ſtill, ſhe gently bares her breaſt!
 Swiftly her Infant ruſhes to his neſt,
And there ſhe claſps her dove.

So ſilently our own dear Mother now,
 Leſt one of her ſtray Sheep ſhould ſuffer loſs,
 Shows us her LORD upon His bitter Croſs—
Shows us the thorn-crowned Brow.

Shows us, frail wanderers in the ways of ſin,
  Our Shepherd bleeding from that piercèd Side—
  Piercèd, that by that entrance opened wide
Sinners might enter in.

Oh! may He grant us to that Home to flee,
  To feel the fulneſs of that Love untold;
  To gaze, and fly unto that One true Fold,
And there for ever be.

Stanzas.

Via, Veritas, Vita.

HAST thou been lured by Pleaſures gay
  From the ſtrait Heavenward path to
    ſtray?
  Seek CHRIST: in Him thou find'ſt the
    Way.

Fain would'ſt thou, in the pride of youth,
The heights of Knowledge climb forſooth?
At CHRIST's Feet ſit thou: He is Truth.

Doſt tremble at the Soul's ſtern ſtrife
'Mid World with deadly dangers rife?
Let CHRIST dwell in thee: He is Life.

The Soul of Man and the Church of Chriſt.

'TWAS night: o'erſtrown with clouds, as
    huge ice-field
  Above me ſpread the vaſty firmament;

Athwart that mafs, which lay as though con-
   gealed,
  Stretched, zigzag-wife, full many a ragged
   rent,
Oping grim gap and unretrieved defcent:
  O'er glacier and crevaffe their onward way
Moon and attendant Stars, majeftic, went;
  She fhone with light lent by the Lord of day,
Within her circling fheen gleamed faint each leffer
   ray.

Thus through this drear dark world, o'er many
   a pit,
  Dread entrance to abyfs of Sin's fad gloom,
The Soul may by the Church of CHRIST be lit
  Onward to regions of eternal bloom;
  Thus, thus will fhe the dangerous path illume,
To them within her pale, throughout the night;
  Thus will her fteady lamp lead on, to whom,
Though hid awhile from earth's expectant fight,
The SUN of Righteoufnefs vouchfafes His glorious
   Light.

Pro Chrifto Mortuus.

SAW amid the lurid fky
   The coward Stars difordered fly;
   I faw with apprehenfion dread
   The troubled Sun and Moon grow red:

E'en in the twinkling of an eye
I saw Creation's wonders die,
As if for them there was no room;
It was, it was the Day of Doom!

I heard the pealing Trump of GOD,
I saw the startled mountains nod,
Earth dropped her brow of ancient pride
And oped her huge foundations wide,
While Ocean at that warning cry
Unbared her inmost channels dry,
Asunder burst was every tomb
Upon this awful Day of Doom.

I saw before a Throne of Light
Than suns ten thousand far more bright,
The quick and dead together stand,
The children of each age and land;
A varied, strange, unnumbered crowd
In mingling woe and terror bowed:
Old Time had bared Creation's womb
To meet upon this Day of Doom.

I saw upon that Throne Divine
One like the SON of MAN recline,
With Eyes so bright that from their blaze
The Universe fled in amaze:
Guilt stood appalled in awe profound
As flashed those beamy terrors round,
That threatened all things to consume
Upon this searching Day of Doom.

One, one alone upon that day
I saw wake up without dismay,
Burst the long fetters of the earth,
As if to claim a second birth;
With tranquil brow and radiant eye
Draw the august Tribunal nigh,
Like a young Star amid the gloom
Of this o'erwhelming Day of Doom.

'Twas one who on his vestment bore
A great red Cross impressed before,
And glistening bright those words outspread,
' Pro Christo mortuus,' I read.
Most wondrous sight! a rainbow form
Amid the universal storm,
A Phœnix true of endless bloom,
The Conqueror of the Day of Doom.

Man.

A Hymn of Alanus.

LIKE a picture all Creation
   Standeth for our contemplation,
     'Tis our mirror and our book:
   Life and death are there presented,
All our pilgrimage imprinted,
   Calling men to pause and look.

For the rose doth paint our story,
And the rose doth glass our glory,
   Readeth all our life's brief hour:

Man.

In the early morn ſhe bloometh;
Agèd, when the evening gloometh,
   Falls off the deflowered flower.

Breathing ſhe her life exhaleth;
Soon her bluſhing beauty paleth;
   Dying came the flower to earth;
Old and new, alike death-laden,
Agèd, yet a youthful maiden,
   Fading in her dawn of birth.

So unto the youthful comer
Miniſters his mortal ſummer;
   Brightly ſmiles the fleeting flower:
But that morning hath its even,
Soon athwart the darkling heaven
   Cometh on life's twilight hour.

Pain is all man's life and being,
Toil without a hope of fleeing,
   Death deſcending covers all:
Sunſhine now is ſtorm hereafter;
Death tracks life, and ſorrow laughter;
   Darkneſs on our day doth fall.

Therefore, when this clauſe thou readeſt,
See that thou the leſſon heedeſt;
   Man, thy life is figured clear;
In what ſtate thou cameſt hither,
What to-day thou art, and whither
   Tend thy ſteps, examine here.

Weep the coſt of paſt tranſgreſſion,
Wail thy ſin, tame pride and paſſion,
   Caſt thy haughtineſs away;
Reinſman of the mind and maſter,
Guard thy truſt, leſt foul diſaſter
   Find thee unawares aſtray.

Chriſt Triumphant.

WHO cometh here from Edom's rocks,
   From Bozrah's haughty tower,
That journeyeth glorious in array,
   Majeſtic in His Power?
With Garments red from fields of blood
   A Conqueror He doth ſeem!
" I come, Who ſpeak in Righteouſneſs,
   The Mighty to redeem!"

And why is Thine Apparel red,
   Like his who treads the vine?
And why, like his who treads the vat,
   Do all Thy Garments ſhine?
" The winepreſs I have trodden out,
   Have trodden it alone;
And in that bloody vintage-hour
   With Me there ſtood not one.

" In Anger did I trample them,
   In Fury did I tread;
Their blood is ſprinkled on My Robe,
   My Raiment all is red;

The awful day is in Mine Heart
    Of vengeance on My foes,
The year is come when I redeem
    My People from their foes.

" And I beheld—but none could save
    His brethren by his hand;
I wondering saw no Child of man
    In that dread day could stand;
Therefore Mine own right Arm alone
    My great Salvation brought;
And by My Strength of zeal upheld
    The conquest I have wrought!"

Yes! Thou hast conquered mightier foes
    Than Edom's hostile power,
Hast Victor come from stronger holds
    Than Bozrah's haughty tower!
For Thou hast burst the gates of Death,
    And laid beneath Thee low,
By Thy right Hand and holy Arm,
    Thine Israel's hellish foe!

Thou didst behold no Child of man
    His brother's Soul could save,
Or make agreement unto GOD
    To free him from the grave;
A costlier price their Souls demand
    Than man hath power to pay;
And therefore Thou, O CHRIST, wouldst die
    That we might live for aye!

And therefore, when the appointed year
    Of Thy redeemèd came,
Thou didſt aſſume the Fleſh of man,
    Didſt take a mortal Frame;
Thou didſt the bloody wineprefs tread
    Of ſuffering from Thy foes,
To ſave Thy People from their ſins,
    From Hell's eternal woes.

And therefore, when o'er Hell and Death
    The conqueſt Thou hadſt won,
Thou didſt aſcend to God's Right Hand,
    And take Thy glorious Throne;
There ſtill doſt Thou retain, O Lord,
    The Mediator's Seat,
Until the Lord ſhall make Thy foes
    The footſtool for Thy Feet.

Gird then, O Thou moſt mighty One,
    Thy Sword upon Thy Thigh!
Ride forth! Avenge Thee on Thy foes
    Who ſtill Thy Name defy!
But when that wineprefs of God's Wrath
    Thy conquering feet ſhall tread,
Help us, Thy Children, Lord, for whom
    Thy precious Blood was ſhed!

Thou art our Father! though not us
    Hath Abraham begot;
Though Iſaac, and though Iſrael
    Our names acknowledge not!

Martyrs' Song.

Thou art our Father still! O Christ,
  And our Redeeming Lord,
The Righteousness of God most High,
  The One Eternal Word!

Martyrs' Song.

E meet in joy, though we part in sorrow;
We part to-night, but we meet to-morrow.

Be it flood or blood the path that's trod,
All the same it leads home to God:

Be it furnace-fire voluminous,
One like God's Son will walk with us.

What are these that glow from afar,
These that lean over the golden bar,

Strong as the lion, pure as the dove,
With open arms and hearts of love?

They the blessed ones gone before,
They the blessed for evermore:

Out of great tribulation they went
Home to their home of Heaven-content;

Through flood, or blood, or furnace fire,
To the Rest that fulfils desire.

What are these that fly as a cloud,
With flashing heads and faces bowed,

In their mouths a victorious psalm,
In their hands a robe and a palm?

Welcoming Angels these that shine,
Your own Angel, and yours, and mine;

Who have hedged us both day and night
On the left hand and on the right,

Who have watched us both night and day,
Because the Devil keeps watch to slay.

Light above light, and Bliss beyond bliss,
Whom words cannot utter, lo! Who is This?

As a King with many crowns He stands,
And our names are graven upon His Hands;

As a Priest, with GOD-uplifted Eyes,
He offers for us His Sacrifice;

As the LAMB of GOD for sinners slain,
That we too may live He lives again;

As our own Champion, behold Him stand
Strong to save us at GOD's Right Hand.

GOD the FATHER give us Grace
To walk in the Light of JESUS' Face.

GOD the SON give us a part
In the hiding-place of JESUS' Heart.

God the Spirit so hold us up
That we may drink of Jesus' Cup.

Death is short and Life is long;
Satan is strong, but Christ more strong.

At His Word, Who hath led us hither,
The Red Sea must part hither and thither;

At His Word, Who goes before us too,
Jordan must cleave to let us pass through.

Yet one pang searching and sore,
And then Heaven for evermore;

Yet one moment awful and dark,
Then safety within the Veil and the Ark;

Yet one effort by Christ His Grace,
And then Christ for ever Face to face.

God the Father we will adore,
In Jesus' Name, now and evermore:

God the Son we will love and thank
In this flood and on the further bank:

God the Holy Ghost we will praise,
In Jesus' Name, unto endless days:

God Almighty, God Three in One,
God Almighty, God Alone.

The Starry Night.

From the Spanish of Luis de Leon.

WHEN nightly through the sky
 I view the stars their files unnumbered
  leading,
   Then see the dark earth lie
  In deathlike trance, unheeding
How Life and Time with those bright orbs are
  speeding:

  Strong love and equal pain
Wake in my heart a fire with anguish burning;
  The tear-drops fall like rain,
   Mine eyes to fountains turning,
And my sad voice pours forth its tones of mourning:

  O Mansion of high state,
Bright Temple of bright Saints in beauty dwelling,
  The Soul, once born to mate
   With these, what force repelling
Hath bound to earth, its light in darkness quelling?

  What mortal disaccord
Hath exiled so from Truth the mind unstable?
  Why, of its blest reward
   Forgetful, lost, unable,
Seeks it each shadowy fraud and guileful fable?

The Starry Night.

  Man lies in slumber dead,
Like one that of his danger hath no feeling,
  The while with silent tread
  Those restless orbs are wheeling,
And as they fly his hours of life are stealing.

  O Mortals, wake and rise;
Think of the loss that on your lives is pressing;
  The Soul, that never dies,
  Ordained for endless blessing,
How shall it live false shows for Truth caressing?

  Ah, raise your fainting eyes
To that firm sphere which still new glory weareth,
  And scorn the low disguise
  The flattering world prepareth,
And all the world's poor thrall hopeth or feareth.

  O what is all earth's round,
Brief scene of man's proud strife and vain endeavour,
  Weighed with that deep profound,
  That tideless Ocean-river,
That onward bears Time's fleeting forms for ever?

  Once meditate, and see
That fixed accord in wondrous variance given,
  The mighty harmony
  Of courses all uneven,
Wherein each star keeps time and place in heaven.

  Who can behold that store
Of light unspent, and not with very sighing

Burst earth's frail bonds, and soar,
With Soul unbodied flying,
From this sad place of exile and of dying?

There dwelleth sweet Content;
There is the reign of Peace; there, throned in splendour,
As one pre-eminent,
With dove-like eyes so tender,
Sits holy Love—honour and joy attend her.

There is revealed whate'er
Of Beauty thought can reach; the source internal
Of purest Light, that ne'er
To darkness yields; eternal
Bloom the bright flowers in clime for ever vernal.

There would my Spirit be,
Those quiet fields and pleasant meads exploring,
Where Truth immortally,
Her priceless wealth outpouring,
Feeds through the blissful vales the Souls of Saints adoring.

Index

OF THE SOURCES OF THE HYMNS.

BLEW, W. J., M.A. CHURCH HYMN AND TUNE BOOK. *Rivingtons.* 1855. No. 92.
Bridges, Matthew, Esq. THE PASSION OF JESUS. *Richardson.* 1852.
W. B. ATHANASIUS. *Masters.* 1858.
Churton, Archdeacon. GONGORA. *Murray.* 1862. No. 137.
Clergyman, A. MORNING THOUGHTS. *J. H. Parker.* 1854.
Coxe, A. Cleveland, Bishop-Elect. ATHANASION. *New York.* 1842.
Croswell, W., D.D. POEMS. *Boston.* 1861.
Faber, F. W., D.D. HYMNS. *Richardson.* 1862.
Hawker, R. S., M.A. ECCLESIA. *J. H. Parker.* 1840
Jackson, E. D., M.A. LAYS OF ANCIENT PALESTINE. No. 28.
Kennaway, C. E., M.A. POEMS. *Rivingtons.* 1846.
King, J. M., M.A. LAYS OF PALESTINE. *Rivingtons.* 1851. No. 91.
Kynaston, Herbert, D.D. OCCASIONAL HYMNS. 1826-64.

F F

Lowe, Helen. THE PROMPECY OF BALAAM. *Murray.* 1841.

Newman, Dean. THE MARTYRS. *Longmans.* 1847.

Oxenham, H. N., M.A. THE SENTENCE OF KAÏRES. *Shrimpton.* 1854. No. 124, pts. 1 and 2.

Procter, A. A. A CHAPLET OF VERSES. *Longmans* 1862.

Rossetti, C. G. GOBLIN MARKET. *Macmillan.* 1862. No. 59.

Trench, Archbishop. GENOVEVA. *J. W. Parker.* 1851.

De Vere, Aubrey, Esq. POEMS. *Burns.* 1855.

Worsley, P. S., Esq. POEMS AND TRANSLATIONS. *Blackwood.* 1863. Nos. 51, 134.

Index

OF THE FIRST LINES OF THE HYMNS.

No. 69.*   Page

	A LONELY Woman's feeble hand . .	229
112.	A Wilderness of barren sand . .	367
79.	Ah, whither flee, or where abide?	263
49.	All of you shall soon forsake Me .	163
130.	Almighty Father, Lord of all .	417
92.	Amid the whirlwind and the thunder-cloud .	309
31.	And comest Thou to me?	103
102.	Arise and sing a joyful Lay	342
13.	Arise! ye Children chosen of the Lord . .	43
96.	Arm me to-day	321
10.	As eager homebound Traveller to the goal .	33
81.	As rippled, by the sickle prest	271
47.	As when from off some precipice	155
79.	At dead of night	266
66.	Away, below the Earth's broad breast . . .	220
74.	Beautiful is Noon	245
81.	Before those bones unshrouded	270
89.	Behold! all things await	297

* The Hymns are not numbered in the Text; but, by a reference to the Page they can at once be found, both in the Index of the First Lines and Table of Contents.

Index of the First Lines.

No.		Page
42.	Beyond the barren Mountain-range	135
104.	Blanched in the blaze of light	348
127.	Blessed City, Holy Salem!	409
16.	Bright upon the vested Altar	53
70.	Brother! now thy toils are o'er	231
71.	Child of My Grief and Pain	236
20.	CHRIST with mighty Triumph rises!	65
25.	Clad in the Panoply of Heaven.	78
107.	Clearly he sang, as only Angels sing.	356
58.	Come! let us wander by the silent beach	196
33.	Could Creatures all their voices raise	109
85.	Day of bright illumination.	283
18.	Dead is thy Daughter	60
48.	Die to thy root, sweet Flower!	161
39.	Eternal WORD! GOD'S True and Only SON.	125
23.	Faith is the dawning of a Day	73
15.	FATHER, One in Gospel-story.	52
75.	First and Last of faith's receiving.	49
71.	Follow to Calvary	233
30.	For forty years was Israel fed.	100
87.	For the Fount of Life eternal	289
78.	Fount of all Mercies, lo! I come.	262
31.	Give me Children, or else I die	101
27.	Glad Zion's halls are sounding	86
92.	Go where your Master's Glory	310
101.	GOD hath sent a MAN before thee	338
38.	GOD is a Sun and Shield	124
15.	GOD, of Glory unabated	51
105.	GOD, Who in Wisdom sweetly ordereth all	350
78.	Hark! yon white-robed Angel-choir	261
132.	Hast Thou been lured by Pleasures gay?	419
60.	He Who with His mighty Hand.	203
125.	Health of the helpless	402
6.	Heaven is no world of self-sufficing Bliss	20
35.	Here we have many fears	113
44.	His Face is flushed with Boyhood's glow	145
45.	Ho! Watchman, what of the night?	151

Index of the First Lines.

No.		Page
75.	How by shining Forms attended	248
25.	How feebly we adore Thee now	80
43.	How I tremble, filled with fear	140
63.	How loved Thy Halls and Dwelling-place	211
62.	How pleasant are thy Paths, O Death!	209
33.	How shall worthy praise and honour	106
128.	How strong are her foundations	410
100.	I am fading from you	336
103.	I heard the voice of Harpers	347
66.	I know not what I could desire	218
124.	I loved the beauty of the earth	396
133.	I saw amid the lurid sky	420
107.	I see the Sun go down behind the wood	355
82.	I stood in the shade of a stately Tree	274
62.	I wish to have no wishes left	207
30.	In anxious haste, at GOD's Command	100
81.	In Blessing parted from the King	269
129.	In careless childhood's sunny hours	414
64.	In dreams I slept where Israel wept of old	214
71.	In His own Raiment clad	233
77.	In My FATHER's House	254
99.	In my last long slumber lying	335
48.	In Spring the green leaves shoot	162
109.	In the Abbot's oaken Chamber	360
2.	In the Camp where flares the watch-fire	3
123.	In the dim morn I wake	394
129.	In the silent midnight watches	412
17.	In Wisdom, GOD the LORD	57
24.	In Youth I died	76
60.	Into the fiery Furnace flung	204
41.	Into Thy Hands, O LORD	133
40.	Is there no Balm in Gilead?	130
14.	It is not true that unto us	48
111.	Jerusalem! thou City towering high	365
3.	JESUS, Beautiful in Form	9
115.	Kings, with triple Gifts provided	376
134.	Like a picture all Creation	422
39.	Lo! He cometh, Meek and Lowly	128
15.	Next in Revelation's sequel	50

No.		Page
39.	No work of Man was e'er complete before	126
9.	Nothing now is left to do	31
92.	Now CHRIST had climbed the ſtarry ſkies	307
55.	Now with vivid deſire	186
57.	O Bliſs beyond telling	191
39.	O Croſs of ſhame! our boaſt and glory	129
43.	O how dreadful when that Word	141
36.	O Human-kind, your voices raiſe	117
76.	O LORD, my GOD, the way is rough and long	252
84.	O Power irreſiſtible	281
72.	O ſtay the obſequious fingers	239
52.	O Thou, EMMANUEL	177
52.	O Thou, the Central Orb of righteous Love	176
52.	O Thou, the Eſſential WISDOM	173
52.	O Thou, the King of Nations	177
52.	O Thou, the Root of Jeſſe	174
52.	O Thou That beareſt David's wondrous Key	175
11.	O Thou uncovered Corſe	36
52.	O Thou, Who ever ruleſt Iſrael's Race	174
124.	Of old, O LORD, Thy Word was plight	398
118.	Of the Higheſt generated	382
28.	Oh, for that day	88
71.	Oh, I will follow Thee	236
119.	Oh, no! we may not whiſper now	385
106.	Oh! ſay not that we die	352
28.	Oh! there were banners	91
71.	On the Croſs lifted	234
97.	On this feſtal Day we ſing	326
22.	Once, amid the wondrous Story	70
72.	Over each tower and minaret	237
110.	One bleſſed noon in Autumn's ſweeteſt weather	362
91.	Ready for battle's grim array	302
67.	Region of Life and Light	223
131.	Riſe! Mother, riſe!	418
92.	Round roll the weeks	308
19.	Samaria, proud and glorious	63
101.	Shew me a Tree, my Gracious LORD	339
108.	Silence reigned at eventide	357
88.	Siſter, once more with fairy touch	293
56.	Silent we reſted where a towering Croſs	188

Index of the First Lines.

No.		Page
80.	Sin hardens, all the heart with ice encrusting	267
129.	Since o'er Thy Footstool here below	416
8.	So spake the hoary Thyme.	27
94.	Springtide birds are singing	316
81.	Stern Remembrancer of error	272
15.	Stronghold safe of Judah's Lion	52
90.	Sun was shining bright and fair	300
59.	Sweet, thou art pale	199
59.	Sweet, thou art young	199
76.	Tell not abroad another's faults	251
99.	Ten thousand stars were burning bright	333
54.	The Christian must on Holy-days	182
34.	The Christmas Eve is waning	111
7.	The evening shadows thickly fall	23
86.	The Graves grow thicker	287
129.	The lilied fields behold!	413
122.	The Music of Heaven	392
113.	The same: hear all that spurn!	368
38.	The Stars are out in their eternal youth	124
30.	The Tree of Life in Eden stood	97
60.	The tuneful sound of music	202
99.	The Universe is shaking	334
46.	There is a spot	152
45.	There is light on Hebron now	148
45.	There is light on Hebron's towers!	150
4.	There is sound of war in Judah	11
14.	There was silence in the Heavens	47
50.	They bound him well in the dungeon cell	168
103.	They trod not now the perilous ground	346
114.	This Day which JESUS calls His Own	371
86.	Thou art gone Home	286
59.	Thou drinkest deep	200
51.	Thou from FATHER, SON, proceeding	170
48.	Thou gavest me no Kiss	159
98.	Thou sayest to us, "Go!"	329
5.	Thou Spotless LAMB of GOD	15
126.	Though for me the tongues of Angels	406
93.	Though thou art lowly now	312
68.	Time hath no brighter jewel on his brow	224
73.	Thrice blessed Land of Hevenly gladness	244
95.	To cull the gems of such a theme	319

Index of the First Lines.

No.		Page
124.	To die and be at rest	400
132.	'Twas night: o'er strewn with clouds	419
32.	'Twas night! still night!	104
61.	'Twas on the Mount of Olives	205
30.	Two Brothers each an Offering made	98
86.	Two Days, by contrast linked together	288
65.	Two thousand years have well nigh passed	215
1.	Upon the SAVIOUR's Birthday blest	1
28.	Wake, Deborah! wake	93
117.	We came not in with broad full canvass	380
60.	We keep the Feast of Pentecost	201
136.	We meet in joy, though we part in sorrow	427
107.	We named our flower-crowned Vessel 'Home'	357
120.	What are these Sighs?	387
21.	What earth appeared to Angel eyes	67
25.	What! left my LORD the Realms of Light?	81
38.	What love I, when I love Thee?	123
26.	What wouldst thou have, O Soul	83
129.	When adverse winds and waves arise	414
30.	When conquering Abram Salem sought	99
43.	When I dwell on Death's dread day	139
48.	When I have said my quiet say	162
43.	When I see with heartfelt pain	138
43.	When I think what shall befall	142
137.	When nightly through the sky	430
29.	When of His Grace the SON of GOD	95
83.	When the LORD JESUS Crucified	276
103.	Where is the Land he saw in glorious Vision?	344
12.	Wherefore doth the circling Sun?	38
135.	Who cometh here from Edom's rocks	424
128.	Who is it clad in garments radiant white?	411
73.	Who neither loves, nor seeks for JESUS' Love	242
53.	Who would not burn with strong desire?	178
121.	Why lies the darkness on the deep?	389
37.	Within a Garden's bound	119
116.	Within the cool Quadrangle's welcome shade	378

CHISWICK PRESS:—PRINTED BY WHITTINGHAM AND WILKINS,
TOOKS COURT, CHANCERY LANE.

Second edition, lately published, uniform with "Lyra Messianica," price 7s. 6d., cloth, antique.

Lyra Eucharistica:
Hymns and Verses on the Holy Communion.

EXTRACTS FROM REVIEWS.

"This is a Manual which we owe to the taste and research of Mr. Orby Shipley. It consists of Hymns, Poems, and Verses, Proses and Sequences, all connected with the great Christian Mystery, and these are collected from all sources, ancient and modern. Both as a book of devotion, and in a merely literary point of view, this is a very important little work."—*The Christian Remembrancer.*

"The first edition of *Lyra Eucharistica* was a success as great as it was deserved. The second edition is in every respect as admirable, while it contains no fewer than 130 additional hymns upon the Holy Communion. Some ninety of these additional hymns are either new or new translations, and they are one and all worthy of having been incorporated in this volume. But as we noticed the first edition at sufficient length we need hardly do anything now but congratulate the editor on his well-earned success and commend his work without reserve to our readers."—*The Morning Herald.*

"This Volume is a real gain to English Literature. . . . Besides collecting together [the Translations of several Authors] and others which are less well known, Mr. Shipley has been able, by the help of friends, to add both original Hymns and new Translations to a very considerable extent. Here then we have a volume, which will supply food to the devout mind, in connection with the great Act of Christian Worship, such as certainly did not exist before; and to many minds, we apprehend, there will be found to be more of edification in these Hymns, than in Treatises of a directly doctrinal or didactic nature."—*The Ecclesiastic.*

"The Collection before us is one of the most valuable, perhaps, which is extant in our language. [The Eucharistic] is a department of Hymnology which hitherto has been only too much neglected in the English Church. . . . This great defect, then, is here, in some measure, supplied—most ably supplied as far as it goes—though, of course, it could only, within the necessary limits of such a Collection, be a gleaning from the vast stores which are available to the Church. . . . . A second edition has since appeared in the same familiar and attractive typography and binding, and enriched by the addition of 120 new and for the most part hitherto unpublished poems, which now form the concluding or *Miscellaneous Section* of the work. If any of our readers have not yet made themselves acquainted with its contents, we can assure them that they have a great pleasure still in store."—*The Church Review.*

" The Volume before us is the last addition to the number [of Books on Hymnology]. But it will be observed, as its title indicates, that the Hymns contained in this Work are all devoted to one subject. Some idea of the labour incurred by the Editor may be gathered from the fact, that the Book contains [304] Hymns devoted to the Holy Communion. These have been selected from every available Source, many of them being Translations from Mediæval Hymns, while others are original compositions. There are copious Indices, and an explanatory Preface which is not the least interesting part of the work. It would be absurd to say a word of praise in favour of the Hymns themselves: we cannot gild refined gold."—*The Church Times.*

" The present beautiful Volume will probably be the most popular of the many Collections and Translations relating to the Holy Communion edited by Mr. Shipley. Those who possess his *Divine Liturgy*, will have learnt to appreciate some of the special beauties of Eucharistic Hymns, as aids to devotion, from the choice specimens, chiefly ancient and mediæval, collected in that Publication. The comparatively few there given have gradually expanded in the Editor's hands into the present Volume."—*John Bull.*

" Works like the *Lyra Eucharistica* are in two ways useful. In this Volume are brought together a great number of beautiful Hymns, original and translated, which for private use will doubtless be grateful to many. But it is also a valuable contribution towards the Hymnal of the future. Eucharistic Hymns are needed: here we have [304], some of which are of a very high order. Mr. Shipley has gathered in his stores from every side: but we conceive the most valuable part of the Volume to be the translations of Ancient Hymns. It must be a subject of congratulation to the Author to have secured for his collection in so short a time the demand for a second edition. The choice of hymns neither goes beyond nor falls short of the teaching of the Church of England."
—*The Press.*

" *Lyra Eucharistica* has a long and learned preface concerning Hymns and Hymnology, taking note of the chief Collections, ancient and modern, in various languages. . . . . All [the Contributions] are worthy to be preserved, and the Volume is a proof that the highest and most passionate human feeling does not necessarily express itself in the worst poetry. . . . This *Lyra* is another contribution to the yearly increasing number of good Sacred Poems. In outward show [it is a] model of ecclesiastical elegance. The sober, imitation-antique style of ' get up' is one of the pleasantest affectations of the day, to eyes wearied with the ' innumerable cheap stains and splendid dyes,' in which the modern book-cover makers delight."—*The Globe.*

" There is nothing more remarkable than the wonderful advance which has been recently made in the Anglican Communion with regard to a true belief in the Real Presence . . . Evidences of this are not wanting on all hands. One such is the publication of a very handsome Volume of Hymns and Verses, called *Lyra Eucharistica*, edited by Mr. Orby Shipley. The Book reflects great credit on the Compiler, who has been assisted by many known writers, and is exceedingly well arranged and printed . . . . Many of the Poems are original, and of singular ability and interest."—*The Union Review.*

" That this work has so soon reached a second edition is no mean proof of its excellence, and the need that there was for its compilation. Mr. Shipley has considerably enlarged it, taking especial care that the additions harmonize with the rest, and thus justifying us in again saying that for reverence in tone and beauty of expression the Volume is indeed worthy of the great mystery that forms its theme."—*Gentleman's Magazine.*

" We are glad to see a second edition of this beautiful Volume,— beautiful in its external features, but still more so in its contents. It is a pleasant sign of the times that so large a Collection of pieces, many quite out of the *rut* of ordinary sacramental poems, should find so large a circle of readers. We are glad of this also for the sake of the Compiler, whose indefatigable labours in the field of devotional literature deserve to be rewarded. This edition is much enlarged with original and selected pieces."—*Clerical Journal.*

" We are glad to see that this Collection of Hymns and Verses has attained to the honour of a Second Edition. This fact must be gratifying to Mr. Shipley, and a significant testimony to the worth of his judgment . . . . From the large quantity of matter which was no doubt placed at Mr. Shipley's disposal, he has made an excellent selection, and produced as delightful a book for devotional purposes as the most cultivated reader could desire."—*Public Opinion.*

"*Lyra Eucharistica* and the *Divine Liturgy*, both of them compilations by the Rev. Orby Shipley, are got up with great typographical *luxe*, and are edited with Mr. Shipley's usual care."—*The Ecclesiologist.*

"The peculiar stamp and beauty of the binding of this Hymnal [*Lyra Eucharistica*], which has been evidently designed with most exquisite taste, in accordance with the strictest rules of mediæval art, is the first circumstance which strikes the Reader on taking it into his hands. Opening the Volume, everything is in character with the exterior—mediæval title-page—mediæval designs, vignettes, and illustrations—mediæval printing—and the Hymns themselves abundantly mediæval and antique."—*The London Review.*

Lately published, uniform with "Lyra Eucharistica," price 7s. 6d., antique, cloth.

Lyra Messianica:

Hymns and Verses on the Life of Christ.

EXTRACTS FROM REVIEWS.

"The *Lyra Messianica* of Mr. Shipley is tuned on the principle that, in the happily revived taste for Hymns and sacred Verse, it is at once more loyal and more politic in Churchmen to seek to satisfy such literary craving from the well-nigh exhaustless stores of ancient Hymns which are in existence. *Lyra Eucharistica* was Mr. Shipley's first experiment in this direction. It met with some success; but if we are not much mistaken, the second attempt will be crowned with far more satisfactory results. He now addresses himself much more directly to the general heart of Christendom .... The Poems follow one another, each marked only by its own heading, like so many variations of a single air. It is delightful to let our thoughts follow the stream of song as it floats on in gently varied melody; it is both delightful and surprising to find on examination from how many different instruments this tide of song proceeds."—*The Guardian.*

"The selection of **Sacred Poetry** is decidedly the best of the kind, and forms a suitable companion to the *Lyra Eucharistica*, which we have before **noticed briefly**. There is, however, this difference: one volume is of necessity more entirely devotional, intended to supply meditation to the devout mind on the great Act of Christian Worship; whereas the *Lyra Messianica*, following the chief events in the Life of our LORD on earth, is more distinctive and dogmatic in its tone. .... In conclusion, we heartily thank Mr. Shipley for this valuable addition to **Catholic Poetry**. It is a real boon to the Church: and it will, we are sure, be appreciated, as it deserves, by all who have her welfare at heart."—*The Ecclesiastic*.

"It is impossible, in a brief notice, to give any adequate idea of the complete and satisfactory manner in which almost every detail and aspect of Christian doctrine has been illustrated or expanded by the varied contributions here gathered together; but we may be confident in our judgment, affirming that this volume is in every respect a worthy companion to the *Lyra Eucharistica*, and will become permanently popular."—*The Union Review*.

"Mr. Orby Shipley's *Lyra Messianica* is not only a beautifully printed book, but it contains some poems—chiefly translations from mediæval sources—which are not to be found elsewhere. It claims companionship to another interesting Volume, *Lyra Eucharistica*, collected by the pious diligence of the same Editor."—*The Christian Remembrancer*.

"We have here another beautiful **Volume of sacred Poetry**, put forth, under the same able editorship, with the same tasteful and attractive embellishments of type and binding, by the same eminent publishers, as the *Lyra Eucharistica*, which we commended to our readers' favourable notice a year ago. The plan of the present compilation, if less unique and specific in its character, admits of a less limited range of choice and a more diversified interest in the variety of its subjects."—*John Bull*.

"We cannot say that, upon the whole, we like *Lyra Messianica* so well as we did *Lyra Eucharistica*; and yet we are at a loss for a justification for this opinion. .... However, we can easily understand that there are many for whom *Lyra Messianica* will have greater charms than its elder sister. *De gustibus*—and it is a small difference after all. The same principle, as Mr. Shipley tells us, underlies both collections. .... If the criticism which we ought to have put into words has not been insinuated by these specimens we are at fault. Our chief difficulty in quoting these samples has been not the finding them, but the rejecting others almost, if not quite, as good in every respect."—*The Church Times*.

"This handsomely-got-up Volume consists of English and Foreign Hymns. The latter are from Greek, Latin, and mediæval sources. Swedish, Spanish, Italian, and German authors have also been translated; and, of the purely English Hymns, ninety are original. The Collection is a very complete one, and will make an admirable companion to a similar compilation by the same industrious Editor, which he calls Lyra Eucharistica."—*The Reader.*

"We are glad to observe that the present work, from the care displayed in its compilation, will be likely to secure a large share of public attention. . . . We have looked carefully through the book, and find in it much to admire. There is a relief in turning from secular poetry to really good poetry setting forth the goodness and majesty of the Creator. Mr. Shipley has exhibited much taste in his editorial duties, and has presented us with a Volume full of beautiful and sublime lays, that will be read with pleasure and profit."—*Public Opinion.*

"This is the companion Volume to the *Lyra Eucharistica*, noticed by us some time since,—its companion not merely in outward appearance, but in that reverence of tone and beauty of expression which we then earnestly commended. If we knew of terms that would more adequately convey our sense of the value of the work before us, we would employ them. Like its precursor, it is intended for devotional reading at home, and not for public use in the Church."—*The Gentleman's Magazine.*

"This Volume looks at once elegant and ecclesiastical. It is a sort of sequel to the *Lyra Eucharistica*, and is collected by the same Editor. The Hymns in the present collection chiefly concern the Life of CHRIST, and are ancient and modern, English and translated. Very few Hymns belong to a high class of poetry; in these, as in other religious matters, it is thought wrong to apply the severe rules of criticism which are enforced in ordinary mundane literature and art. Mr. Shipley has inserted some fine compositions, real sacred songs in this volume."—*The Globe.*

"We are indebted for this admirable collection of Hymns and Verses on the Life of our Blessed Lord to the success which has been so well achieved for a kindred collection, entitled *Lyra Eucharistica*. The former Volume, in fact, has not only led to this, but it must have prepared for an appreciation of it. There is here a good development of much which was there suggested."—*The Church Review.*

"Mr. Shipley's two handsome volumes [*Lyra Messianica* and *Lyra Eucharistica*] are most valuable contributions to the everyday literature of the Church. Neither trouble nor expense appear to have been spared in their compilation, and the result is well worthy of the pains bestowed."—*The Church and State Review.*

"Mr. Shipley has done good service to the Church by editing this Volume. It is a compilation from various sources, English and Foreign, of Hymns and Verses on the Life of our Blessed Saviour. The Book is divided into sections corresponding with the great Seasons of the Christian Year. Every one seems to have willingly allowed Mr. Shipley to use their original Verses or translations of old Hymns, and the consequence is that we possess in this Book a perfect treasure-house of 'Hymns and Spiritual Songs' on the Life of Christ. As regards typography and 'get up' the volume is sumptuous, though perhaps a trifle too mediæval for some tastes. However, it is on the whole a very pleasing volume, and is enriched by an interesting Preface from Mr. Shipley's pen. It must have been the result of much practical labour and research on the part of the Compiler."—*The Churchman*.

"*Lyra Messianica* seems to us the most beautiful collection of Poems which Mr. Orby Shipley has brought together."—*The Monthly Packet*.

"The reverend Author of the *Lyra Messianica* is already favourably known as a hymn collector by his previously-published volume, *Lyra Eucharistica*. He has gone to the source of the fountain for his inspiration, and dug into the mine whence the true metal is to be extracted..... The Hymns are mostly of an objective character, and group themselves around the various events in the Life and History of our Blessed Lord, accompanying Him through the successive stages of His humiliation to the record of His glory as an Ascended Man, 'exalted with great triumph into His kingdom in Heaven.' The Author has furnished a rich source of enjoyment to that now happily numerous class of readers who find pleasure in these elevating and cheering poetical illustrations."—*The Press*.

"This volume, like its predecessor, *Lyra Eucharistica*, published under the same editorship, consists for the most part of a translation of ancient and mediæval Hymns of the Church..... It cannot be questioned that Mr. Shipley's volume contains much of antiquarian interest, poetic beauty, and religious expression."—*The London Review*.

"Mr. Shipley's Collection is full of fine pieces, but its very principle is to give us poetry that does not express our mode of faith now, so much as the 'definite and dogmatic truth,' and the mode of translation is often needlessly stiff. It is a fine collection of old Hymns, which by their rendering into English, generally increase, instead of diminishing the distance between ourselves and them."

The Spectator.

BY THE SAME EDITOR.

Second Thousand, small 8vo. 2s. 6d.

THE DIVINE LITURGY: *A Manual of Devotions for the Holy Communion; for daily use.* From Ancient Sources.

Royal 18mo. Toned paper and plate. 3s.

LUIS DE GRANADA: *Considerations on Mysteries of the Faith.* Newly translated and abridged from the original Spanish.

Royal 18mo. Toned paper and plate. 4s.

AVRILLON: *Eucharistic Meditations for a Month.* Newly translated and abridged from the French.

Royal 18mo. Toned paper and plate. 2s.

RODRIGUEZ: *A Treatise of the Virtue of Humility.* Abridged from the Spanish.

Royal 18mo. Toned paper and plate. 2s.

DAILY MEDITATIONS FOR A MONTH: *On some of the more moving Truths of Christianity.* From Ancient Sources.

Small 8vo. Toned paper and plates. 3s. 6d.

DAILY MEDITATIONS FOR THE SEASONS: *For Advent, Christmas, Epiphany, Lent, Easter, Ascension, Whitsuntide, and the Season of Trinity.* From Ancient Sources.

Small 8vo. 2s. 6d.

EUCHARISTIC LITANIES. From Ancient Sources.

Second Thousand, small 8vo, with plate. 2s. 6d.

THE DAILY SACRIFICE: *A Manual of Spiritual Communion; for daily use.* From Ancient Sources.

8vo. 4d.

THE RESURRECTION: *An Easter Sermon; by Luis de Granada.* Translated from the Spanish.

LONDON: J. MASTERS, ALDERSGATE STREET, AND 78, NEW BOND STREET.

www.ingramcontent.com/pod-product-compliance
Lightning Source LLC
Chambersburg PA
CBHW022115300426
44117CB00007B/714